NASCAR Winston Cup
2000

ACKNOWLEDGMENTS

The adage about good things coming to those who wait certainly rang true for both Bobby Labonte and his team owner, Joe Gibbs, in 2000. Nine years of thoughtful planning by the former professional football coach and eight seasons of hard competition on the part of a very talented race driver finally paid off for both men in the form of the crown jewel of American motorsports — the NASCAR Winston Cup Series championship.

UMI Publications, Inc., is pleased and gratified to be able to present for your enjoyment this reminiscence in words and photos of the 2000 NASCAR Winston Cup Series season. Its main highlight, naturally, was the 36-year-old Texas native and North Carolina resident capturing the title in a most convincing manner. Behind the wheel of Joe Gibbs Racing's Interstate Batteries Pontiacs, Labonte took the lead in points following the year's third race at Las Vegas. He held it through the eighth event at Martinsville, lost it briefly (one race), and once he regained it after finishing second at California Speedway in April, the point lead was his for someone else to try and take away. No one could, though, and Labonte was able to claim the championship at the season's next-to-last race in Homestead, Fla.

It was a year that also saw 1999 NASCAR Winston Cup Series Champion Dale Jarrett win his third Daytona 500; Rusty Wallace vow to "fix" things he saw wrong with his race team and live up to that promise with four memorable race victories and a season high nine Bud Pole Awards; Dale Earnhardt seemingly come out of nowhere to take a stunning win in the Winston 500 at Talladega Superspeedway; Matt Kenseth claim the Raybestos Rookie of the Year Award; and three-time NASCAR Winston Cup Series Champion Darrell Waltrip embark on his "Victory Tour" and bring to a conclusion a driving career that began in 1972.

Without help and guidance from a lot of fine folks, publication of this book would not be possible. At NASCAR, we'd like to recognize the efforts of Bill, Jim and Brian France; Mike Helton; Paul Brooks; George Pyne; John Griffin; Kelly Crouch; Jennifer White, Paul Schaefer and Tracey Eberts. Working with them has been a pleasure.

Obviously, the NASCAR Winston Cup Series wouldn't be what it is today without the overwhelming support of the R.J. Reynolds Tobacco Company over the years. So, we'd also like to recognize and thank key members of the company for their assistance along the way in our efforts here. They include: Rick Sanders; Greg Littell; Rich Habegger; Dennis Dawson; Denny Darnell; Mitch Cox; Rob Goodman; Sean Kinder; Mark Clodfelter; Mark Rutledge and Chad Willis.

UMI is once again thankful to have been able to rely on master storyteller Bob Kelly, who diligently put words to paper and produced everything you'll read on the following pages. We cannot thank him enough for his insight and accuracy.

The same thing goes when it comes to the efforts of our "shooters." The photographers for this year's edition of the NASCAR Winston Cup Series story are again Don Grassman, Ernie Masche and Gary Eller of CIA Stock Photography and veteran freelancer David Chobat. They enjoy a high degree of respect among those who comprise the NASCAR Winston Cup Series, and we're most fortunate for their contributions here.

However, without NASCAR's legions of fans and followers, everything we do here would be for naught. Therefore, we dedicate this publication to you, the fans of the sport.

Please enjoy.

U M I   P U B L I C A T I O N S   S T A F F

President and Publisher: **Ivan Mothershead**; Vice President and Associate Publisher: **Charlie Keiger**; Associate Publisher: **Rick Peters**; Controller: **Lewis Patton**; National Advertising Manager: **Mark Cantey**; Advertising Executive: **Paul Kaperonis**; Managing Editor: **Ward Woodbury**; Associate Editor: **Gary McCredie**; Senior Editor: **Bob Kelly**; Art Director: **Brett Shippy**; Senior Designer: **Paul Bond**; Manager of Information Systems: **Chris Devera**; Administrative Staff: **Mary Flowe, Dorothy Gates, Linda Goltz, Sean McCartney, Christine Petrasko, Joanie Tarbert.**

FOREWORD

The 2000 NASCAR Winston Cup Series season can be defined in two words: highly competitive.

The tone for the season was set right out of the box this year, when we opened with 13 consecutive different race winners. As the season developed, some pretty significant modern-era records were matched... 14 different winners in a single season (1988, 1990, 1991, 2000), and for the first time since 1988, we had four first-time winners in Dale Earnhardt, Jr., Matt Kenseth, Steve Park and Jerry Nadeau.

Kenseth won the 2000 NASCAR Winston Cup Series Rookie of the Year Award among an outstanding rookie field which included Earnhardt, Jr., Dave Blaney, Scott Pruett, Stacy Compton and Mike Bliss. In addition, 11 different drivers made their first career NASCAR Winston Cup Series starts.

But the 2000 NASCAR Winston Cup Series season will be remembered for the stout performance of Joe Gibbs Racing's Interstate Batteries Pontiac team, lead by crew chief Jimmy Makar and driver Bobby Labonte.

After finishing second to Dale Jarrett in the 1999 championship chase, the Gibbs team confidently went about their 2000 season in workman-like style. They were unflappable.

Labonte captured four victories, and added 19 top-5s and 24 top-10s in 34 starts en route to the richest championship in American motorsports. True to the competitive nature of the 2000 NASCAR Winston Cup Series season, however, Labonte was the only driver in the top-40 drivers in the points chase to have "locked-in" his finishing position in points prior to the season ending event at Atlanta on November 20. Adding to the prestige of Labonte's title, seven time NASCAR Winston Cup Series champion Dale Earnhardt, climbed into second in the season's final standings.

Labonte won the title in his eighth full-time season of competition, and became the 24th different driver to win the NASCAR Winston Cup Series championship. Bobby joins his brother, Terry, the series' 1984 and 1996 champion, as the only brothers to win the title. Bobby is also the first NASCAR Winston Cup Series champion to have previously won a NASCAR Busch Series, Grand National Division title in 1991.

To all the members of the Labonte family who head to the NASCAR tracks each week, we offer our congratulations. And to those who pressured Labonte to the championship at varying times throughout the season, including Mark Martin, Dale Jarrett, Jeff Burton, and Dale Earnhardt, we extend our congratulations.

A new era dawns in 2001, with new tracks in Chicago, Ill., and Kansas City, Kan., set to host us, and new television network partners prepared to bring NASCAR fans closer to the action than ever.

As Bobby Labonte and the Joe Gibbs team lead us into our new era, they join NASCAR in saluting our drivers, teams and tracks, and most of all, the best fans in professional sports.

We know you will enjoy this chronicle of the 2000 NASCAR Winston Cup Series season.

Sincerely,

Bill France
Chairman
NASCAR

TABLE OF CONTENTS

PREFACE 2000

After battling Dale Earnhardt Jr. for the NASCAR Busch Series, Grand National Division championship over the past two seasons, Matt Kenseth prepares to make his bid for NASCAR Winston Cup Series Rookie of the Year honors.

A s NASCAR and its flagship NASCAR Winston Cup Series prepared to begin a new century of competition, the list of unanswered questions was lengthy, to say the very least.

Would this be the season that a rejuvenated Dale Earnhardt and the Richard Childress Racing team celebrated a championship, denied to them since 1994? Would Earnhardt's off-season back surgery prove successful and allow the seven-time titlist another chance to grab stock car racing's greatest achievement?

Would Mark Martin finally score the breakthrough season that would reward one of the best drivers in stock car history with his long-sought title? Would his oft-postponed, but finally undertaken back surgery allow him to compete pain-free for the first time in years?

Would former champions Rusty Wallace and Bill Elliott find the winning edge needed to return to the head table at the Waldorf-Astoria Hotel in December?

Or would this be the season that Bobby Labonte or Jeff Burton — or even last year's sensational rookie, Tony Stewart — put together the season of consistency that brings the championship?

Robert Yates solidified his organization by adding a new pit crew for Dale Jarrett's "88" team and bringing veteran Ricky Rudd on board to pilot the "28" car.

Three-time NASCAR Winston Cup Series Champion Darrell Waltrip announced that 2000 would be his last year behind the wheel. As he began the season, Waltrip's 28-year career included 780 starts, exactly half of which ended with top-10 finishes, and 84 wins, placing him in a tie for third with Bobby Allison on the all-time winners list.

Could Dale Jarrett — the sport's workman-like driver and extremely popular 1999 title-holder — be able to assemble another championship with the Robert Yates Racing team that had performed like a Swiss watch in 1999?

Was it possible to pull together an almost totally new cast of characters and watch Jeff Gordon — sans guidance from crack crew chief Ray Evernham — return to his recent dominant position in the sport? Could Terry Labonte, reunited with crew chief Gary DeHart, create another title-winning season for Hendrick Motorsports as they had in 1996?

Would the new Chevrolet Monte Carlos, under development for nearly two years, become the dominant cars on the track, as many expected? Would the new nose and rear of the Ford Taurus be able to bring the Dearborn, Mich., manufacturer another title? Or would this be the season the Pontiacs forged to the front of the manufacturer's championship battle?

Who would join the Dodge camp, led since the fall of 1999 by Evernham, in preparation for that marque's return to competition in 2001?

Would the driver and crew chief switching at the end of the '99 season produce the chemistry needed to challenge for a championship? Would new car owners in the sport immediately establish a competitive presence? Would new sponsors find themselves making victory lane visits in their first year on the hoods, deck-lids and quarterpanels of their chosen teams' mounts?

Could one of a stellar field of rookies be able to follow the overall brilliance of Tony Stewart's 1999 season?

Would eligible drivers again find the recipe for success to claim $1-million bonuses for their teams and for a selected sweepstakes entry in

any or all of the five Winston No Bull 5 events of the year, this year including the Daytona 500, the CarsDirect.com 400 at Las Vegas, Charlotte's Coca-Cola 600, the Chevrolet Monte Carlo 400 at Richmond and the Winston 500 at Talladega?

And who would emerge to claim the huge $3-million champion's bonus from the post-season point fund, doubled to an enormous $10 million by series sponsor Winston for the 2000 season?

As teams prepared for the season-opening event at Daytona International Speedway, these were just a few of the questions facing prognosticators as they tried to sort the wheat from the chaff and attempted to determine who would emerge on top over the 10-month season. The competitive level of the sport, higher than ever before, offered many drivers the opportunity to go to victory lane during the season. The key to the championship would again be a season of consistency and the ability to score maximum points on race days when the handling, the horsepower and the circumstances of the event did not provide for a chance to win that particular race.

No team or driver had been better prepared to provide the championship consistency in 1999 than Dale Jarrett and the Quality Care Ford team fielded by Robert Yates Racing. Jarrett had taken what he could at every race and had been given solid chassis and engines with which to do his job on Sunday. He responded by claiming his first title, and in the process gave the greatly respected Yates his initial championship.

The team had taken what it hoped to be a huge step in the off-season taking on most of the race-day pit crew from Gordon's No. 24 DuPont team. The former "Rainbow Warriors" would move to the red, white and blue of the Quality Care effort after approaching Yates and offering their services as a group. Yates reasoned he could use his former "over-the-wall" crew in more beneficial ways within his team and took on this crew of speedy specialists. The quiet but thoughtful car owner hoped it would be the key to repeating the championship.

Yates also made changes with the No. 28 Texaco-backed team, hiring Ricky Rudd to replace Kenny Irwin as the driver of the "Star Car." Rudd abandoned the job of owner/driver he'd assumed in 1994 and sold his team at auction. He chose to return to a driver-only role and believed the opportunity with Yates offered his best chance to win a long-sought

team changed, as well, and Gordon and Loomis also chose replacements for the departed "over the wall" group. None, however, were race-day-only specialists. With a new Chevrolet to work into shape, a new crew chief to communicate with and a nearly new crew to work with, Gordon had his work cut out for him in his quest to return to the champion's seat at the head table at the Waldorf-Astoria for a fourth time.

The other two Hendrick teams also underwent changes. Gary DeHart returned to work with Labonte on the Kellogg's team, with several new crew members blended into the mix. At the No. 25 team, Jerry Nadeau took over the controls of the Chevrolets from Wally Dallenbach, while the painters were busy changing all the equipment from Budweiser red to the blue and white of Michael Holigan Homes.

(Top) Among the new sponsors entering the sport in 2000 were NorthernLight.com, offering support for Roush Racing's Kevin Lepage, and Conseco, which put its funding behind A.J. Foyt's newly formed team.

(Above) After claiming two consecutive NASCAR Busch Series titles, Dale Earnhardt Jr. joined his dad in the big league. In addition to fielding teams for Dale Jr. and Steve Park, Dale Earnhardt entered the season determined to challenge for a record eighth title.

(Right) Bobby Labonte had to be considered one of the favorites to win the 2000 crown after he showed tremendous strength and consistency in 1999 and finished second to Dale Jarrett in the final points.

championship. Mike McSwain was named crew chief for the "28" car, continuing his association with Rudd.

Gordon, on the other hand, found himself facing a total reorganization of his Hendrick Motorsports team. Evernham had left to head up DaimlerChrysler's Dodge Division's return to the sport, and during the off-season, team owner Rick Hendrick hired Robby Loomis from Petty Enterprises to be Gordon's new crew chief. The faces within the

Both Earnhardt and Martin had undergone back operations following the final race of 1999, with Martin's the more serious. He had spent nearly the entire off-season flat on his back, letting the fusion surgery heal properly. By the time Daytona opened its gates, the health-conscious Roush Racing driver had recovered, returned to his daily workouts and was rarin' to race again. He hoped the changes to the Taurus would further improve the competitiveness of his Valvoline-sponsored team and that at year's end, he would finally claim the NASCAR Winston Cup Series title he had chased for so long.

Earnhardt was also ready for the season to begin. Rested and recovered from his own surgical experience, he felt his team's return to competitiveness in the second half of the 1999 season would enable him to lay siege to an unprecedented eighth championship.

The biggest question facing Earnhardt, Gordon and others in the Chevrolet camp was how good the new Monte Carlo would be as a race car. Under development for nearly two years, the "Bowtie Brigade" had its collective hopes pinned on the latest design. But there was some concern, based on testing speeds, that the Monte

(Above) Robby Gordon brought Turtle Wax and Ingersol-Rand into the sport with his new effort, while veteran open-wheel driver Scott Pruett picked up longtime sponsor Tide for his new Fords fielded by Cal Wells.

(Left) Rusty Wallace confers with Mike Helton, who had completed his first year as NASCAR Chief Operating Officer and Senior Vice President. While serving, since 1993, as vice president of competition, Helton established strong relationships with all of the competitors in the garage.

(Bottom) After sustaining the rigors of being an owner/driver since 1994, Ricky Rudd sold the assets of his team and went to work for Robert Yates, bringing with him crew chief Mike McSwain (left).

Carlo would not be as competitive as the reworked Taurus and Pontiac's tried-and-true Grand Prix. Only time — and on-track results — would tell the tale.

In the Pontiac camp, the Joe Gibbs Racing teams were expected to again carry the battle to Ford and Chevrolet. Bobby Labonte's outstanding 1999 effort and Tony Stewart's brilliant rookie season had captured headlines throughout the year. Expected first-year mistakes had cost Stewart and his orange-clad, Home Depot-sponsored team a couple of opportunities to notch victories. At the same time, though, Stewart had set new standards of success for rookies of the future to aim at. On the other side of the enormous garage bay at Gibbs' state-of-the-art shop, Labonte's green-and-black Interstate Batteries mounts had taken the Texan to second place in the final 1999 standings. If a little more consistency could be found,

Tony Stewart entered the 2000 season with his game face on, determined not to suffer a sophomore slump after posting the most successful rookie season in the sport's modern era.

Labonte felt he would have an excellent chance to claim the championship in 2000.

Many teams were working with new key components — drivers, sponsors, crew chiefs, shop personnel — and all hoped the new combinations would bring increased success.

Stacy Compton was the new driver for Melling Racing, while Kodiak settled in as the primary sponsor for the team. Joe Nemechek moved to Andy Petree's No. 33 team, with sponsorship from Oakwood Homes, while Ken Schrader carried his helmet over to the M&M's-sponsored Pontiacs fielded by MB2 Racing.

Michael Waltrip's Chevrolets would be painted in the black-and-yellow colors of Nation's Rent, Brett Bodine found funding from Ralphs Supermarkets for the season and Junie Donlavey's Richmond, Va.-based Ford team would carry Hills Brothers Coffee colors in events during the 2000 season. Kmart stepped up its sponsorship to include both Travis Carter-owned teams, putting its colors on Jimmy Spencer's renumbered "26" cars and also supporting three-time NASCAR Winston Cup Series Champion Darrell Waltrip in his final season of competition.

At Petty Enterprises, Greg Steadman was named crew chief of John Andretti's STP Pontiac, and the team faced a strange situation. STP would be the primary sponsor of the team for the first half of the season, but beginning with the July 1 Pepsi 400 at Daytona, the team's colors would change to the yellow and blue of Cheerios.

Several new teams provided even more questions to be answered during the 2000 season. Budweiser moved its sponsorship dollars to back Dale Earnhardt Jr.'s rookie season, and "Junior" appeared ready to equal — or perhaps top — Stewart's brilliant rookie season records after claiming back-to-back NASCAR Busch Series titles. Robby Gordon again left the open-wheel ranks and returned to NASCAR. He put together a team with owners Mike Held and John Menard and secured sponsorship money from a variety of

Joe Nemechek stands ready to take the wheel and begin the 2000 season after moving to Andy Petree racing to drive the No. 33 Chevrolets with new sponsor Oakwood Homes.

sources. Matt Kenseth, with DeWalt sponsorship, moved up from the NASCAR Busch Series ranks to battle in one of Jack Roush's Fords at the NASCAR Winston Cup Series level.

Cal Wells, with Tide sponsorship, would provide Scott Pruett with a solid effort in NASCAR Winston Cup Series racing, and Bill Davis "grew" Dave Blaney's NASCAR Busch Series team into an Amoco-sponsored NASCAR Winston Cup Series program. A.J. Foyt put together a new NASCAR Winston Cup Series team with Conseco as the sponsor and ultimately hired journeyman Rick Mast as the driver.

With Earnhardt Jr., Kenseth, Pruett and Blaney all in solid rides for the season, there was little question that this crop of rookie drivers would provide plenty to watch not only in their battle for the rookie title, but also in the overall finishes of events throughout the season.

Winston's staggering announcement that it would double the post-season point fund provided additional inspiration to teams. With the champion's bonus now at $3 million and the runner-up now receiving over $1 million, the battle for the NASCAR Winston Cup Series title had taken on even greater dimensions.

After months of testing, adding, changing and fine-tuning, teams finally loaded their transporters and headed for Daytona and the season-opening Daytona 500 — where questions about the new season would begin to be answered.

NASCAR WINSTON CUP SERIES
CHAMPION

BOBBY LABONTE

The dream came true for all of us at Joe Gibbs Racing.

And I couldn't be happier for everyone involved — from our sponsors to our car manufacturers to our office staff to the guys who work on every part of the Interstate Batteries Pontiacs we put on the starting line at each race.

It's been an incredible season, and to know that we have won the NASCAR Winston Cup Series championship in one of the most competitive years the sport has seen — and in the first season of the new millennium — is something that we are all truly proud of.

Last year, we learned so much chasing Dale Jarrett and not being able to stop him in his quest for the title. We watched it happen, week after week, while we were parked beside his transporter. And although we made a good run, we just didn't have the consistency we needed throughout the season to beat him and Robert Yates' team.

When the 1999 season was over, Jimmy Makar and I sat down and went over the entire season, race by race, and tried to figure out exactly where we needed to improve to make an even stronger run for the title this year.

(Right) The likeable Bobby Labonte's popularity had increased steadily since his rookie season of 1993, but with the visibility of being the point leader for most of the season, it soared, as fans clamored for autographs from the championship contender.

(Below) Team owner Joe Gibbs (far left), Bobby Labonte and crew chief Jimmy Makar (far right) were joined by Norm Miller (right of Labonte), Interstate Batteries chairman of the board, and Norm's son, Interstate President Tommy Miller, during victory lane celebrations during the year. The sponsor's principals have become an integral part of the team during their nine-year association with Joe Gibbs Racing.

We found some weak places in the program, and we made plans to test at some of the tracks where we could make a better effort. Most of all, however, we felt we needed to improve our consistency and not get into a situation where we had poor results because of mistakes we had made. That included the team in its preparation and work at the track as well as on pit road — and it also included the driver.

We fought to a sixth place at Daytona — the highest finishing non-Ford — and then came out and won at Rockingham in the second race of the season. That win gave our team a lot of confidence — that we could come out early in the season and win. Part of the win was directly attributable to the work the crew did on pit road throughout the day, and particularly in the closing stages of the race.

(Above) The Interstate Batteries crew lived up to its billing as the reigning world champions after winning the Union 76-Rockingham Pit Crew Championship in October 1999. Indeed, Bobby attributes much of the team's success over the 2000 season to consistently superior work on pit road.

(Left) Bobby exuded confidence as the season progressed, due in part to the fact that the team arrived at the race track each week with well prepared and reliable race cars — a testament to the work being done behind the scenes that helps win championships.

Two races later, at Atlanta, we nearly scored our second victory of the season, finishing second by mere inches to Dale Earnhardt, and I think that cemented our confidence that we were really going to be a factor in the point battle. We might not win the title, but it was clear that we were going to be highly competitive after those first four races of the year.

For the first third of the season, it was a dogfight among ourselves, Dale Jarrett, Mark Martin, Ward and Jeff Burton and others, as we saw an incredible string of 10 consecutive different winners. While that was going on, there was a huge battle within the top five in the point standings. We were at the top of that ladder after the third race of the season, falling to second just once, after Talladega, but it was clear that no one had a real advantage.

In the second third of the season, we never felt we were in command of the point lead at all. We had consistent finishes, but we didn't win a race for the longest time. Still, we managed to maintain a point lead that ranged from 45 to 98 points, but no one on our team felt we were at a real advantage. One slip, one problem on the racetrack, one cut tire, one anything, and the complexion of the point battle would change.

Then, beginning in August, we seemed to find the answer when we needed it most. We went into Indianapolis with a 53-point lead over Dale Jarrett, and it was beginning to look like D.J. and his team were ready to make a run at defending their title. But we had a great car at The Brickyard and, in the closing laps, we ran down Rusty Wallace, passed him and drove away to the victory. That punched our lead up to 87 over D.J. and gave us a little breathing room.

Less than a month later, at Darlington, we were able to take the wind out of the sails of our closest competitors. I wrecked the primary car in practice, and we had to take the backup out of the transporter and use a provisional start. But we came from 37th through

top five and took fifth — but the Monster Mile changed the point race. We went into that event with a 168-point lead over Jeff Burton, and in that race, Jeff, Dale Jarrett and Dale Earnhardt all had problems of one kind or another. When the race was over, we found ourselves with a 249-point lead over Dale Earnhardt.

Earnhardt cut our lead to 213 after Martinsville, and we knew he was making noises about catching us. The last person you want getting close to you in the late stages of a championship battle is Earnhardt. They don't call him "The Intimidator" for nothing, so Charlotte became an incredibly important race for us, as it turned out. We sat on the outside pole for the race and were able to win it,

Bobby Labonte's confidence behind the wheel was evident throughout the season, even on the road courses — not typically his forte. Bobby took fourth place at Sears Point in June and followed that with a strong fifth-place finish at Watkins Glen in August.

the field, and on the final pit stop, the crew turned me out of the pits in first place — and then the rain came. We were able to win the Pepsi Southern 500 despite being forced to a backup car, and if our confidence wasn't high before that point, it certainly was after Darlington.

Three races later, at Dover, it seemed like the season really turned. We didn't have a great car — we were good enough to finish in the

while Dale had problems. When it was over, we were 252 points ahead of Jeff Burton.

It seemed that those four races — one in August, two in September and one in October — really sealed the championship battle for us. After Charlotte, we simply needed to race smart and not make mistakes, and if our luck held, we could win the championship.

And that's what happened.

Homestead turned out to be an incredible weekend for Joe Gibbs Racing. Tony Stewart and the Home Depot team were totally plugged in for the weekend. They had everything going for them and were clearly the class of the field. We did everything we had to do, and when Tony won the race for the second straight year and we finished fourth, it was simply great. Tony had the win — giving him six for the season — and we had the championship. That lap — when the two Joe Gibbs-owned cars circled around the track and the crews of both teams gathered on pit road to celebrate the success of the entire organization — was an awesome thing to have happen and be a part of. I was grinning from ear to ear, and I know Tony was too.

Looking back at the season, it's a testament to the team that we had the results we had. Our last DNF was at Bristol in the fall of 1999. While others struggled from time to time, we were able to go the entire season without a DNF until we clinched the title in Homestead. That's an unbelievable string of success in a world that is as highly competitive as NASCAR Winston Cup Series racing is today.

By the time we clinched the title, we had 18 top-five finishes in 33 races, including four victories. The work we began last year in the off-season had paid off.

From a personal standpoint, there were some things that came with the title that make me extremely proud. By winning the championship, my brother, Terry, and I became the first brothers to ever win NASCAR Winston Cup Series championships. We're proud of that accomplishment, but I think our parents are even more proud than we are. At the same time, I became the first NASCAR Busch Series champion to go on to win the NASCAR Winston Cup Series title. In the years to come, I hope others are able to emerge from the NASCAR Busch Series ranks to join me on that page in the record book.

It's pretty amazing to me that over the years, only 24 drivers have been able to win the NASCAR Winston Cup Series championship and that Terry and I are part of that group. I can't begin to tell you how hard it is to win the title and to have the dream come true.

Nothing is easy. Believe me. And I had to get a little chuckle the other day when I listened to a message on my answering machine. The call was from my banker, and he left me a message of congratulations — and then jokingly added, "It's a long way from worrying about how you were going to pay for the tires at Caraway Speedway, isn't it?" The important part of the message was that it was only half-joking. I did have to worry about paying for tires, and I had to come through the sport the hard way, earning my way.

That's what makes this championship all the sweeter. It shows — like many others have shown by winning the title before me — that if you work hard enough, you can accomplish the goal you set for yourself in any walk of life.

The championship is obviously a wonderful fulfillment for me and my family, but it is much, much more than that. In many ways, the pleasure of being the champion comes from what it represents.

It means that Joe Gibbs, and Joe Gibbs Racing and Interstate Batteries are also the champions. To me, that's more important than my name being in the record book.

It's so hard to get all the right parts and pieces of the championship puzzle. Everything has to come right, and for a long period of time. The title isn't decided over the course of four or five races, or a few weeks. It is a long, extended, 10-month battle that is waged almost every weekend. One slip-up and you can be toast. You have so many people, all with different personalities, who are working a hundred hours a week, seven days a week, month after month, traveling, not seeing their families, totally immersed in winning this championship. It is a pressure-cooker of the highest order and one little remark, one bad attitude, one problem personality can ruin the dream for everyone.

That's where we have been fortunate. We have a group of people at Joe Gibbs Racing who all work together with such outstanding chemistry it is hard to explain. You have to be there, see it, feel it, to understand it. Joe Gibbs hired some great people, and Jimmy Makar

Sweet gratification finally came for the Interstate Batteries team at Homestead-Miami, the season's penultimate event.

has found the way to get all these different personalities to work for the common goal of winning the championship.

At the same time, the folks at Pontiac have been great to work for, and they gave us good equipment to work with. They helped in every possible way, and between our team and the Pontiac personnel, we found ways to massage the product to make it even better for the racetrack.

Part of the delight for all of us is to win the championship for Interstate Batteries. Norm and Tommy Miller have put their hearts into the team since Joe Gibbs Racing was formed. Their company's advertising budget is keyed on racing. It spends nearly its entire advertising budget with our sport. They have been so devoted with their time, their lives and their company to NASCAR Winston Cup Series racing and Joe Gibbs Racing that winning the title for them is even more special. They are so much more than business partners with us. They are family. And that's what makes it so great for all of us.

I'm sure that during the days ahead I will look back at this season and some of the events will stand out more than others: The Rockingham win that gave the team confidence; Winning the Brickyard 400, one of the biggest races of the year and helping Interstate Batteries with that great victory; Winning the Southern 500 at Darlington, one of the greatest races a driver can win in his career; Winning at Charlotte in the fall, always an important race because it is where nearly all of the teams call home; Making the best of races where we didn't have the best car, or got involved in someone else's problems and still came home with good finishes.

All of these things are the parts of a season a driver has to have if he is going to win the NASCAR Winston Cup Series championship. A great car owner, a wonderful sponsor and a fabulous crew chief. A team of people working behind the scenes to make the cars the very best they can be, and a talented group of people traveling week to week on the road, making the cars even better at the track. A pit

crew that doesn't know how to quit and gets the job done stop after stop on pit road.

Every one of those parts is crucially important. Even more important, in some ways, is to have good racing luck, and we had everything going for us this year.

As we get ready to go to New York and accept the NASCAR Winston Cup Series championship, I need to thank all of the people at Joe Gibbs Racing for their hard work this year, and in the past, that laid the groundwork for our successful run at this year's championship. Everyone had an important role in this title.

And that includes my wife, Donna, and our two children, Tyler and Madison. Without their support and their love, I doubt any of this would be possible.

I am looking forward to all of the changes that will come to the sport in the next few years. We embark on a new journey with different television partners and new tracks added to the schedule. We're going to miss some of the familiar faces from CBS, ESPN and TNN who have been with us for so long and who have become part of our NASCAR family. I know everyone in the garage area would join me in saying "thank you" to all of them for their incredible work through the years that has helped our sport grow to the level it is today.

And while thanking people, I would like to say a special "thank you" to the fans who have supported Joe Gibbs Racing through the years, and to the millions who have followed and support our sport. We are blessed to have fans like you, and I hope you will continue in your support of NASCAR Winston Cup Series racing.

I hope to be a worthy champion during the years to come. Most of all, I look forward to seeing you at the tracks on the circuit during the coming season.

Bobby Labonte
2000 NASCAR Winston Cup Series Champion

Posing with the newest addition to the Labonte household's trophy room are wife Donna, daughter Madison and son Tyler. "Without their support and love," Bobby says, "none of this would be possible."

DAYTONA 500

(Left) Dale Earnhardt Jr. (8) protects the low line with Jeremy Mayfield (12) and Ward Burton (22) dueling on his right. Earnhardt finished 13th in the first race of his rookie season.

(Right) Dale Jarrett opened defense of his championship by dominating Speedweeks, including wins in the Bud Shootout and the Daytona 500.

With new color schemes, a host of new faces, new crewmen, different drivers and new Monte Carlos and Tauruses all ready for competition, Daytona International Speedway's garage gates opened for the initial event of the season — and of the new millennium.

And as though those were not enough changes, NASCAR had also issued new rules for teams to follow regarding shock absorbers and springs, mandating that teams use a standard set of shocks that were handed to crew members during pre-event inspection. Teams also had to follow a new rule that specified a minimum spring rate, which was also checked during inspection.

The purpose of the new mandate was to keep the cars from "squatting" down on the track and to make competition more equal for all teams. The changes also alleviated some of the white-knuckled, teeth-jarring setups many teams had resorted to over the last year. The new rules turned the emphasis, particularly during qualifying sessions, back to horsepower and aerodynamics — to the delight of some teams and the displeasure of others.

With 57 teams on hand, there was no question that some would be hugely disappointed when Bud Pole qualifying was completed at The Beach. Only 43 cars would make the field, leaving some 14 teams by the wayside after months of preparation for what many consider the biggest race of the

Ricky Rudd rocketed to an uncontested victory in his Gatorade Twin 125, answering any questions regarding his off-season move to Robert Yates Racing.

season. All knew that qualifying times were of utmost importance, and many teams hoped that the Gatorade Twin 125s would offer the opportunity to race into the 500 if they were unable to post fast qualifying times. The first 15 finishers in each of the Gatorade Twins would automatically make the field.

With his engine department working day and night, and using his airplane to fly motors back and forth daily from Daytona to Charlotte, Robert Yates was determined to wring every bit of available horsepower out of his Ford powerplants. The crews of the Quality Care "88" and the Texaco "28" had worked 15-hour days during the month of January, and when the first round of Bud Pole qualifying was completed, all the effort had paid off.

Dale Jarrett, who failed to win a single Bud Pole on the way to his first NASCAR Winston Cup Series championship in 1999, had claimed the pole for the Daytona 500. And his teammate,

(Above) Bill Elliott, looking very much like the Elliott of old, posted the third-fastest lap in Bud Pole qualifying, snatched the win from Jarrett in his Gatorade Twin 125, and then took third in the "500."

(Right) Jeff Burton (99) and Roush teammate Mark Martin (6) work the outside of Tony Stewart (20) with Joe Nemechek in tow. The Roush Fords were in contention for the win, but when Martin made his move, Burton turned from friend to foe, leaving Mark hung out on the high side to fight for a fifth-place finish. Burton came home second behind Jarrett.

(Below) Joe Nemechek's Andy Petree-owned Chevrolet gets outfitted with new shocks before entering inspection. NASCAR officials supplied the newly mandated suspension parts to all the teams upon their arrival at Daytona.

In his NASCAR Winston Cup Series debut, Scott Pruett raised some eyebrows by posting the ninth-fastest qualifying speed in a Taurus fielded by the new Cal Wells team. In the race, Pruett handled the tight traffic and brought the Tide Ford home on the lead lap in 19th place.

Ricky Rudd, was right beside him on the front row — the first time teammates had claimed the front row for the Daytona 500 since 1992 when Bill Elliott and Sterling Marlin turned the trick for Junior Johnson's team. Jarrett would not have to wait all year to know he was in the 2001 Bud Shootout.

Even more impressive was the fact that rookie Scott Pruett, with a Yates motor under the hood of his Tide Ford, was ninth fastest after the first round, ensuring a solid start in the 500 for the new Cal Wells team.

Bill Elliott surprised many by posting the third-fastest lap, nearly knocking Rudd off the front row in the process. Mike Skinner and Mark Martin were fourth and fifth fastest ahead of Ward Burton and Rusty Wallace, while John Andretti was eighth fastest. Rookie Dave Blaney gave his new Bill Davis-owned team a jump-start by turning the 10th-fastest lap in his Amoco Pontiac.

With the first round of qualifying complete, Jarrett then switched to his other Quality Care Taurus and blistered the field in the qualifying race for Bud Shootout — held for those who had failed to win a Bud Pole in 1999 — to earn the final starting position in the lucrative main event. Jarrett then used a fast pit stop from his new over-the-wall gang to put himself in the position to power to victory in the 25-lap Bud Shootout. Not a bad accomplishment for one who had to earn his way into the field the hard way!

Many expected Jarrett to run away with his Gatorade Twin, while others were sure that Dale Earnhardt would find a way to extend his incredible string of Twin victories that went back to 1989. Few expected the winner to be Elliott, who had reworked his team during the off-season. But "Awesome Bill" rocketed to victory — his first since 1994 — leading every lap on the way to handing Jarrett his first loss of Speedweeks 2000.

In the second Gatorade Twin, Rudd rolled to an uncontested victory over Mike Skinner, leading the entire distance and showing to all he had made the right decision to sell his team and join forces with Robert Yates Racing.

After the completion of the Gatorade Twins, NASCAR officials used qualifying results and provisionals to complete the field for the Daytona 500. Making the starting lineup with provisionals were

(Above) Rookie Matt Kenseth fit right in at The Beach, taking a top-10 finish in the Daytona 500 to gain the early lead in rookie points.

(Left) Robby Gordon (13) finds himself caught in the middle with Johnny Benson (10) on the low side and Terry Labonte (5) up high. Benson and the Tyler Jet team came to Daytona without a sponsor and were able to sign Lycos.com to a one-race contract just in time for the Daytona 500. After Benson nearly won the event, the deal turned into a season-long package.

(Below) Elliott Sadler (21) and Michael Waltrip (7) were the only two cars to post DNFs due to accident damage after getting together off turn four with less than 10 laps to go. Dave Blaney (93) managed to avoid major damage by scooting by on the apron and went on to finish the race in 27th place.

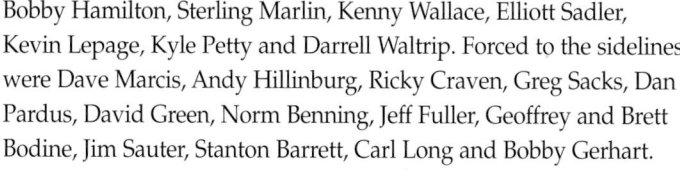

Bobby Hamilton, Sterling Marlin, Kenny Wallace, Elliott Sadler, Kevin Lepage, Kyle Petty and Darrell Waltrip. Forced to the sidelines were Dave Marcis, Andy Hillinburg, Ricky Craven, Greg Sacks, Dan Pardus, David Green, Norm Benning, Jeff Fuller, Geoffrey and Brett Bodine, Jim Sauter, Stanton Barrett, Carl Long and Bobby Gerhart.

Despite the victories by Elliott and Rudd in the Gatorade Twins, most garage watchers were willing to plunk down their bets on Jarrett to win his third Daytona 500. Then, during "Happy Hour," the final practice session, Jarrett's Ford was involved in a multi-car accident on the track. The rocker panels, exhaust pipes and rear bumper of the red-white-and-blue Ford were damaged, but more importantly, the nose of the Taurus was also in disarray. Team owner Yates immediately dispatched his plane back to Charlotte to pick up three of the team's fabricators and body specialists, and when they

He may be a rookie, but he sure knows how to use the horn! Earnhardt Jr. closes up on Jimmy Spencer in a 200 mph game of tag while Jeremy Mayfield (12) tries to close the gap on Kenseth.

arrived at Daytona they immediately fell to work making repairs to the pole-winning car.

By race morning, the team felt the car was back to its original aerodynamic state, but there would be no true answer until Jarrett pushed the pedal in anger. After feeling the car out for the first four laps, Jarrett moved past Skinner to take the point, and with the help of fellow Blue Oval drivers Elliott and Rusty Wallace, he immediately began to separate himself from the field. A broken oil line in Jeff Gordon's Chevrolet brought out the yellow flag and erased his lead, but Jarrett felt comfortable in the Ford and knew his crew's hard work late Saturday evening and early Sunday morning had the Taurus back to where it had been before the Saturday accident.

Jarrett ran with the leaders for the remainder of the event before it all came down to a strategy call during a late-race caution: Some cars were given two tires and others took on four. Jarrett found himself fifth in line for the restart with four fresh Goodyears.

With 16 laps to go, Johnny Benson was the upstart leader after taking just two tires, with Mark Martin second, Jarrett third and Jeff

Burton fourth. Dale had agreed to go with Mark in an effort to pass Benson's Pontiac, but when Martin went high, Jarrett looked in his mirror and saw Burton making a move toward the inside lane. Jarrett immediately turned down, taking second place while Martin, alone on the outside, fell to sixth.

With less than 10 laps left in the race and Jarrett unable to get past Benson, the final caution of the race fell for a six-car accident on the frontstretch. Jarrett knew his Taurus was better on the restarts than Benson's Pontiac, and when the green flag fell for the final time on lap 197, he faked high and went low, pulling into the lead for the last time exiting the second turn. Another multi-car accident forced the event to end under caution, but there was no doubt that Jarrett had enough muscle under the hood of his Taurus to win the event had it finished under green.

Burton came home in second place ahead of Elliott and Rusty Wallace, with Martin rallying to fifth ahead of Bobby and Terry Labonte. Ward Burton was eighth, Ken Schrader ninth, and Matt Kenseth completed the top 10, claiming the highest finish by a rookie.

(Right) Sterling Marlin (40) chases Matt Kenseth (17) with Bobby Hamilton on the inside. The Kodak Chevrolet took Marlin to two straight Daytona 500 wins in 1994 and '95, but this year would finish last, forcing Hamilton to the garage with a blown motor.

(Below Right) The Quality Care crew greets Dale Jarrett along pit road before they all head for victory lane. Most of Jarrett's "new" pit crew had been there before, when they were better known as the Rainbow Warriors.

Jarrett's total winnings for Speedweeks was nearly $2.5 million, including a bonus of $1 million for himself with another $1 million awarded to race fan Melissa Brown as part of the Winston No Bull 5 program. He was extremely proud of his team's accomplishments, but also chagrined to have to give his car to Daytona USA, to be put on display for the next year. The Taurus had won at Talladega in 1998 and had claimed the Pepsi 400 at Daytona last July, in addition to finishing second in both Talladega events last year.

Still, a third Daytona 500 victory, the NASCAR Winston Cup Series point lead and almost $2.5 million in winnings made for an extremely successful opening to the defense of his NASCAR Winston Cup Series championship.

DAYTONA 500 • final results

Even after 500 miles of competition, Dale Jarrett has no problem hoisting the Harley J. Earl trophy. In addition to his third Daytona 500 prize, Jarrett also collected winnings of nearly $2.5 million for his work during Speedweeks 2000.

Fin. Pos.	Start Pos.	Car No.	Driver	Team
1	1	88	Dale Jarrett	Quality Care/Ford Credit Ford
2	14	99	Jeff Burton	Exide Batteries Ford
3	3	94	Bill Elliott	McDonald's Ford
4	5	2	Rusty Wallace	Miller Lite Ford
5	9	6	Mark Martin	Valvoline/Cummins Ford
6	13	18	Bobby Labonte	Interstate Batteries Pontiac
7	25	5	Terry Labonte	Kellogg's Chevrolet
8	6	22	Ward Burton	Caterpillar Pontiac
9	23	36	Ken Schrader	M&M's Pontiac
10	24	17	Matt Kenseth	DeWalt Tools Ford
11	19	12	Jeremy Mayfield	Mobil 1 Ford
12	27	10	Johnny Benson	Lycos.com Pontiac
13	8	8	Dale Earnhardt Jr.	Budweiser Chevrolet
14	18	42	Kenny Irwin	BellSouth Chevrolet
15	2	28	Ricky Rudd	Texaco/Havoline Ford
16	4	31	Mike Skinner	Lowe's Chevrolet
17	7	20	Tony Stewart	Home Depot Pontiac
18	17	13	Robby Gordon	Turtlewax/Duracell/CD2 Ford
19	15	32	Scott Pruett	Tide Ford
20	32	77	Robert Pressley	Jasper Engines Ford
21	21	3	Dale Earnhardt	GM Goodwrench Service Chevrolet
22	30	43	John Andretti	STP/Cheerios Pontiac

Fin. Pos.	Start Pos.	Car No.	Driver	Team
23	29	97	Chad Little	John Deere Ford
24	38	40	Sterling Marlin	Coors Light Chevrolet
25	42	44	Kyle Petty	Hot Wheels Pontiac
26	33	9	Stacy Compton	Kodiak Ford
27	31	93	Dave Blaney	Amoco Pontiac
28	28	41	Rick Mast	Big Daddy's BBQ Sauce Chevrolet
29	39	55	Kenny Wallace	Square D Chevrolet
30	22	26	Jimmy Spencer	Big Kmart Ford
31	36	1	Steve Park	Pennzoil Chevrolet
32	43	66	Darrell Waltrip	Big Kmart/Route 66 Ford
33	35	14	Mike Bliss	Conseco Pontiac
34	11	24	Jeff Gordon	DuPont Automotive Finishes Chevrolet
35	20	25	Jerry Nadeau	MichaelHoligan.com Chevrolet
36	41	16	Kevin Lepage	NorthernLight.com Ford
37	26	90	Ed Berrier	Hills Brothers Coffee Ford
38	40	21	Elliott Sadler	CITGO Ford
39	10	7	Michael Waltrip	Nations Rent Chevrolet
40	34	75	Wally Dallenbach	Turner Broadcasting Ford
41	12	15	Derrike Cope	Fenley-Moore Motorsports Ford
42	16	33	Joe Nemechek	Oakwood Homes Chevrolet
43	37	4	Bobby Hamilton	Kodak Chevrolet

DURA LUBE/KMART *400*

(Left) Wally Dallenbach waits for new tires and fuel in his second race for Galaxy Motorsports, the first with new sponsor Rotozip.

(Right) Pole-winner Rusty Wallace holds the early lead with eventual race winner Bobby Labonte trailing closely.

With the new Ford Tauruses finishing 1-2-3-4-5 and with Terry Labonte's new Monte Carlo the highest finishing Chevrolet in seventh place in the season-opening Daytona 500, the engines had barely been shut off at The Beach before the politicking began.

Chevrolet drivers, car owners, crew chiefs and mechanics all joined in the posturing, asking NASCAR for something to make the brand new Monte Carlos more competitive with the reworked Fords. NASCAR countered by saying it would take a look at the situation, and when the crews arrived at North Carolina Speedway the next weekend, the focus was on how both the Fords and Chevrolets would do on an intermediate-sized track with unrestricted engines.

A total of 47 teams were on hand and Ted Musgrave found himself behind the wheel of the No. 60, substituting for Geoffrey Bodine. Bodine had been injured in an accident during the NASCAR Craftsman Truck Series event at Daytona, and although he was on the mend, he would be out of Joe Bessey's Power Team cars for the next few races. Musgrave agreed to help out until Bodine was ready to return.

Rockingham's 1.017-mile oval offers a huge challenge to drivers trying to post fast laps around the track. Drivers have to toe a very fine line between being aggressive and being overaggressive when

With no cautions over the second half of the event, NASCAR flagman Jimmy Howell stayed very busy directing lapped traffic with the "move over" flag.

ond straight race, put the Texaco "Star Car" on the outside of the front row.

Behind the Ford front row, Bobby Labonte put the spurs to his Interstate Batteries Pontiac to claim the inside of the second row, with Dale Earnhardt alongside after earning his first top-10 start at Rockingham since February 1993. Jeff Gordon and Matt Kenseth made up the third row, with Dale Earnhardt Jr. and Joe Nemechek right behind. Bolstered by his Daytona 500 finish, Bill Elliott claimed the ninth-fastest lap with his McDonald's Ford, and Darrell Waltrip was gleefully jumping

---

(Above Left) Reunited for the 2000 season, the 1996 championship team of Terry Labonte and crew chief Gary DeHart arrived in Rockingham feeling as good as any Chevrolet team could. Their seventh-place finish at Daytona was best among the Monte Carlos.

(Left) John Andretti has a good chuckle before taking to the track for a solid, 12th-place performance.

(Below) In his second start with Hendrick Motorsports, a pensive Jerry Nadeau considers his strategy for moving through the field from his 22nd starting spot at Rockingham.

putting their cars into the turns. Tiptoeing around the track brings a slow speed, but throwing the car hard into a corner causes it to push up the banking, costing precious time. Somewhere in the middle is the key to a quick lap, and it often means having total trust in your car.

The one who found the best combination of driving his car into the corners — and having it stick there — was Rusty Wallace, who claimed his second career Rockingham pole and set a new track record of over 158 miles per hour in the Miller Lite Ford. He was more than a mile per hour faster than Ricky Rudd who, for the sec-

(Top) Bill Elliott's Taurus sports a commemorative paint scheme to celebrate the 25th anniversary of Elliott's NASCAR Winston Cup Series debut in the 1976 Carolina 500.

(Above) Jeff Gordon (24) eases past Ricky Rudd along Rockingham's frontstretch, after Rudd qualified on the outside pole for the second straight week. Both Rudd and Gordon scored top-10 finishes in the event.

(Right) Mark Martin gets four tires and fuel amidst a flurry of pit-road activity during one the day's four caution periods. Mark fought his way through the field from his 33rd starting position and led on three occasions before settling to an 8th-place finish, one lap off the winning pace.

up and down after claiming the final top-10 starting position.

Several of the sport's big names — Mark Martin, Daytona 500 winner Dale Jarrett, Jeff Burton, Terry Labonte and Tony Stewart, to name a few — were missing from the top 10 after Bud Pole qualifying, but all made it into the field. Bobby Hamilton, Chad Little, Ted Musgrave, Wally Dallenbach, Robert Pressley, Dave Marcis and Ed Berrier used provisionals to make the 43-car field, leaving Ricky Craven, Scott

Childress Racing teammates Mike Skinner (31) and Dale Earnhardt had occasion to race together during the day, before Earnhardt went on to wage a stirring run in pursuit of race-leader Bobby Labonte.

Pruett, Dave Blaney and Mike Bliss out of the starting lineup for the second race of the season.

After Dale Jarrett's dominant performance at Daytona, tens of thousands of fans arrived on Sunday morning for the Dura Lube/Kmart 400 hoping to see the fender-to-fender excitement that typifies racing at The Rock. They were in for a treat.

There were eight lead changes before the first third of the race was in the books, and it was clear this would not be a Ford parade as Daytona had been, as Ward Burton, Bobby Hamilton, Mark Martin, Sterling Marlin and pole-sitter Rusty Wallace all swapped the lead. It began to look like Hamilton and Ward Burton had the best cars in the field, but Hamilton's challenge eventually ended with engine problems. In the second half of the event, Bobby Labonte made his moves to get to the front of the pack, and he took over the point with just over 100 laps remaining. The Texan seemed to have the race in hand ... until he heard on his radio that the wily seven-time champion, Dale Earnhardt, was making a charge.

Dale was up over the steering wheel, for sure, and steadily chopped at Labonte's seemingly insurmountable 5.91-second lead. Labonte saw him coming and knew that Earnhardt's Chevrolet was stronger over a long run than his own Pontiac. It had been that way throughout the afternoon, and Bobby could only hope he had enough of an edge to make it to the line before the black Chevrolet closed on his rear bumper.

This time it was Labonte's turn to manage his tires the best and hold onto his lead. Earnhardt managed to buzzsaw the margin

The last time they raced at Rockingham, Ward Burton (22) finished second to brother Jeff (99). This time, Ward finished third, but way ahead of Jeff, who took 32nd place. Ward's finish, combined with an eighth place at Daytona, bumped him up to third in the point standings.

(Left) Bobby Labonte's championship pit crew was on form at Rockingham, providing fresh tires, fuel and the necessary adjustments to get their driver to the front of the field.

(Below Left) Labonte brings the Interstate Pontiac to the finish line just over a second ahead of a charging Dale Earnhardt. Even though Earnhardt was on the move, Labonte's win was a convincing one, having led the final 113 laps, all under green.

down to just over a second, but he ran out of laps. Four or five more and he would have been gnawing at the rear bumper of the Pontiac. But the race was 393 laps, not 402 or 403.

Ward Burton put together a rock-solid third place while Stewart claimed fourth place, the final driver on the lead lap at the conclusion of the event. Jarrett was fifth ahead of Robert Yates Racing teammate Ricky Rudd. Jeremy Mayfield, Mark Martin, Steve Park and Jeff Gordon completed the top 10, all a lap behind the leaders.

Pole-sitter Wallace finished 11th, and Musgrave, in his first outing as a substitute for Geoffrey Bodine, drove to a 16th-place finish.

After two races, the point standings had a familiar look at the top, with Jarrett just five points ahead of Bobby Labonte. With Las Vegas next on the schedule, both drivers hoped the dice would continue to roll in their favor in the third race of the season.

DURA LUBE/KMART 400 • final results

Labonte smiles for photographers after collecting his first Rockingham trophy. The win moved Bobby into second place in the standings, five points behind Jarrett.

Fin. Pos.	Start Pos.	Car No.	Driver	Team	Fin. Pos.	Start Pos.	Car No.	Driver	Team
1	3	18	Bobby Labonte	Interstate Batteries Pontiac	23	24	7	Michael Waltrip	Nations Rent Chevrolet
2	4	3	Dale Earnhardt	GM Goodwrench Service Chevrolet	24	19	55	Kenny Wallace	Square D Chevrolet
3	11	22	Ward Burton	Caterpillar Pontiac	25	9	94	Bill Elliott	McDonald's Ford
4	15	20	Tony Stewart	Home Depot Pontiac	26	35	26	Jimmy Spencer	Big Kmart Ford
5	23	88	Dale Jarrett	Quality Care/Ford Credit Ford	27	28	16	Kevin Lepage	NorthernLight.com Ford
6	2	28	Ricky Rudd	Texaco/Havoline Ford	28	26	21	Elliott Sadler	CITGO Ford
7	27	12	Jeremy Mayfield	Mobil 1 Ford	29	22	25	Jerry Nadeau	MichaelHoligan.com Chevrolet
8	33	6	Mark Martin	Valvoline/Cummins Ford	30	8	33	Joe Nemechek	Oakwood Homes Chevrolet
9	18	1	Steve Park	Pennzoil Chevrolet	31	13	44	Kyle Petty	Hot Wheels Pontiac
10	5	24	Jeff Gordon	DuPont Automotive Finishes Chevrolet	32	16	99	Jeff Burton	Exide Batteries Ford
11	1	2	Rusty Wallace	Miller Lite Ford	33	29	41	Rick Mast	Big Daddy's BBQ Sauce Chevrolet
12	20	43	John Andretti	STP Pontiac	34	21	9	Stacy Compton	Kodiak Ford
13	36	36	Ken Schrader	M&M's Pontiac	35	32	11	Brett Bodine	Ralphs Supermarkets Ford
14	34	10	Johnny Benson	Lycos.com Pontiac	36	43	90	Ed Berrier	Hills Brothers Coffee Ford
15	14	40	Sterling Marlin	Coors Light Chevrolet	37	6	17	Matt Kenseth	DeWalt Tools Ford
16	39	60	Ted Musgrave	Power Team Chevrolet	38	25	13	Robby Gordon	Turtlewax/Duracell/CD2 Ford
17	17	5	Terry Labonte	Kellogg's Chevrolet	39	10	66	Darrell Waltrip	Big Kmart/Route 66 Ford
18	38	97	Chad Little	John Deere Ford	40	37	4	Bobby Hamilton	Kodak Chevrolet
19	7	8	Dale Earnhardt Jr.	Budweiser Chevrolet	41	42	71	Dave Marcis	Realtree Chevrolet
20	40	75	Wally Dallenbach	Rotozip Ford	42	30	27	Jeff Fuller	Pfizer/Viagra Ford
21	12	31	Mike Skinner	Lowe's Chevrolet	43	41	77	Robert Pressley	Jasper Engines Ford
22	31	42	Kenny Irwin	BellSouth Chevrolet					

CARSDIRECT.COM *400*

(Left) Joe Nemechek (33) feels some pressure from Ward Burton (22), with Rusty Wallace and Dale Earnhardt on the inside.

(Right) Jeff Burton shields his eyes while watching the track during Saturday practice. The sun's absence on Sunday worked in his favor — again.

By thwarting Dale Earnhardt's charge at The Rock, Bobby Labonte moved to within five points of leader Dale Jarrett in the early battle for this year's NASCAR Winston Cup Series title. Labonte celebrated his victory with the obligatory champagne shower, but knew that it was far too early to be thinking about championships.

After all, there were just two events in the books and months of competition ahead before anyone would be grinning about their title chances. At the same time, however, Labonte also knew that his Joe Gibbs-owned team had been through the battle in 1999 and had learned that consistency delivers championships. The Interstate Batteries-sponsored team had spent the winter months planning how to better take advantage of points in every race, and Labonte was determined to gain every point he could in every single event.

Ward Burton was sandwiched between Labonte and fourth-place Mark Martin in the point standings after the first two races, while Penske teammates Rusty Wallace and Jeremy Mayfield held down the fifth and sixth places. A rejuvenated Dale Earnhardt was in seventh ahead of Ricky Rudd and Tony Stewart, while Ken Schrader was 10th as the teams headed for the glitz and glamour of Las Vegas.

Jimmy Spencer wonders what it will take to get his season on track: His best finish so far was a 26th at Rockingham.

It hadn't taken Las Vegas long to become one of the most popular stops on the circuit. "Glitter Gulch" offers something for everyone — from top-notch hotels to restaurants to nightlife. It is a mecca for sponsors, offering great opportunities for hospitality. And the racing at Las Vegas Motor Speedway has been competitive, to say the least, since the NASCAR Winston Cup Series regulars began competing there just three years ago.

Jeff Gordon arrived in Vegas hoping his luck would take a turn for the better. He was 22nd in the point standings, 140 points behind Jarrett. Although it was far too early to be pushing the panic button, Gordon also knew that he couldn't afford to fall much further behind. As far as he was concerned, there was no better place to get his season back on track. With his rebuilt crew working as hard as

A trip to Las Vegas always seems to bring out the special paint schemes. Among the brightest and the best were Sterling Marlin's Coors Chevrolet (above) and Steve Park's Pennzoil Monte Carlo (below). Unfortunately for Park, the new colors did not prove lucky: His engine let go after 92 laps forcing him to a last-place finish.

any other team in the garage area and with the chemistry on track between himself and new crew chief Robbie Loomis, Gordon hoped to emerge from Bud Pole qualifying with his first pole position of the season.

Instead, Gordon was only the fourth-fastest Chevrolet driver following the first qualifying session and found himself 10th on the rundown sheet, almost two miles per hour slower than pole sitter Ricky Rudd.

Ricky's Texaco Ford set a new track record during qualifying at 172.563 miles per hour — and he needed all of that speed to keep rookie Scott Pruett off the pole after the Tide Ford driver posted the best

(Below) Covered race cars line the starting grid on Sunday morning under a gray overcast sky — a sky that would eventually dictate the outcome of the race.

qualifying performance of his young stock car racing career. Dale Earnhardt Jr. continued his torrid qualifying performances to claim the inside of the second row, with Bobby Labonte alongside. Martin and Jarrett made up the third row, while Michael Waltrip and surprising Johnny Benson were seventh and eighth fastest. Jerry Nadeau barely nosed out Hendrick Motorsports teammate Jeff Gordon for the

(Left) Veteran drivers Brett Bodine (left) and Darrell Waltrip have a chance for some lighthearted conversation in the LVMS garage area, but the rest of the weekend was not altogether pleasant for them. Waltrip had to use the Former Champion's provisional to make the field, while Bodine failed to qualify for the race.

(Below) Scott Pruett leads this pack trailed by Mike Skinner (31), Kenny Irwin (42) and Terry Labonte (5). Pruett qualified on the front row in only his third NASCAR Winston Cup Series start, but went from next-to-first to next-to-last in the race.

LAS VEGAS · U.S.A.

(Above) Mark Martin (6) follows teammate Jeff Burton (99) with Sterling Marlin (40) in between. Later, Jeff would get help from Mark in lapped traffic, and then have to overtake him for the win.

(Left) The Quality Care crew cranks off a strong pit stop for driver Dale Jarrett. Dale and Bobby Labonte swapped the top two positions in the point standings, with Labonte finishing fifth in the race, two spots ahead of Jarrett.

ninth-fastest lap, while Jeff Burton and Robby Gordon had solid runs that barely missed the top 10.

Ward Burton, John Andretti, Bill Elliott, Kenny Wallace, Kyle Petty, Wally Dallenbach and Darrell Waltrip used provisionals to make the field, leaving Rick Mast, Mike Bliss, Ed Berrier, Brett Bodine, Dave Marcis and Austin Cameron on the sidelines for the CarsDirect.com 400.

After rolling to victory in Saturday's NASCAR Busch Series race, Jeff Burton zipped from the victory lane ceremonies to the NASCAR Winston Cup Series garage for "Happy Hour" in his Exide Ford. Arriving at his car, he found his crew members going about their

work with bigger smiles than they usually carried. They had already seen the weather report for Sunday — and there was a strong possibility of rain.

Rain? In Las Vegas? Yes, rain.

No wonder the crew members were smiling: Last spring, Burton won the rain-shortened race at Darlington. Then at the Southern 500 it rained again — and who happened to be at the point that time? Yep. Burton. That Darlington race was a Winston No Bull 5 event, and Jeff pocketed the $1-million bonus. This week, the CarsDirect.com 400 was also a Winston No Bull 5 event, and that combined with rain in the forecast had the Exide team feeling lucky.

Race morning, it was apparent that the weather would, indeed, play a part in the outcome of the CarsDirect.com 400. Burton and Roush Racing teammate Mark Martin made it clear from the start they were not going to wait around, and by lap 19, Martin was at the

point with Burton right behind him as the first rainsqualls swept across the track. The red flag was displayed and the event was held up for more than an hour. When the green flag waved again, it was clear to everyone that more rain was coming, and Burton was determined to be at the point when the rain arrived.

He moved to the lead for the first time on lap 60 and established himself there, giving up the point only during a round of green-flag pit stops. Shortly after the 100-lap mark, Burton encountered his brother, Ward, and became frustrated trying to put a lap on the Caterpillar Pontiac. Jeff let Martin into the lead, hoping Mark could find a way to get past the yellow-and-black Grand Prix, and eventually Martin did. At that point, with the skies turning darker by the minute and the halfway point of the race fast approaching, Burton knew it was time to make his move and try to find a way around Martin.

He worked and worked, and finally eased past Martin to regain the point on lap 136. Stewart also pushed his Home Depot Pontiac past Martin's Valvoline Ford, and on lap 148, the event had to be stopped for the second time due to rain. With the forecast promising sustained precipitation, NASCAR officials were finally forced to call

the race, and Burton claimed yet another rain-shortened event. In the process, he also won the Winston No Bull 5 $1-million bonus and helped Joyce Williams of Port Isabel, Texas, become an instant millionaire as the fan paired with Burton in the Winston No Bull 5 program.

Stewart held on to second, with Martin third ahead of Bill Elliott. Bobby Labonte finished fifth, with Johnny Benson sixth and Dale Jarrett seventh. Earnhardt was eighth, with Joe Nemechek ninth and Dale Earnhardt Jr. 10th. Jeff Gordon, who had hoped to get his season back on track at Vegas, finished 28th, a lap behind.

CARSDIRECT.COM 400 • final results

Giant screen TV monitors are being used more and more frequently at NASCAR events, and they are very popular among the fans in attendance.

Fin. Pos.	Start Pos.	Car No.	Driver	Team	Fin. Pos.	Start Pos.	Car No.	Driver	Team
1	11	99	Jeff Burton	Exide Batteries Ford	23	37	22	Ward Burton	Caterpillar Pontiac
2	16	20	Tony Stewart	Home Depot Pontiac	24	25	42	Kenny Irwin	BellSouth Chevrolet
3	5	6	Mark Martin	Valvoline/Cummins Ford	25	38	43	John Andretti	STP/Cheerios Pontiac
4	39	94	Bill Elliott	McDonald's Ford	26	28	60	Ted Musgrave	Power Team Chevrolet
5	4	18	Bobby Labonte	Interstate Batteries Pontiac	27	20	31	Mike Skinner	Lowe's Chevrolet
6	8	10	Johnny Benson	Lycos.com Pontiac	28	10	24	Jeff Gordon	DuPont Automotive Finishes Chevrolet
7	6	88	Dale Jarrett	Quality Care/Ford Credit Ford	29	41	44	Kyle Petty	Hot Wheels Pontiac
8	33	3	Dale Earnhardt	GM Goodwrench Service Chevrolet	30	35	26	Jimmy Spencer	Big Kmart Ford
9	18	33	Joe Nemechek	Oakwood Homes Chevrolet	31	24	5	Terry Labonte	Kellogg's Chevrolet
10	3	8	Dale Earnhardt Jr.	Budweiser Chevrolet	32	32	9	Stacy Compton	Kodiak Ford
11	14	16	Kevin Lepage	FamilyClick.com Ford	33	7	7	Michael Waltrip	Nations Rent Chevrolet
12	1	28	Ricky Rudd	Texaco/Havoline Ford	34	31	4	Bobby Hamilton	Kodak Chevrolet
13	12	13	Robby Gordon	Turtlewax/Duracell/CD2 Ford	35	42	75	Wally Dallenbach	WCW/Red Cell Batteries Ford
14	21	17	Matt Kenseth	DeWalt Tools Ford	36	22	27	Jeff Fuller	Pfizer/Viagra Pontiac
15	19	2	Rusty Wallace	Miller Lite Ford	37	26	15	Derrike Cope	EverythingCommerce.com Ford
16	34	36	Ken Schrader	M&M's Pontiac	38	43	66	Darrell Waltrip	Big Kmart/Route 66 Ford
17	15	12	Jeremy Mayfield	Mobil 1 Ford	39	40	55	Kenny Wallace	Square D Chevrolet
18	30	40	Sterling Marlin	Coors Light Chevrolet	40	29	50	Ricky Craven	Midwest Transit Chevrolet
19	27	97	Chad Little	John Deere Ford	41	17	21	Elliott Sadler	CITGO Ford
20	9	25	Jerry Nadeau	MichaelHoligan.com Chevrolet	42	2	32	Scott Pruett	Tide Ford
21	13	77	Robert Pressley	Jasper Engines Ford	43	23	1	Steve Park	Pennzoil Chevrolet
22	36	93	Dave Blaney	Amoco Pontiac					

CRACKER BARREL
OLD COUNTRY STORE 500

MARCH 12, 2000 • ATLANTA MOTOR SPEEDWAY

(Left) Dale Earnhardt (3) and Bobby Labonte flash across the line in a near photo finish.

(Right) Earnhardt, joined by wife Teresa, celebrates the thrilling win that led Chevrolet back to victory lane.

J eff Burton's rain-shortened $1.3-million Las Vegas victory pushed the Exide Ford driver to fifth place in the point standings and made him the third different driver to win in the first three events of the season. But it also opened the door to changes for the Chevrolet teams.

Based on the results of the first three events combined with the findings from wind tunnel tests, NASCAR made the decision to give some help to the Bowtie Brigade, allowing crew chiefs to extend the bottom of the front air dams of the Monte Carlos two inches to create additional downforce on the front of the cars. Some crew chiefs automatically said the change was not enough, while others nodded quietly, knowing the changes at the front of the cars would give the teams what they needed to be ultra-competitive at the high-speed Atlanta Motor Speedway, the next stop on this year's NASCAR Winston Cup Series tour. With only one Chevrolet driver represented in the top 11 in the point standings after the first three races of the season, it was high time for the Bowtie Brigade to begin putting some victories on the board.

The combination of Bobby Labonte's fifth place at Las Vegas and Dale Jarrett's seventh place created a new leader in the NASCAR Winston Cup Series point standings, with Labonte now on top by a mere

Jeff Gordon managed a ninth-place finish at Atlanta — his best of the season so far.

four points. Mark Martin held down third place, nine points behind Jarrett, while Tony Stewart's second place at Vegas moved him to fourth, 48 behind Labonte and 15 ahead of Vegas winner Jeff Burton.

Bill Elliott remained a surprising sixth place in the standings, while Dale Earnhardt continued to impress with his seventh place, just a single point behind Elliott. Rusty Wallace was eighth, four behind Earnhardt, while Ward Burton was now ninth, 84 behind Labonte and a single point ahead of Ricky Rudd.

Bobby Labonte tried to deflect discussions about his chances of winning a championship, telling reporters that there was so much of the season left there was no way to even think of titles yet. But Bobby liked his chances at Atlanta: His record at the track has simply been outstanding in recent races, with four victories in the last seven events at Ed Clark's speed plant. The Interstate Batteries Pontiac selected for competition by Labonte and crew chief Jimmy Makar was the same one he had won with at Atlanta last year. That particular chassis had also posted a win at Michigan, was second at Charlotte and Indianapolis, and had also won the pole position for the fall Charlotte event. He knew he had a strong mount under him when the first round of Bud Pole qualifying took place at Atlanta.

At the end of the session, however, Bobby wondered just how good his chances were going to be in the race. He qualified 22nd, almost 2.5 miles per hour slower than pole-winner Jarrett, while Dale Earnhardt Jr. continued his strong qualifying performances to grab the outside of the first row. Steve Park turned in the third-fastest time, while

Clear skies and bright sunshine welcomed the Atlanta fans — quite a contrast to the stormy Nevada desert of a week ago.

(Above) Bobby Labonte charges into the first turn on a restart followed closely by Mike Skinner and Dale Earnhardt. Skinner led the most laps in the race and appeared headed for his initial NASCAR Winston Cup Series win.

(Right) Kevin Lepage (16), running alongside John Andretti, posted a sparkling qualifying effort that was good enough for fifth place on the starting grid. From there, Lepage jumped to an early lead before problems dropped him out of contention.

rookie Matt Kenseth kept pace with "Little E" by notching the fourth-fastest lap. Kevin Lepage and Jerry Nadeau made up the third row, with Jeff Gordon and Joe Nemechek seventh and eighth fastest. Dave Blaney, yet another rookie, qualified ninth, with Elliott beating Martin for the final starting position in the top 10.

It was obvious the changes made to the Chevrolets were good ones: Five of the fastest 10 cars wore Monte Carlo nameplates.

The second round of Bud Pole qualifying fell victim to rain, so first-round times and provisionals were used to fill the remainder of the field. Terry Labonte, Bobby Hamilton, Sterling Marlin, Kyle Petty, Ted Musgrave and Ken Schrader used provisional spots to make the starting lineup, and Darrell Waltrip used the Former Champion's provisional for the third time in the first four races of the season.

Elliott Sadler's Wood Brothers Ford, running here with Ken Schrader, sports a retro look. Sadler fought to 14th from his 31st-place start, while Schrader took the M&M's Pontiac to a top-five finish.

The Kodak Chevrolet got a little heated up at the rear, but Bobby Hamilton still managed a 13th-place finish after having to use a provisional to make the field.

The fact that this was the final event in which 1999 point standings were used to determine provisionals left some strong-running cars out of the event. Johnny Benson, 11th in the driver standings after the first three races, went home, with Tyler Jet Motorsports finishing the 1999 season 35th in the owner point standings. Robby Gordon had no provisionals with his new team although he currently sat 22nd in the point standings, and Mike Bliss had no provisionals to use with A.J. Foyt's new team. Dave Marcis and Ed Berrier, in Junie Donlavey's Ford, were the other drivers to miss the race.

On a cool and sunny Sunday afternoon, the green flag dropped and the field rumbled up to speed. Labonte left no doubt he would be a contender, immediately fighting his way up through the field. His Interstate Batteries Pontiac was set up for long runs, and as other cars began slipping and sliding on the track, Labonte inexorably closed in on the leaders. No matter how good Labonte was, however, it appeared this race was going to go to Mike Skinner, whose Lowe's Chevrolet was simply the class of the field.

Several times in the past, Skinner has appeared to be within reach of his first career NASCAR Winston Cup Series victory, but this time it looked as though the engraver was already at work on the winner's trophy.

Then, with 20 laps left in the race, Skinner lost the engine in his Lowe's Monte Carlo, and the event took on an entirely new com-

Eventual winner Dale Earnhardt manages to avoid a spinning Wally Dallenbach — an incident that brought out the second caution flag of the race. Wally later was involved in an accident that ended his day in the garage.

The two drivers blasted out of the fourth turn with Earnhardt high and Labonte low. Bobby gave it all he had, but he came up just inches short, with Earnhardt shoving the Monte Carlo across the line on sheer will power. The victory was the 75th of his storied career and the first for him at Atlanta since the spring race in 1996.

Mark Martin was third, with Park posting a great run to finish fourth ahead of Nemechek. Chad Little and Todd Bodine also had sparkling runs to claim sixth and seventh, ahead of Ward Burton, Jeff Gordon and Bill Elliott.

Earnhardt was bursting with joy and pride in his accomplishment. He had underscored the fact that his team was, in his eyes, a bona fide championship contender, and he was proud to be hoisting the beautiful trophy symbolic of the Atlanta victory. What he liked best was his "hoisting partner," General Colin Powell, the event's Grand Marshal. There are few drivers who have a deeper appreciation for patriotism than Earnhardt. To share victory lane with one of his longtime heroes made his 75th NASCAR Winston Cup Series victory one he would remember for the rest of his career.

plexion. Dale Earnhardt was at the point, and his GM Goodwrench Service Chevrolet was perfect on short runs. Behind him, Labonte knew there probably weren't enough laps for him to reel in the black Chevrolet. One thing about Labonte, though — there's no quit in the young Texan.

He fought and scratched and clawed, and little by little he chopped at Earnhardt's margin, closing onto the rear bumper of the Chevrolet in the final laps. Finally, on the last time around the 1.5-mile track, he pulled alongside Earnhardt.

CRACKER BARREL OLD COUNTRY STORE 500 • final results

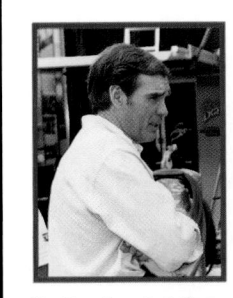

Ray Evernham took time out from building his Dodge teams to attend Atlanta. Earlier in the week, he and Bill Elliott announced their union that will put Elliott behind the wheel of a Dodge in 2001.

Fin. Pos.	Start Pos.	Car No.	Driver	Team	Fin. Pos.	Start Pos.	Car No.	Driver	Team
1	35	3	Dale Earnhardt	GM Goodwrench Service Chevrolet	23	42	36	Ken Schrader	M&M's Pontiac
2	22	18	Bobby Labonte	Interstate Batteries Pontiac	24	32	42	Kenny Irwin	BellSouth Chevrolet
3	11	6	Mark Martin	Valvoline/Cummins Ford	25	28	7	Michael Waltrip	Nations Rent Chevrolet
4	3	1	Steve Park	Pennzoil Chevrolet	26	40	44	Kyle Petty	Hot Wheels Pontiac
5	8	33	Joe Nemechek	Oakwood Homes Chevrolet	27	41	60	Ted Musgrave	Power Team Chevrolet
6	13	97	Chad Little	John Deere Ford	28	33	12	Jeremy Mayfield	Mobil 1 Ford
7	24	91	Todd Bodine	KMC Telecom Chevrolet	29	2	8	Dale Earnhardt Jr.	Budweiser Chevrolet
8	18	22	Ward Burton	Caterpillar Pontiac	30	14	31	Mike Skinner	Lowe's Chevrolet
9	7	24	Jeff Gordon	DuPont Automotive Finishes Chevrolet	31	43	66	Darrell Waltrip	Big Kmart/Route 66 Ford
10	10	94	Bill Elliott	McDonald's Ford	32	30	2	Rusty Wallace	Miller Lite Ford
11	34	28	Ricky Rudd	Texaco/Havoline Ford	33	12	77	Robert Pressley	Jasper Engines Ford
12	39	40	Sterling Marlin	Coors Light Chevrolet	34	27	20	Tony Stewart	Home Depot Pontiac
13	38	4	Bobby Hamilton	Kodak Chevrolet	35	17	9	Stacy Compton	Kodiak/Cougar Ford
14	31	21	Elliott Sadler	CITGO Ford	36	1	88	Dale Jarrett	Quality Care/Ford Credit Ford
15	37	5	Terry Labonte	Kellogg's Chevrolet	37	26	55	Kenny Wallace	Square D/Cooper Lighting Chevrolet
16	16	11	Brett Bodine	Ralphs Supermarkets Ford	38	5	16	Kevin Lepage	FamilyClick.com Ford
17	19	26	Jimmy Spencer	Big Kmart Ford	39	21	75	Wally Dallenbach	Turner Broadcasting Ford
18	23	43	John Andretti	STP/Cheerios Pontiac	40	4	17	Matt Kenseth	DeWalt Tools Ford
19	36	15	Derrike Cope	EverythingCommerce.com Ford	41	20	32	Scott Pruett	Tide Ford
20	9	93	Dave Blaney	Amoco Pontiac	42	6	25	Jerry Nadeau	MichaelHoligan.com Chevrolet
21	25	41	Rick Mast	Big Daddy's BBQ Sauce Chevrolet	43	29	99	Jeff Burton	Exide Batteries Ford
22	15	27	Jeff Fuller	Pfizer/Viagra Pontiac					

MALL.COM 400

MARCH 19, 2000 • DARLINGTON RACEWAY

(Left) Ward Burton is joined by Tommy Baldwin (left), who's making his first trip to a NASCAR Winston Cup Series victory lane as a crew chief.

(Right) Fourth in the points after Atlanta, Bill Elliott is focused and determined to continue his best start to a season in several years.

After the first four races of the season, there were plenty of reasons for raised eyebrows among many of the garage dwellers as practice began at Darlington's venerable egg-shaped oval for the Mall.com 400.

With a victory, a fifth and a second place in the last three races, Bobby Labonte had established his Interstate Batteries Pontiac at the top of the point ladder, and the Texan gave every appearance of being poised to win his first NASCAR Winston Cup Series title.

Mark Martin was solidly in second place despite not having won a NASCAR Winston Cup Series race yet this year, and clearly, his back surgery had been successful. Mark was not disappointed with the fact that his team had yet to visit victory lane, knowing the Valvoline Tauruses coming from the Jack Roush shop were ultra competitive and that his wins would come before much more of the season passed.

Dale Earnhardt's hard-fought Atlanta victory vaulted him to third place in the point standings, 68 markers behind Martin, and had shown everyone in the garage area that he was a valid contender to win the championship. His drive exhibited the old Earnhardt flair, and once again underlined the fact

Crew chief Scott Eggleston (left) makes his point with Sterling Marlin in Darlington's garage.

(Left) Mark Martin (left), second in points and feeling better than he has in years, chats with good friend and teammate Jeff Burton, winner of both Darlington events last season. Burton bested his friend in the Mall.com 400 with a top-five finish. Martin scored in the top 10.

(Below Left) One of Martin's crewmembers tears a plastic film away from the windshield — a much more effective technique than the older "spray and wipe" method.

McDonald's sponsorship on Elliott's Fords. Bill found himself just 40 points behind Earnhardt after the first four races, and he had that competitive look in his eyes again.

Ward Burton was just nine points behind Elliott, and there was every indication that the Bill Davis owned Caterpillar team would be in victory lane soon. The team was competitive every week, and Ward expected he would join brother Jeff as winners of races in 2000 before many more events were in the books.

Robert Yates Racing teammates Dale Jarrett and Ricky Rudd were sixth and seventh in the point standings but in a virtual lock for fifth place with Ward Burton. Jarrett, in defense of his championship, was two points behind the Caterpillar Pontiac driver, while Rudd trailed Jarrett by nine points. Tony Stewart was eighth in the point standings, 32 behind Rudd and 23 ahead of Rusty Wallace, while Ken Schrader was 10th with his M&M's Pontiac, just nine points behind his close friend Wallace.

After failing to qualify for a race since the season-opener at Daytona, A.J. Foyt and team manager Waddell Wilson decided to make a driver change for Darlington. Mike Bliss was out of the car

he had not lost a single iota of his talent. Given competitive machinery, he proved he could win — and perhaps win often — and battle for a record eighth championship.

Right behind Earnhardt was perennial Most Popular Driver Bill Elliott, and Bill was enjoying his return to the front of the field. After struggling for several seasons, Elliott had made the decision to join Ray Evernham's Dodge effort in 2001 — and his early-season performances were showing the evidence of Ray's behind-the-scenes involvement with Bill Elliott Racing in the final season of

and Dick Trickle signed to wheel the Conseco Pontiac at Darlington and Bristol. At that point, Foyt said, he would evaluate the team's progress and needs, and make a final decision regarding a driver for the remainder of the year.

Trickle responded by putting the Conseco Pontiac solidly in the field with the 12th-fastest lap during Bud Pole qualifying, and when the session was completed, Jeff Gordon had scored his third pole at stock car racing's pioneer superspeedway, the 31st pole of his career and his first since the Brickyard 400 last year at Indianapolis.

Gordon needed everything he could get from the DuPont Chevrolet, besting Kevin Lepage's FamilyClick.com Ford by less than a tenth of a second for the pole. Ward Burton was third fastest, a tick in front of Earnhardt, while Martin was on the inside of the third row with Elliott Sadler on his right in the CITGO Ford fielded by the Wood Brothers.

Bobby Labonte and Elliott made up the fourth row ahead of Stewart and Dale Earnhardt Jr., while John Andretti just missed the final top-10 starting position. Chad Little, Kyle Petty, Ted Musgrave (substituting for the recovering Geoffrey Bodine in the Power Team Chevrolet), Robby Gordon, Rick Mast and Stacy Compton used provisionals to get into the field along with Darrell Waltrip, who was forced to use a Former Champion's provisional. That left Derrike

---

(Above Left) Earnhardt is right where he loves to be at Darlington — ready to drop low and sweep past Jeff Burton (99) coming off the turn. Earnhardt, a nine-time Darlington winner, had a strong run to third place in the race to remain third in points.

(Left) A torch and chisel are sometimes the best method to clean off a used tire so it can be properly checked for wear or damage.

(Below) Robby Gordon pilots his No. 13 Taurus down the center of the frontstretch with Rick Mast (41) and Ricky Rudd (28) ready to make their moves on either side.

(Above) In his first race behind the wheel of A.J. Foyt's Pontiac, Dick Trickle (14) shows he hasn't lost his nerve as he tries to best Rusty Wallace (2) and Michael Waltrip (7) on the bottom of the track — a tenuous move at Darlington. Johnny Benson watches the action from behind.

(Left) Jerry Nadeau got tangled up with Kenny Irwin and Jeremy Mayfield before 10 laps were completed in the event. Despite the damage, the Hendrick crew was able to get Jerry back on the track where he finished the race, although 61 laps off the pace.

(Below Left) The race's third caution flew on lap 19 when Ted Musgrave got into the third-turn wall in the Power Team Chevrolet. Ted continued, but his day worsened when the engine failed, ending Ted's effort for the day.

Cope, Ricky Craven, Scott Pruett, Wally Dallenbach and Ed Berrier out of the field, relegated to watching the event from the sidelines.

The opening of the Mall.com 400 at Darlington saw yellow flags govern 15 of the first 22 laps, but that barely deterred Ward Burton, who pushed his yellow-and-black Pontiac to the point after just five laps of green-flag racing. It was the place where fans would see the driver and car for much of the remainder of the event. The Virginian led 188 of the race's 293 laps in a dominating performance that no one in the field could match. Finally, Ward had captured his long-sought second career win.

(Right) Bobby Labonte chases Ward Burton down the frontstretch. The two Pontiac drivers swapped the point four times over the first half of the event, before Burton proved the stronger of the two.

(Below Right) Ward Burton claims victory, the second of his career and the first since Rockingham in October 1995, breaking a winless string of 132 races.

His first victory came at Rockingham in 1995, and many had expected him to return to victory lane much sooner than this. Three times last year he finished second — to his brother Jeff each time — but this time he had everything he needed to take his team to the win.

He beat Jarrett by nearly 1.5 seconds, and handed crew chief Tommy Baldwin his first career NASCAR Winston Cup Series victory. It also was the first time a Pontiac had been to victory lane at Darlington since Joe Weatherly won there in 1963.

Earnhardt continued his strong performances with a third-place finish ahead of Stewart, while Jeff Burton was fifth. Rookie Matt Kenseth had a superb showing, coming home sixth, while Bobby Hamilton was seventh, celebrating a renewal of Kodak's sponsorship for the next five years with the Morgan-McClure team. Jeff Gordon was eighth ahead of Martin and Lepage, making it four Jack Roush cars among the top 10 finishers.

MALL.COM 400 • final results

Rookie Dave Blaney had a good run to 26th place and was both happy and encouraged about the success of Ward Burton, his Bill Davis Racing teammate.

Fin. Pos.	Start Pos.	Car No.	Driver	Team	Fin. Pos.	Start Pos.	Car No.	Driver	Team
1	3	22	Ward Burton	Caterpillar Pontiac	23	24	26	Jimmy Spencer	Big Kmart Ford
2	17	88	Dale Jarrett	Quality Care/Ford Credit Ford	24	29	10	Johnny Benson	Lycos.com Pontiac
3	4	3	Dale Earnhardt	GM Goodwrench Service Chevrolet	25	38	44	Kyle Petty	Hot Wheels Pontiac
4	9	20	Tony Stewart	Home Depot Pontiac	26	15	93	Dave Blaney	Amoco Pontiac
5	27	99	Jeff Burton	Exide Batteries Ford	27	32	11	Brett Bodine	Ralphs Supermarkets Ford
6	16	17	Matt Kenseth	DeWalt Tools Ford	28	40	13	Robby Gordon	Menards/Turtlewax Ford
7	33	4	Bobby Hamilton	Kodak Chevrolet	29	42	9	Stacy Compton	Kodiak/Cougar Ford
8	1	24	Jeff Gordon	DuPont Automotive Finishes Chevrolet	30	41	41	Rick Mast	Big Daddy's BBQ Sauce Chevrolet
9	5	6	Mark Martin	Valvoline/Cummins Ford	31	12	14	Dick Trickle	Conseco Pontiac
10	2	16	Kevin Lepage	FamilyClick.com Ford	32	35	7	Michael Waltrip	Nations Rent Chevrolet
11	34	11	Terry Labonte	Kellogg's Chevrolet	33	26	71	Dave Marcis	Realtree Chevrolet
12	6	21	Elliott Sadler	CITGO Ford	34	21	12	Jeremy Mayfield	Mobil 1 Ford
13	7	18	Bobby Labonte	Interstate Batteries Pontiac	35	25	55	Kenny Wallace	Square D/Cooper Lighting Chevrolet
14	23	31	Mike Skinner	Lowe's Chevrolet	36	14	27	Jeff Fuller	Pfizer/Viagra Pontiac
15	37	97	Chad Little	John Deere Ford	37	19	25	Jerry Nadeau	MichaelHoligan.com Chevrolet
16	20	2	Rusty Wallace	Miller Lite Ford	38	18	42	Kenny Irwin	BellSouth Chevrolet
17	22	28	Ricky Rudd	Texaco/Havoline Ford	39	31	1	Steve Park	Pennzoil Chevrolet
18	13	77	Robert Pressley	Jasper Engines Ford	40	10	8	Dale Earnhardt Jr.	Budweiser Chevrolet
19	8	94	Bill Elliott	McDonald's Ford	41	30	33	Joe Nemechek	Oakwood Homes Chevrolet
20	11	43	John Andretti	STP/Cheerios Pontiac	42	39	60	Ted Musgrave	Power Team Chevrolet
21	28	40	Sterling Marlin	Coors Light Chevrolet	43	43	66	Darrell Waltrip	Big Kmart/Route 66 Ford
22	36	36	Ken Schrader	M&M's Pontiac					

FOOD CITY *500*

MARCH 26, 2000 • BRISTOL MOTOR SPEEDWAY

(Left) Rusty Wallace cracks a big-time smile in front of his Bristol trophy — the eighth in his collection.

(Right) Rusty's Miller Lite Taurus was on a rail when it counted: He led the final 76 laps of the race.

It's been a while, but there was a time when Darrell Waltrip ruled Bristol. Waltrip didn't just come to Thunder Valley with hopes of finding a win. He arrived at the half-mile oval knowing that every other competitor in the pit area would more than likely go home from the event empty-handed, while Darrell — driving Junior Johnson's Chevrolets — would add yet another monster trophy to his collection.

He made the most of those trips, collecting a dozen Bristol trophies, which included an incredible string of seven consecutive victories. Although his last Bristol win came back in 1992 when he took his own car to victory lane, Thunder Valley has always remained important to him. It was where he proved beyond a shadow of a doubt that he belonged in NASCAR Winston Cup Series racing. Several times he came to Bristol needing a victory to get his title runs into the right gear, or to end a winless streak. Time after time, he was able to do what he needed to do while adding to his victory total.

Ah, but the years march on. Those brilliant Bristol victories are but treasured memories of Waltrip fans throughout the sport. This year Darrell arrived at Bristol with hopes of finding some luck in his final season of NASCAR Winston Cup Series competition. He had struggled in both qualifying and in the races in the first five events of the season. He was tired of needing provisionals to make the field, and even more disappointed with his team's — and his own — race-day performances.

Mike Skinner gets a few tips from his team-mate, Dale Earnhardt, a 10-time Bristol winner.

Could the old Bristol magic be brought out of the bottle once more?

It was altogether fitting that Darrell was honored during the Bristol weekend at the Children of Bristol Benefit Auction. His triumphs of past years have not been forgotten by those who have battled with him on the high banks in the past, and among those feting him at the charity event were Dale Earnhardt, Bobby Allison, Rusty Wallace, Jimmy Spencer, Bill Elliott, Dale and Ned Jarrett, former car owner Johnson and Darrell's younger brother Michael. All had witty things to say — and Waltrip made sure his wife Stevie and daughters Jessica and Sarah were with him to share in the evening.

It was even more fitting that Waltrip put his Ford solidly in the field with the 13th-fastest lap during Bud Pole qualifying for the Food City 500. Now, if he could just wring a solid race-day performance out of the Taurus. After all, there had been five winners in the first five events of the season. Why, Waltrip pondered, couldn't he find the magic and become the sixth, particularly at a track that had been so kind to him in the past.

At the conclusion of Bud Pole qualifying, Waltrip's lap wasn't the only surprise. Steve Park claimed the first pole of his brief NASCAR Winston Cup Series career, and the first for a car fielded by Dale and Teresa Earnhardt in their team's short existence. Park ripped to a new record of more than 126 miles per hour around the concrete high

Front-row starters Steve Park (1) and Kenny Wallace (55) bring the field down the backstretch just seconds before taking the initial green flag. Park led the first 40 laps from the pole, the first of his career, and drove to an admirable seventh-place, lead-lap finish.

(Right) Jeff Gordon (24) and Dale Earnhardt put their fenders in play while Dick Trickle (14) looks on. The two former champions battled at the front, until both were bitten by bad Bristol luck.

(Below) The final caution flag flew on lap 464 when Dave Blaney (93), John Andretti (43) and Rick Mast (41) tangled in the first turn. None of the three cars were able to continue before the checkered flag fell.

banks and plunked the Pennzoil Chevrolet on the inside of the front row for the start of his 62nd career event. Kenny Wallace put the Square D Chevrolet on Park's right, while Jeff Gordon and Mike Skinner made it a 1-2-3-4 sweep for the Bowtie Brigade. Ward Burton was fifth fastest, while Rusty Wallace wheeled the quickest Ford with the sixth-fastest lap. Terry Labonte and hometown favorite Bobby Hamilton made up the fourth row ahead of a solid performance from Elliott Sadler in the Wood Brothers Ford and

Bobby Labonte. Dale Earnhardt and son Dale Jr. shared the sixth row, just ahead of Waltrip and Joe Nemechek.

Bill Elliott, Kevin Lepage, Kenny Irwin, Robby Gordon, Rick Mast, Wally Dallenbach and Jeff Fuller were the provisional starters, sending Dave Marcis, Ricky Craven, Ed Berrier and Scott Pruett to the sidelines for the race.

As the event got underway, Waltrip began searching for the old magic while Dale Earnhardt started hunting for his second victory of

get his season on track — and getting to 50 before Rusty did would be a nice little arrow to have in his quiver the next time the two drivers began joking and trading jibes.

It appeared that Jeff was on his way, taking over the point on lap 52 and then leading all but one of the next 153 circuits around the track. Earnhardt fought his way past Gordon on lap 206, but The Intimidator held the lead for just two laps before being collected by a sliding Irwin. Earnhardt spent more than 125 laps in the pits before returning to competition.

That put Gordon in the lead, but his luck ended when he hit a tire left on pit road by one of Park's crewmembers during a pit stop, and the aerodynamic damage to the front of the DuPont Chevrolet ended Gordon's hopes.

Wallace, a contender throughout the afternoon, emerged as the strongest in the field, and after taking the lead for the final time

the season. Jeff Gordon and Rusty Wallace had their own little struggle going on between two of the sport's superstars: Both had 49 career victories, and each wanted to be the first to win the long-sought 50th. Wallace had hoped to reach the 50-win mark during NASCAR's 50th Anniversary season, but had been unable to do so. Gordon, working with his new crewmembers, was simply trying to

on lap 425, rolled to a 2.6-second victory over Johnny Benson's Lycos.com Pontiac. Not only was it his milestone 50th career victory, but it also extended his string of winning at least one race per year to 15, one shy of Ricky Rudd's record of 16.

Fresh from his Darlington victory, Ward Burton came home third ahead of Jeremy Mayfield and Terry Labonte. NASCAR Winston

Long shadows, dirty cars and bent sheet metal tell you this is a late-race restart, with Rusty fronting lead-lap runners Ward Burton (22), Bobby Labonte (18) and Jeremy Mayfield in the Mobil 1 Ford.

Cup Series point leader Bobby Labonte stretched his lead in the standings with a sixth-place finish, while pole-winner Park was seventh ahead of Gordon and Jeff Burton. Sterling Marlin beat Michael Waltrip for the final position in the top 10.

For Darrell Waltrip, Bristol became another disappointment. He suffered a collision with Dale Earnhardt Jr. during the second lap of the race, and his Big Kmart Ford wasn't right the rest of the afternoon. He finished a very disappointing 31st in the field.

FOOD CITY 500 • final results

Wallace hoists the "Big 50" to signify his long-awaited milestone win. It's fitting that it came at Bristol, the site of his first career NASCAR Winston Cup Series victory, nearly 14 years ago.

Fin. Pos.	Start Pos.	Car No.	Driver	Team	Fin. Pos.	Start Pos.	Car No.	Driver	Team
1	6	2	Rusty Wallace	Miller Lite Ford	23	31	97	Chad Little	John Deere Ford
2	33	10	Johnny Benson	Lycos.com Pontiac	24	35	44	Kyle Petty	Hot Wheels Pontiac
3	5	22	Ward Burton	Caterpillar Pontiac	25	14	33	Joe Nemechek	Oakwood Homes Chevrolet
4	17	12	Jeremy Mayfield	Mobil 1 Ford	26	25	36	Ken Schrader	M&M's Pontiac
5	7	5	Terry Labonte	Kellogg's Chevrolet	27	21	14	Dick Trickle	Conseco Pontiac
6	10	18	Bobby Labonte	Interstate Batteries Pontiac	28	29	9	Stacy Compton	Kodiak/Cougar Ford
7	1	1	Steve Park	Pennzoil Chevrolet	29	42	75	Wally Dallenbach	Rotozip Ford
8	3	24	Jeff Gordon	DuPont Automotive Finishes Chevrolet	30	38	16	Kevin Lepage	FamilyClick.com Ford
9	15	99	Jeff Burton	Exide Batteries Ford	31	13	66	Darrell Waltrip	Route 66/Big Kmart Ford
10	28	40	Sterling Marlin	Coors Light Chevrolet	32	40	13	Robby Gordon	Menards/Turtlewax Ford
11	23	7	Michael Waltrip	Nations Rent Chevrolet	33	32	43	John Andretti	STP/Cheerios Pontiac
12	22	17	Matt Kenseth	DeWalt Tools Ford	34	41	41	Rick Mast	Big Daddy's BBQ Sauce Chevrolet
13	4	31	Mike Skinner	Lowe's Chevrolet	35	26	93	Dave Blaney	Amoco Pontiac
14	27	28	Ricky Rudd	Texaco/Havoline Ford	36	37	94	Bill Elliott	McDonald's Ford
15	8	4	Bobby Hamilton	Kodak Chevrolet	37	43	27	Jeff Fuller	Pfizer/Viagra Pontiac
16	34	6	Mark Martin	Valvoline/Cummins Ford	38	12	8	Dale Earnhardt Jr.	Budweiser Chevrolet
17	18	77	Robert Pressley	Jasper Engines Ford	39	11	3	Dale Earnhardt	GM Goodwrench Service Chevrolet
18	30	26	Jimmy Spencer	Big Kmart/Route 66 Ford	40	39	42	Kenny Irwin	BellSouth Chevrolet
19	16	25	Jerry Nadeau	MichaelHoligan.com Chevrolet	41	9	21	Elliott Sadler	CITGO Ford
20	2	55	Kenny Wallace	Square D/Cooper Lighting Chevrolet	42	19	20	Tony Stewart	Home Depot Pontiac
21	20	88	Dale Jarrett	Quality Care/Ford Credit Ford	43	36	60	Ted Musgrave	Power Team Chevrolet
22	24	11	Brett Bodine	Ralphs Supermarkets Ford					

DIRECTV 500

(Left) Rear-tire changer Carl Moore times his jump onto pit road perfectly as the Power Team Chevrolet enters its pit box.

(Right) Flanked by crew chief Tony Eury Sr. (left) and Tony Eury Jr., Dale Earnhardt Jr. celebrates his first career NASCAR Winston Cup Series win.

Rusty Wallace's Bristol victory vaulted him from 10th in the point standings to sixth after the first six races of the season, and the Miller Lite driver was the first to say he felt he was a true contender for a second NASCAR Winston Cup Series championship.

More than a decade after he won the title for the first time, Wallace hoped his early-season strength would translate into a full-fledged effort enabling him to win a second championship. At the same time, he knew the year was young and there were many others who showed the same type of early-season competitiveness and could also challenge for the crown.

Bobby Labonte's perch atop the NASCAR Winston Cup Series point ladder continued following the Bristol event. He held a 41-point advantage over Ward Burton, who pushed Mark Martin from second to third in the standings after Mark's 16th-place finish at Bristol. Dale Jarrett climbed from fifth in the standings to fourth after Bristol, while Dale Earnhardt slid from third to fifth, 13 points behind Jarrett.

Ricky Rudd climbed a notch from eighth to seventh place, while Jeff Burton moved up a position to eighth place after finishing ninth at Bristol. Terry Labonte's fifth place at Thunder Valley and Jeff Gordon's eighth place moved those two drivers into ninth and 10th in the point standings after six races, while Bill Elliott and Tony Stewart fell out of the top 10.

"Texas Terry" Labonte got some hometown momentum for Bud Pole qualifying and turned a record lap at 192.137 miles per hour.

the thousands of campers that had arrived early in the week for the race. It appeared ready to damage the track, but as it neared the Speedway, it split, and although some areas within a few miles of the track suffered damage, the facility was spared and fans were unscathed.

Although thousands in the area were struggling with the after-effects of the storm, the event went on as scheduled. There were some minor inconveniences for fans and competitors with many

(Above) Ward Burton leads Rusty Wallace with Dale Jarrett on the outside after a mid-race restart. The gray skies remained around Fort Worth following the storms earlier in the week, but weather was not a factor during the 500-mile event.

(Above Right) With 12 caution flags during the race, crewmembers got little chance to rest. Kelly Pryor — carb specialist, engine tuner and race-day crewmember for Terry Labonte — stays focused on the action, ready to perform at a moment's notice.

(Right) Point leader and Texas native Bobby Labonte greets his fans during driver introductions. Bobby's third-place finish in the race kept him atop the standings for the fifth straight week.

The DirecTV 500 at Texas Motor Speedway was the seventh race in as many weekends at the start of the season — but it narrowly escaped having to be postponed due to an Act of God in the days preceding the event. A weather front that spawned tornadoes swept through Texas, ravaging Fort Worth and causing some $500 million in damage. The Fort Worth twister was headed directly for TMS and

(Left) Richard Childress Racing teammates Dale Earnhardt (3) and Mike Skinner (31) take the tri-oval side by side. Both drivers finished on the lead lap with Earnhardt seventh and Skinner in 12th.

(Below) Ricky Rudd (28) and Elliott Sadler (21) found a chance to match their Fords at Texas. Of the two, Rudd had the better day, notching his second top-10 finish of the year.

Winston Cup Series Champion Terry, always seem to find a way to claim the headlines in the Lone Star State's newspapers when the tour arrives at the 1.5-mile track. This year was no different.

Terry emerged from Bud Pole qualifying at the top of the speed chart, grabbing his first pole position of the season and his first in nearly four years. The last time he fronted the field was at Sears Point in May 1996. Talk about some Longhorn Magic! He beat Kevin Lepage by just over two-hundredths of a second for the pole and ensured himself of a starting position in the Bud Shootout next February at Daytona.

having to find alternative housing for the weekend when their primary hotels and motels were damaged by the storm. But those problems paled in comparison to those suffered by thousands of nearby residents.

There seems to be something about TMS that brings out the best in the Labontes. Bobby and older brother, two-time NASCAR

Scott Pruett and Dale Earnhardt Jr. continued the surprising qualifying results with the third- and fourth-fastest laps, while Dale

Jeff Gordon has never had much luck at Texas, and this year was no different. Here, his crew makes repairs to the DuPont Chevrolet after Bill Elliott's Ford landed on the left front. The accident also sent Hendrick teammate Jerry Nadeau to the garage in last place.

NASCAR officials stayed busy on pit road, enforcing penalties for violating the new tire rule, enacted to increase safety. Even reigning champion Dale Jarrett was not exempt, being held here by NASCAR Official Hoss Berry.

Jeff Burton, Tony Stewart, Sterling Marlin, John Andretti, Jimmy Spencer, Bobby Hamilton and Robert Pressley were the provisional starters, leaving Robby Gordon, Dave Marcis, Wally Dallenbach and Todd Bodine on the sidelines. Kyle Petty also failed to make the field. The Texas race marked the debut of Adam Petty, and Kyle had planned for a long time to race with his son. It would have to wait for another event.

Many drivers with high hopes for victory in Texas found themselves victim of a variety of gremlins during the running of the DirecTV 500. Gordon nudged teammate Jerry Nadeau, triggering a multicar accident that included Bill Elliott's McDonald's Ford landing atop the DuPont Chevrolet's left front. Tony Stewart's crew let a tire get loose on pit road, bringing a penalty to the Home Depot Pontiac driver. Jarrett spun and whacked the wall after he and

Jarrett and Steve Park claimed the third-row positions. Jeff Fuller and Jerry Nadeau made up the fourth row ahead of Ward Burton and Mark Martin, with Mike Skinner and Joe Nemechek just missing the final top-10 starting spots.

If some of the faces in the top 10 were surprising, so were some of the drivers who were forced to use provisionals to make the field.

(Right) Despite some cosmetic damage to the Texaco Ford, Ricky Rudd leads the field for the lap 175 restart after the seventh caution of the day. Matt Kenseth leads the line of lap-down cars on the inside. Rudd managed a top-10 finish in the race, good enough to keep seventh place in the point standings.

(Below) Scott Pruett's Tide Ford gets a nudge from Steve Park's Pennzoil Chevrolet, a bump that triggered the first caution of the race on lap 18. Pruett qualified third and led 13 laps in the early going before this incident took place.

Dale Earnhardt Jr. flashes under the flagstand on his way to writing his name in the history book. His initial win came in just his 12th career start, the earliest of any driver in the sport's Modern Era.

teammate Ricky Rudd got too close for comfort. Dale Earnhardt struggled through several pit stops while a battery was changed in the GM Goodwrench Service Chevrolet. Some drivers gambled with two-tire stops, only to find the combination sent them reeling back from the front of the pack.

While all this was occurring, Dale Earnhardt Jr. was at the front of the field, rolling his Bud Chevrolet away from the other contenders. After struggling with finishes of 29th, 40th and 38th in his last three races, "Little E" was wondering if he should even be in a NASCAR Winston Cup Series ride. Surprisingly, none other than NASCAR's Gary Nelson bolstered his confidence, and Sunday, Dale Junior had it all together. He led seemingly at will, with his final test coming in the last 50 laps.

He was fourth on a restart behind Steve Park, Rusty Wallace and Matt Kenseth, but took just three laps to rocket to the point. From then on, it was a matter of keeping his wits about him until the checkered flag fell. He left the others to battle for the scraps while establishing a margin of victory of almost six seconds to capture his first career NASCAR Winston Cup Series victory. The win came in just his 12th career start, and it also marked the first Cup win for the team owned by father Dale and Teresa Earnhardt.

Jeff Burton beat Bobby Labonte for second place, while Rusty Wallace finished ahead of Lepage for fourth place. Jeremy Mayfield claimed sixth ahead of the elder Earnhardt, with pole-sitter Terry Labonte in eighth. Stewart survived his pit road problems to claim ninth, just ahead of Rudd and Martin.

DIRECTV 500 • final results

Seven-time champion and now winning car owner Dale Earnhardt has much to keep his eyes on. While making his own bid for a record eighth title, the champ oversees the cars he fields for Dale Jr., Steve Park and NASCAR Busch Series driver Ron Hornaday.

Fin. Pos.	Start Pos.	Car No.	Driver	Team	Fin. Pos.	Start Pos.	Car No.	Driver	Team
1	4	8	Dale Earnhardt Jr.	Budweiser Chevrolet	23	25	11	Brett Bodine	Ralphs Supermarkets Ford
2	37	99	Jeff Burton	Exide Batteries Ford	24	30	66	Darrell Waltrip	Route 66/Big Kmart Ford
3	14	18	Bobby Labonte	Interstate Batteries Pontiac	25	23	24	Jeff Gordon	DuPont Automotive Finishes Chevrolet
4	19	2	Rusty Wallace	Miller Lite Ford	26	43	77	Robert Pressley	Jasper Engines Ford
5	2	16	Kevin Lepage	FamilyClick.com Ford	27	3	32	Scott Pruett	Tide Ford
6	31	12	Jeremy Mayfield	Mobil 1 Ford	28	28	60	Dick Trickle	Power Team Chevrolet
7	17	3	Dale Earnhardt	GM Goodwrench Service Chevrolet	29	21	7	Michael Waltrip	Nations Rent Chevrolet
8	1	5	Terry Labonte	Kellogg's Chevrolet	30	22	94	Bill Elliott	McDonald's Ford
9	38	20	Tony Stewart	Home Depot Pontiac	31	13	17	Matt Kenseth	DeWalt Tools Ford
10	20	28	Ricky Rudd	Texaco/Havoline Ford	32	40	43	John Andretti	STP Pontiac
11	10	6	Mark Martin	Valvoline/Cummins Ford	33	5	88	Dale Jarrett	Quality Care/Ford Credit Ford
12	11	31	Mike Skinner	Lowe's Chevrolet	34	39	40	Sterling Marlin	Coors Light Chevrolet
13	16	97	Chad Little	John Deere Ford	35	18	90	Ed Berrier	Hills Brothers Coffee Ford
14	9	22	Ward Burton	Caterpillar Pontiac	36	15	9	Stacy Compton	Kodiak/Cougar Ford
15	41	26	Jimmy Spencer	Big Kmart/Route 66 Ford	37	12	33	Joe Nemechek	Oakwood Homes Chevrolet
16	42	4	Bobby Hamilton	Kodak Chevrolet	38	7	27	Jeff Fuller	Pfizer/Viagra Pontiac
17	27	42	Kenny Irwin	BellSouth Chevrolet	39	35	21	Elliott Sadler	CITGO Ford
18	36	36	Ken Schrader	M&M's Pontiac	40	33	45	Adam Petty	Sprint Chevrolet
19	6	1	Steve Park	Pennzoil Chevrolet	41	29	41	Gary Bradberry	Big Daddy's BBQ Sauce Chevrolet
20	34	14	Rick Mast	Conseco Pontiac	42	26	10	Johnny Benson	Lycos.com Pontiac
21	32	55	Kenny Wallace	Square D/Cooper Lighting Chevrolet	43	8	25	Jerry Nadeau	MichaelHoligan.com Chevrolet
22	24	93	Dave Blaney	Amoco Pontiac					

GOODY'S BODY PAIN 500

APRIL 9, 2000 • MARTINSVILLE SPEEDWAY

NASCAR 2000

(Left) Mark Martin and crew chief Jimmy Fennig make their first trip to victory lane in 2000. Martin became the eighth different winner of the year.

(Right) A sea of equipment and humanity precedes the Goody's Body Pain 500. (Bonus question: Where's Jack?)

D ale Earnhardt Jr.'s dominant performance and victory at Texas Motor Speedway made him the seventh different winner in as many races this season. And like all the others who made their way to victory lane this year, "Little E" found there was little time to savor the triumph.

Dale Jr. did find some time to relax on the couch in his home and spend some time with close friends. But just a few days after his win in Texas, the Budweiser driver and the others who make up the NASCAR Winston Cup Series had to gear up for the Goody's Body Pain 500 at Clay Campbell's flat half-mile oval in southern Virginia to begin the struggle for supremacy in the eighth straight race of the young season.

Every competitor's anticipation of the weekend's events at Martinsville was tempered in mid-week, however, when news of the passing of Petty Enterprises patriarch Lee Petty swept through the motorsports community. Petty, one of the greatest drivers in the history of the sport and perhaps the most famous NASCAR pioneer driver, died at age 86 after being in failing health for some time. He was the founder of Petty Enterprises, a three-time NASCAR Winston Cup Series champion and winner of 55 events — still seventh on the all-time list. His loss was one felt throughout the racing world.

Wallaces dominated Martinsville qualifying. Rusty took the pole with brother Kenny alongside for Sunday's event, while Mike Wallace won the pole for Saturday's NASCAR Craftsman Truck Series race.

Rusty's hot rod spit fire at both ends of the racetrack, but it didn't skip a beat as Wallace was able to dominate the first half of the event. Here, he hunts down Bill Elliott (94) with John Andretti in tow, while Brett Bodine (11) and Jerry Nadeau (25) give him room on the inside.

Martinsville has long been a leader on the NASCAR tour, and when teams unloaded for the beginning of practice for the Goody's Body Pain 500 there was even more evidence of the Virginia track's dedication to the sport. An additional 5,000 seats had been added between the first and second turns, with new concession stands and restrooms for the fans. A new press box had also been completed, flanked by new hospitality suites. Three of the eight suites were completed, with the other five to be ready for the fall event.

Jeff Fuller had been released by Eel River Racing following the Texas event and was immediately replaced by Mike Bliss. It was a reunion for Bliss and crew chief Barry Dodson, and both hoped they could repeat the success they shared in the NASCAR Craftsman Truck Series. In Robby Gordon's camp, crew chief Fred Graves had been released and Jerry Baxter was named as the new head wrench, while at Galaxy Motorsports, Wally Dallenbach was still in search of a new crew chief who he hoped would lead that team out of the wilderness.

After finishing third at Texas, Bobby Labonte saw his margin in the standings jump to 84 points over Mark Martin, while Ward Burton slid to third place following his 14th-place finish. Dale Earnhardt moved to fourth place in the point standings, while Rusty Wallace moved to fifth, just 19 points behind the driver of the GM Goodwrench Service Chevrolet. Jeff Burton jumped from eighth place to sixth, while Ricky Rudd remained seventh in the standings.

(Above) Even the very best get dinged up at Martinsville. Reigning champ Dale Jarrett gets into the back of three-time champ Jeff Gordon, while 1988 champion Bill Elliott muscles in on the inside.

(Left) Brakes are as important as anything when it comes to racing at Martinsville. This "cut away" version of Joe Nemechek's Chevrolet shows some of the extra duct work unique to Martinsville cars to help keep air flowing over the brake system.

Defending NASCAR Winston Cup Series Champion Dale Jarrett suffered the most during the Texas race. His accident relegated him to a 33rd-place finish, sending him plummeting to eighth in the standings. He was now just 17 points ahead of Terry Labonte, while Jeremy Mayfield used his sixth place at Texas to move past Tony Stewart into 10th.

For the fifth time this year, a Ford was the fastest car in Bud Pole qualifying, and this time Rusty Wallace gained the 28th pole of his career and his second of the season. Younger brother Kenny did all he could to oust his older brother from the pole, but came up just hundredths of a second shy. Mike Skinner and Brett Bodine — for Bodine, his first top-10 qualifying effort of the season — made up the second row, with Jeff Burton and Jerry Nadeau claiming the third row. Ricky Rudd and Sterling Marlin were seventh and eighth fastest ahead of Bill Elliott and Bobby Hamilton, while Jeff Gordon and Ken Schrader failed to make the top 10.

Stewart, last year's pole winner here, was forced to use a provisional to make the field, as were Chad Little, Kevin Lepage, Jimmy Spencer, Elliott Sadler, Robby Gordon and Gary Bradberry. Dallenbach, trying to handle both the crew chief and driver roles, failed to qualify, as did Rick Mast, Dave Marcis and Ed Berrier.

From the drop of the green flag, it was evident that Rusty Wallace had the most dominant car in the field. He led 232 of the first 253 laps in brilliant fashion, but in the late going he opted for four tires during a caution and found the new stickers didn't work as well as sets he had used earlier in the race. With others taking two tires and beating the Miller Lite Ford out of the pits, Wallace found himself in

After numerous penalties for tires being left on pit road at Texas, teams took particular care to make sure their tires were safely contained during stops at Martinsville. Note how the tire carrier keeps a spare lug nut, just in case one falls off during the stop.

Mark Martin took the lead for the first time with 64 laps remaining and never relinquished it, finishing with a 1.5-second margin of victory over Jeff Burton. The win, Mark's second at the Virginia half mile (his first coming in 1992), allowed him to close the point gap by 48 on leader Bobby Labonte.

a struggle and wound up battling for a 10th-place finish in a race he had thoroughly expected to win.

With 17 cautions for 112 laps dotting the 500-lap event, the final race results turned on pit strategy. And the beneficiary was none other than the eighth different winner of the season.

Mark Martin made his final pit stop on lap 412, and as the event ground into the closing laps, no one was able to make a move to challenge Martin for the victory. Although he didn't have the fastest car in the field, Martin used track position to glide to the 32nd victory of his NASCAR Winston Cup Series career and edge Roush Racing teammate Jeff Burton by 1.5 seconds.

Michael Waltrip fought to third place in the final results, while Gordon came home fourth. Dale Jarrett put a stop to his bleeding in the points with a fifth place ahead of Stewart and Mayfield. Elliott and Earnhardt were eighth and ninth ahead of Wallace, while Ward Burton just missed the final top-10 position.

GOODY'S BODY PAIN 500 • final results

Jeff Gordon and crew chief Robbie Loomis continue to focus on their team's performance, confident that their steady progress will result in a win before too long.

Fin. Pos.	Start Pos.	Car No.	Driver	Team	Fin. Pos.	Start Pos.	Car No.	Driver	Team
1	21	6	Mark Martin	Valvoline/Cummins Ford	23	27	5	Terry Labonte	Kellogg's Chevrolet
2	5	99	Jeff Burton	Exide Batteries Ford	24	8	40	Sterling Marlin	Coors Light Chevrolet
3	34	7	Michael Waltrip	Nations Rent Chevrolet	25	19	1	Steve Park	Pennzoil Chevrolet
4	11	24	Jeff Gordon	DuPont Automotive Finishes Chevrolet	26	22	8	Dale Earnhardt Jr.	Budweiser Chevrolet
5	28	88	Dale Jarrett	Quality Care/Ford Credit Ford	27	38	97	Chad Little	John Deere Ford
6	37	20	Tony Stewart	Home Depot Pontiac	28	40	26	Jimmy Spencer	Big Kmart/Route 66 Ford
7	24	12	Jeremy Mayfield	Mobil 1 Ford	29	41	21	Elliott Sadler	CITGO Ford
8	9	94	Bill Elliott	McDonald's Ford	30	30	60	Rich Bickle	Power Team Chevrolet
9	17	3	Dale Earnhardt	GM Goodwrench Service Chevrolet	31	14	50	Ricky Craven	Midwest Transit Chevrolet
10	1	2	Rusty Wallace	Miller Lite Ford	32	35	32	Scott Pruett	Tide Ford
11	18	22	Ward Burton	Caterpillar Pontiac	33	43	41	Gary Bradberry	Big Daddy's BBQ Sauce Chevrolet
12	13	18	Bobby Labonte	Interstate Batteries Pontiac	34	39	16	Kevin Lepage	FamilyClick.com Ford
13	12	36	Ken Schrader	M&M's Pontiac	35	33	27	Mike Bliss	Pfizer/Viagra Pontiac
14	26	43	John Andretti	STP/Cheerios Pontiac	36	4	11	Brett Bodine	Ralphs Supermarkets Ford
15	23	77	Robert Pressley	Jasper Engines Ford	37	32	42	Kenny Irwin	BellSouth Chevrolet
16	25	10	Johnny Benson	Lycos.com Pontiac	38	16	44	Kyle Petty	Hot Wheels Pontiac
17	29	33	Joe Nemechek	Oakwood Homes Chevrolet	39	15	9	Stacy Compton	Kodiak/Cougar Ford
18	10	4	Bobby Hamilton	Kodak Chevrolet	40	42	13	Robby Gordon	Menards/Turtlewax Ford
19	3	31	Mike Skinner	Lowe's Chevrolet	41	20	93	Dave Blaney	Amoco Pontiac
20	6	25	Jerry Nadeau	MichaelHoligan.com Chevrolet	42	2	55	Kenny Wallace	Square D/Cooper Lighting Chevrolet
21	31	17	Matt Kenseth	DeWalt Tools Ford	43	36	66	Darrell Waltrip	Route 66/Big Kmart Ford
22	7	28	Ricky Rudd	Texaco/Havoline Ford					

DIEHARD *500*

APRIL 16, 2000 • TALLADEGA SUPERSPEEDWAY

(Left) Veteran independent driver-turned-crew chief Jimmy Means works on the No. 90 Ford driven by Ed Berrier.

(Right) Jeff Gordon negotiates traffic through the middle in search of the leaders at Talladega.

M ark Martin's strategic Martinsville victory coupled with Bobby Labonte's 12th-place finish at the Virginia half-mile track, enabled the Valvoline Ford driver to chop the point gap from 84 to 36 as teams assembled at mammoth Talladega Superspeedway for the ninth round of the season.

Martin had added his name to the list of different drivers to post victories so far this year, and the string now stood at eight. With at least a half dozen others who had threatened to win — but were so far unable to find the key to victory lane — there was much speculation that the DieHard 500 at Talladega would add a ninth different name to the list of 2000 season race winners at the conclusion of the event.

Labonte had good reason to expect an excellent finish at Talladega. In the last seven events at the huge oval, Bobby had finished eighth or better. Martin, on the other hand, had been 15th or worse in four of the last five races at the Alabama superspeedway.

With his 11th-place finish at Martinsville, Ward Burton maintained the third position in the point standings, but behind him, the remainder of the top 10 underwent changes. Jeff Burton's second place at Martinsville moved him to fourth in the standings, dropping Dale Earnhardt from fourth to fifth

Gordon, joined by wife Brooke in victory lane, broke a winless string dating back to the 1999 Brickyard 400.

and Rusty Wallace from fifth to sixth. Dale Jarrett's fifth place at Martinsville moved him up a notch to seventh and forced Robert Yates Racing teammate Ricky Rudd down to eighth. Jeremy Mayfield moved up one spot from 10th to ninth, allowing Tony Stewart to take over the final top-10 position following his sixth place at the Virginia bullring. That left Terry Labonte the odd man out, falling from ninth to 11th place in the standings.

Jarrett and Earnhardt hoped to make further inroads into Bobby Labonte's position atop the standings at Talladega — and both drivers had good reason to be optimistic. Earnhardt swept both races at the superspeedway last year and was the winningest driver in the track's history. Jarrett had posted finishes of third or better in seven of the last nine Talladega events and looked to continue that kind of performance despite being forced to use a brand new Ford after his Daytona 500-winning mount was placed on display at Daytona USA.

Drivers come to Talladega knowing that once qualifying is completed, they will be racing side by side in packs throughout the

(Left) The GM Goodwrench crew services Dale Earnhardt's Chevrolet under green, hurrying to return their driver to the track with drafting partners Steve Park (1) and Rusty Wallace (further down pit road).

(Below) With Earnhardt at the point, the massive pack of cars screams through Talladega's first and second turns.

weekend. With a smaller restrictor place mandated for the DieHard 500, the competition would be even more equal, and the freight train of cars racing around the track would be even closer together. With that in mind, teams searched for the slightest edge in parts and bodywork, hoping to increase their chances for victory.

But when qualifying day turns out to be a rainy one giving NASCAR's inspectors additional time to do their jobs, things can become just a little sticky for teams going through NASCAR's strict inspection procedures. Many teams were forced to do some body work on their cars to pass inspection, and by the time Bud Pole qualifying finally began late in the afternoon, unapproved parts that included fuel cells, hubs, springs, spoilers and carburetors had been taken off of cars by NASCAR inspectors. Earnhardt's black Chevrolet underwent major surgery, with the GM Goodwrench Service crew removing the rear of the car and replacing it with one that would pass inspection.

The smaller restrictor plate meant the qualifying speeds were slower than in the past, but when the Bud Pole session was completed, Mayfield's Mobil 1 Ford was the fastest of the field with a pole speed of 186.969 miles per hour. The difference between his speed and the lap posted by Bill Elliott was a blink of an eye — .009 second — but it was good enough to gain the Kentucky native's third career pole, his first since the 1998 Texas event, 69 races ago.

Jarrett and Earnhardt fortified their hopes for victory by claiming the second row, with Mark Martin and Dale Earnhardt Jr. making up the third row ahead of Sterling Marlin and Mike Skinner. Ward Burton and Ricky Rudd completed the top 10, just ahead of Michael Waltrip and Kenny Irwin. With Jeff Gordon claiming the final position in the field determined by time, Bobby Labonte, Jeff Burton, Tony Stewart, Ken Schrader, Steve Park, Matt Kenseth and Darrell Waltrip were forced to use provisionals to make

Like rush hour on the expressway, Talladega traffic uses four lanes but with little room to spare. Unlike rush hour, however, this pack never stops moving.

Nearly three quarters of the race had been completed with only two quick cautions for debris. But just three laps after the second restart, it happened:

(Above) Scott Pruett (32) and Michael Waltrip (7) touched, with Robby Gordon (13) close behind.

(Left) Waltrip and Gordon, spinning on the infield grass, are joined by Stacy Compton (9) as the approaching pack tries to navigate through their tire smoke.

(Below Left) When the smoke began to clear 17 cars had been significantly involved, including point leader and top-five contender Bobby Labonte and Dale Earnhardt Jr., both of whom limp up pit road and head behind the wall.

the field. Brett Bodine, Kevin Lepage, Gary Bradberry, Rick Mast and Elliott Sadler all failed to make the starting lineup.

When you start 36th in the sardine-can pack that rumbles around Talladega in furious fashion, the fastest route to the front is to work through the middle, splitting the rows of cars and forcing your way past. It also creates a pucker-factor of about 14.8 on a 10-point scale. The tiniest mistake by anyone can create "The Big One," a multicar accident that can take out half the field on the massive track. Jeff Gordon, starting at the back of the pack, felt he had no other choice.

While Mark Martin led the early portion of the event, Gordon was working his way through the pack, mostly

Jeff Gordon scored the win that extended the streak of different winners to nine, and was able to celebrate his 50th trip to victory lane. Jeff reached his milestone win in 232 starts — that's a winning percentage of 21.5 percent over his career, now in its eighth season.

in the middle, and he eventually emerged among the leaders with some well-judged moves. When Rusty Wallace lost the engine in his Miller Lite Ford and Jarrett ran out of fuel, it began to look like either Martin or Roush Racing teammate Jeff Burton would become the first two-time winner of the year.

Then came the slip everyone had hoped would not happen, and when the tire smoke cleared, 17 cars had been involved in the accident, including point leader Bobby Labonte and Joe Gibbs Racing teammate Tony Stewart. Gordon escaped, as did Martin, Jeff Burton and a few others.

Gordon moved to the point on lap 159, but then was shuffled out of the lead and back as far as ninth with just 18 laps remaining in the race. He looked like anything but the ninth different winner of the season.

But you simply can't count Gordon out, particularly on a restrictor-plate track, and with eight laps to go he had fought back to fourth place behind Martin, Mayfield and Skinner. With six laps remaining he was third, and two laps later Gordon found his opportunity to go for the win. When Mayfield went high to pass Martin, Gordon chose to go low and pushed his way into the lead. Skinner tried his best in the final two laps but was unable to find a way past

Gordon, and as the cars flashed to the checkered flag, Jeff maintained his lead to snap a 13-race winless streak.

The ninth different winner of the season, Jeff also claimed his 50th career victory, gaining the same plateau Rusty Wallace had reached three weeks prior.

Skinner beat Earnhardt for second place in the battle of Childress Racing cars, while Kenny Irwin had a fine run to fourth ahead of Jimmy Spencer. Martin emerged sixth ahead of Terry Labonte, with Marlin claiming eighth place. Kyle Petty had a solid performance, coming home ninth in the Hot Wheels Pontiac, with Ward Burton 10th ahead of John Andretti.

DIEHARD 500 • final results

Mark Martin led 98 of the 188 laps, but like at Daytona, couldn't find a friend with five laps to go and was shuffled back to a sixth-place finish.

Fin. Pos.	Start Pos.	Car No.	Driver	Team	Fin. Pos.	Start Pos.	Car No.	Driver	Team
1	36	24	Jeff Gordon	DuPont Automotive Finishes Chevrolet	23	19	77	Robert Pressley	Jasper Engines Ford
2	8	31	Mike Skinner	Lowe's Chevrolet	24	18	27	Mike Bliss	Pfizer/Viagra Pontiac
3	4	3	Dale Earnhardt	GM Goodwrench Service Chevrolet	25	14	97	Chad Little	John Deere Ford
4	12	42	Kenny Irwin	BellSouth Chevrolet	26	43	66	Darrell Waltrip	Route 66/Big Kmart Ford
5	20	26	Jimmy Spencer	Big Kmart/Route 66 Ford	27	10	28	Ricky Rudd	Texaco/Havoline Ford
6	5	6	Mark Martin	Valvoline/Cummins Ford	28	23	90	Ed Berrier	Hills Brothers Coffee Ford
7	33	5	Terry Labonte	Kellogg's Chevrolet	29	32	50	Ricky Craven	Midwest Transit Chevrolet
8	7	40	Sterling Marlin	Coors Light Chevrolet	30	16	93	Dave Blaney	Amoco Pontiac
9	21	44	Kyle Petty	Hot Wheels Pontiac	31	11	7	Michael Waltrip	Nations Rent Chevrolet
10	9	22	Ward Burton	Caterpillar Pontiac	32	41	1	Steve Park	Pennzoil Chevrolet
11	25	43	John Andretti	STP/Cheerios Pontiac	33	22	9	Stacy Compton	Kodiak/Cougar Ford
12	38	99	Jeff Burton	Exide Batteries Ford	34	39	20	Tony Stewart	Home Depot Pontiac
13	13	10	Johnny Benson	Lycos.com Pontiac	35	29	15	Ted Musgrave	Fenley-Moore Motorsports Ford
14	1	12	Jeremy Mayfield	Mobil 1 Ford	36	40	36	Ken Schrader	M&M's Pontiac
15	2	94	Bill Elliott	McDonald's Ford	37	34	13	Robby Gordon	Menards/Turtlewax Ford
16	35	75	Wally Dallenbach	Redcell Ford	38	27	71	Dave Marcis	Realtree Chevrolet
17	3	88	Dale Jarrett	Quality Care/Ford Credit Ford	39	31	60	Dick Trickle	Power Team Chevrolet
18	42	17	Matt Kenseth	DeWalt Tools Ford	40	26	55	Kenny Wallace	Square D/Cooper Lighting Chevrolet
19	30	25	Jerry Nadeau	MichaelHoligan.com Chevrolet	41	17	2	Rusty Wallace	Miller Lite Ford
20	15	32	Scott Pruett	Tide Ford	42	6	8	Dale Earnhardt Jr.	Budweiser Chevrolet
21	37	18	Bobby Labonte	Interstate Batteries Pontiac	43	28	4	Bobby Hamilton	Kodak Chevrolet
22	24	33	Joe Nemechek	Oakwood Homes Chevrolet					

NAPA AUTO PARTS *500*

APRIL 30, 2000 • CALIFORNIA SPEEDWAY

(Left) Race fans were treated to a beautiful day in Southern California for the fourth running of the NAPA Auto Parts 500.

(Right) Jeremy Mayfield congratulates his team in victory lane after a late-race, two-tire pit stop put the Mobil 1 driver in position for the win.

After a break for the Easter holiday — the first weekend off since the season began in February at Daytona Beach — teams arrived at the spectacular two-mile oasis in Southern California to do battle in the NAPA Auto Parts 500.

Nine different drivers had gone to victory lane in the first nine events of the season, and there was little reason to think the streak would not continue in California. After all, "La-La-Land" has traditionally been a place where dreams come true, and what better venue for one of at least a half-dozen teams to sprint to the winner's circle to taste the victory bubbly?

Bobby Labonte's involvement in the multicar accident at Talladega, along with Mark Martin's fighting sixth place, enabled the Valvoline Ford driver to take over the top rung of the point ladder, with Martin 24 points ahead of Labonte. The Talladega results also shuffled others within the top 10 in the standings. Ward Burton remained in third, while Dale Earnhardt moved from fifth to fourth, edging ahead of Jeff Burton. Dale Jarrett moved up a slot from seventh to sixth, while Jeff Gordon's victory moved him all the way from 12th to seventh. Rusty Wallace slid from sixth to eighth after losing the engine in his Miller Lite Ford and finishing 41st at Talladega. Jeremy Mayfield remained

Tony Stewart enjoys the pre-race festivities before racing through the field to a 10th-place finish at California — his sixth top 10 in the first 10 events of the year.

Pole-winner Mike Skinner gets four tires and a chassis adjustment during an early-race caution. Skinner had the car to beat in the early stages of the race, but gave way to Kenseth and others as they improved their cars during pit stops.

ninth, but Terry Labonte moved into the top 10 with his seventh-place finish, dropping Ricky Rudd to 11th, while Bill Elliott and Mike Skinner were 12th and 13th.

During the Easter break, team owner A.J. Foyt rearranged his Conseco-sponsored team. After missing the field in five of the first nine races, it was clear Foyt had seen enough of the status quo, and there were several new faces within the team when the green Pontiac was unloaded in California. Team Manager Waddell Wilson was gone, and Philippe Lopez replaced crew chief Terry Wooten. Three new members were toiling in the engine department, and the shakeup included new members from the Larry Hedrick and Jeff

(Above) Mark Martin (6), Ricky Rudd (28) and Jimmy Spencer all started among the top five and staged an early-race battle that took them three-wide on California's roomy frontstretch. Spencer, who started on the outside pole, ran well until he smacked the wall with just 30 laps remaining.

(Left) Skinner takes the green on a restart in the early going with Matt Kenseth challenging from second place. Kenseth finally worked past the Lowe's Chevrolet on lap 87 and led 120 of the next 134 laps to gain the five-point bonus for leading the most laps in the event.

(Below Left) Rudd, who qualified third for the race, ponders a strategy to capture his first win since joining Robert Yates Racing at the beginning of the season. His Texaco Ford ran well in the race and carried him to a fourth-place finish.

Burton teams, among others. Foyt felt his third driver of the year, Rick Mast, was capable of bringing strong results, and the entire team took on a new sense of purpose for the 10th race of the season.

Lopez wasn't the only new crew chief at work. Newt Moore had been named the new head wrench for Galaxy Motorsports and driver Wally Dallenbach, and Wally was relieved to not have to be driver, crew chief, pit strategist and jack-of-all-trades as he had been for the last few races.

(Above) Kenseth looks for an opening between Johnny Benson (10) and Wally Dallenbach (75) with Ward Burton (22) holding the high line along the frontstretch. Burton, who started fourth, was never able to lead, but stayed among the front-runners to score a sixth-place finish.

(Right) Bill Elliott's Drive Thru Crew greets the McDonald's Ford for a green-flag pit stop on lap 152. The stop handed the lead to Jeff Burton, who held the point briefly before making his stop.

After recording his best career finish at Talladega, Mike Skinner and the Lowe's team headed into California on a high, and when Bud Pole qualifying was completed, the team continued its surge with a new track-record speed in excess of 186 miles per hour. The quick lap brought Skinner his first Bud Pole of the season, the fifth of his career, and gave the team its fifth top-10 starting position this year.

Jimmy Spencer nearly notched his first pole of the season, coming within 17-hundredths of a second of Skinner's time, but he was forced to settle for the outside of the front row. It was Skinner's best qualifying effort since he started second at Phoenix in 1997. Rudd and Ward Burton claimed the second row, with Mark Martin on the inside of the third row. Scott Pruett posted the sixth-fastest lap of the session, while Darrell Waltrip dialed up a lap good enough to claim the inside of the fourth row. Waltrip had gone to California with no provisionals to use and knew he had to find a quick lap to make the field. The old pro did just that. Stacy Compton, Steve Park and John

Andretti completed the top 10, with Rusty Wallace just missing and settling for 11th to start the race.

Several of the point leaders had problems on the two-mile oval, with Tony Stewart qualifying 32nd, Dale Jarrett 33rd, Terry Labonte 34th, Dale Earnhardt 35th and Bobby Labonte 36th, the final driver to make the field with his timed lap. Sterling Marlin, Chad Little,

was forced to watch the battle for victory take place through his windshield.

When Skinner faded, rookie Matt Kenseth headed for the front and began a performance that many expected would make him the 10th different winner of the season. His chance to post the victory ended, however, when Spencer rapped the wall and brought out the

(Above) Jeremy Mayfield hugs the inside line while working past Ken Schrader (36) and Chad Little (97). Mayfield spent most of the day climbing through the field from his 24th starting spot and then benefited from good pit strategy to take the point for the first — and only — time with 25 laps to go.

(Right) Bobby Labonte (18) streaks past the grandstands alongside Ricky Rudd on his charge to the front. After a disappointing qualifying effort that put him 36th on the grid, Labonte battled all the way to a second-place finish — good enough to retake the point lead he had held for most of the season.

Kenny Irwin, Kevin Lepage, Kenny Wallace, Dick Trickle and Mike Bliss all used provisionals to get into the race, while Dave Marcis, Ed Berrier and Dwayne Leik were forced to the sidelines.

During the first portion of the NAPA Auto Parts 500, Skinner appeared to be headed for his first NASCAR Winston Cup Series victory. But, like several other events in the last two years, Skinner had the right combination to dominate early, but then watched his chances go away during the final portion of the event. The handling of his Chevrolet disappeared in the second half of the race, and he

fourth yellow flag of the day, offering other teams a chance to erase the lead Kenseth had painstakingly built.

During that fateful caution, Martin remained on the track to take the point. Jeremy Mayfield, who had regained a lap lost earlier while his crew worked on a malfunctioning oil cooler, took just two tires and emerged in second place for the restart. Penske teammate Rusty Wallace also took just two tires, as did both Jeff and Ward Burton.

Mayfield hoists his California trophy for photographers in victory lane. Jeremy's second career victory broke a 61-race winless streak that dated back to June 1998.

Kenseth was in line in sixth place with four new tires, and when the green dropped, he found he could not force his way back to the front.

On the first lap under green, Mayfield went past Martin to take the point — but the race wasn't over yet. When Dick Trickle slapped the wall with less than 10 laps remaining to bring out the final yellow, Mayfield found himself looking in the mirror at Bobby Labonte, who had fought his way through the field to have one last chance at victory. When the green dropped for the final four-lap sprint, Mayfield felt his Ford falter. He immediately hit the switch for the backup ignition and was able to keep Labonte at bay for the final laps around the track. His margin of victory was just three car-lengths, while Kenseth fought his way to third behind Bobby Labonte. Ricky Rudd came home fourth ahead of Jeff and Ward Burton, while Skinner was seventh. Rusty Wallace finished eighth ahead of Dale Jarrett, with Tony Stewart edging Gordon for 10th place.

Mayfield climbed from his car and jumped up and down with elation after scoring his second career NASCAR Winston Cup Series victory. It would prove costly to him and his team, however. Shortly after the event, the team was notified that the car did not make the 51-inch minimum height rule and would be impounded and taken to Charlotte for further examination. Already under a cloud after NASCAR inspectors found problems with a fuel sample at Talladega, Mayfield and crew chief Peter Sospenzo could only wait to be told what penalties would occur.

Still, Mayfield had driven a great race to become the 10th different winner of the season.

NAPA AUTO PARTS 500 • final results

A race that featured 20 lead changes among 15 different drivers, in large part, came down to strategy and performance on pit road, with Mayfield's two-tire stop proving to be the difference in the race.

Fin. Pos.	Start Pos.	Car No.	Driver	Team
1	24	12	Jeremy Mayfield	Mobil 1 Ford
2	36	18	Bobby Labonte	Interstate Batteries Pontiac
3	23	17	Matt Kenseth	DeWalt Tools Ford
4	3	28	Ricky Rudd	Texaco/Havoline Ford
5	13	99	Jeff Burton	Exide Batteries Ford
6	4	22	Ward Burton	Caterpillar Pontiac
7	1	31	Mike Skinner	Lowe's Chevrolet
8	11	2	Rusty Wallace	Miller Lite Ford
9	33	88	Dale Jarrett	Quality Care/Ford Credit Ford
10	32	20	Tony Stewart	Home Depot Pontiac
11	26	24	Jeff Gordon	DuPont Automotive Finishes Chevrolet
12	20	8	Dale Earnhardt Jr.	Budweiser Chevrolet
13	25	25	Jerry Nadeau	MichaelHoligan.com Chevrolet
14	5	6	Mark Martin	Valvoline/Cummins Ford
15	38	97	Chad Little	John Deere Ford
16	9	1	Steve Park	Pennzoil Chevrolet
17	35	3	Dale Earnhardt	GM Goodwrench Service Chevrolet
18	12	4	Bobby Hamilton	Kodak Chevrolet
19	27	94	Bill Elliott	McDonald's Ford
20	28	33	Joe Nemechek	Oakwood Homes Chevrolet
21	16	77	Robert Pressley	Jasper Engines Ford
22	40	16	Kevin Lepage	FamilyClick.com Ford

Fin. Pos.	Start Pos.	Car No.	Driver	Team
23	14	10	Johnny Benson	Lycos.com Pontiac
24	18	36	Ken Schrader	M&M's Pontiac
25	10	43	John Andretti	STP/Cheerios Pontiac
26	30	44	Kyle Petty	Hot Wheels Pontiac
27	22	75	Wally Dallenbach	TBS Dinner & A Movie Ford
28	8	9	Stacy Compton	Kodiak/Cougar Ford
29	7	66	Darrell Waltrip	Route 66/Big Kmart Ford
30	21	7	Michael Waltrip	Nations Rent Chevrolet
31	29	13	Robby Gordon	Menards/Turtlewax Ford
32	37	40	Sterling Marlin	Coors Light Chevrolet
33	34	5	Terry Labonte	Kellogg's Chevrolet
34	6	32	Scott Pruett	Tide Ford
35	43	27	Mike Bliss	Pfizer/Viagra Pontiac
36	41	55	Kenny Wallace	Square D/Cooper Lighting Chevrolet
37	42	60	Dick Trickle	Power Team Chevrolet
38	17	93	Dave Blaney	Amoco Pontiac
39	15	14	Rick Mast	Conseco Pontiac
40	2	26	Jimmy Spencer	Big Kmart/Route 66 Ford
41	31	11	Brett Bodine	Ralphs Supermarkets Ford
42	39	42	Kenny Irwin	BellSouth Chevrolet
43	19	21	Elliott Sadler	CITGO Ford

PONTIAC EXCITEMENT *400*

(Left) The starting field roars to life for the 46th running of the Pontiac Excitement 400 as dusk settles over Richmond International Raceway.

(Right) With finishes of 26th, 42nd and 12th since his initial win at Texas, Dale Earnhardt Jr. arrived at Richmond focused and intent on having a strong performance.

Jeremy Mayfield and his Mobil 1 teammates celebrated their first win in over two years following the California victory. After becoming the 10th different winner in as many races this year, Mayfield found himself seventh in the point standings, just five points behind defending NASCAR Winston Cup Series Champion Dale Jarrett.

By the time the teams assembled for the Pontiac Excitement 400 the following weekend, however, Mayfield was 14th in the driver standings and his Ford team had been taken behind the woodshed for a thorough whipping.

Based on test results of the fuel sample taken from the catch-can at Talladega, the team was hit with a $50,000 fine, crew chief Peter Sospenzo was suspended for a month, and the team's owners, Michael Kranefuss and Roger Penske, were docked 151 owner points. Mayfield was penalized the same number of driver points, causing his plummet from seventh to 14th in the standings. As if that wasn't enough, Jeremy's triumphant dance on the top of the car in California's victory lane had made the Taurus too low going through post-race technical inspection, and the team received another fine to the tune of $25,000.

"Little E" gets a congratulatory hug from Dad and team owner Dale Earnhardt. After the final restart, Dale Jr. fought past the seven-time champ to take the lead for the final time in the race.

of the season with a fourth place in California, Rudd found himself out of The Winston, the sport's upcoming all-star race. Mayfield's victory had dropped Rudd from automatic entry and into the field for the Winston Open. The Richmond race — at a track where Ricky had a chance to perform in front of his Virginia fans — was the last chance for Rudd to re-earn an automatic berth in The Winston. If he failed to win on the three-quarter mile "mini-super-speedway," he would have to triumph in the preliminary events to The Winston

(Above) A wounded Jeremy Mayfield is chased by teammate Rusty Wallace. Trying to shake off penalties incurred after last week's win in California, Mayfield cut a tire and smacked the wall, leaving him with a 36th-place finish.

(Right) Wallace enjoyed lightning-fast pit stops that helped the pole-winner stay out front for much of the race. Ironically, a stop for tires during the seventh caution of the evening cost him dearly when many of the lead-lap cars decided not to pit, dropping Rusty back into the pack.

(Below Right) Although Richmond is considered a short track, its wide, smooth racing surface allows two and three-abreast racing, as demonstrated by Michael Waltrip (7), Chad Little (97) and Robby Gordon (13).

Members of the team shouldered the responsibility, the fines and the point loss levied by NASCAR officials, and they arrived in Richmond hoping to put the affair behind them. Mayfield and his teammates hoped solid runs during the second two-thirds of the season would enable Jeremy to climb back to the position he had held immediately following the California race.

While Mayfield and his team arrived in Richmond with their personal mission, Ricky Rudd had his own. Despite posting his first top-five finish since joining Robert Yates Racing at the beginning

Ricky Rudd sticks his Texaco Ford on the inside to get past Mike Skinner (31) with Jeff Burton (99) applying pressure from behind. Rudd was fighting for a win that would restore his status in The Winston, but fell a little short finishing fourth behind teammate Dale Jarrett.

to regain a spot in the field for the all-star race. He was one of only three drivers who have competed in all of the 15 previous runnings of the event, and he was determined to maintain that string.

Bobby Labonte had moved back to the point lead after Mark Martin's 14th place in California, with Martin 20 points behind Labonte and 53 ahead of Ward Burton. Jeff Burton trailed his brother by 47 points and held a slim, 12-point margin over Dale Earnhardt.

Jarrett held sixth place, with Jeff Gordon seventh after Mayfield's penalty. Rusty Wallace was eighth, with Rudd now ninth, 57 points ahead of Mike Skinner. Tony Stewart (11th) and Terry Labonte (12th) were right on Skinner's tail.

Although he failed to approach the track record set a year ago by Jeff Gordon, Rusty Wallace slipped around the track fast enough to gain his third Bud Pole Award of the season and the 29th of his career. He needed every bit of speed he could muster with the Miller Lite Ford to push Steve Park onto the outside of the front row, while Skinner was third fastest. Geoffrey Bodine made a superb return to action after

Mark Martin brings out the final caution of the night on lap 363 after a cut tire sent him into the wall. Unable to return to action, Martin dropped to 32nd in the finishing order and fell a spot to third in the points.

(Left) Tony Stewart (20) and Dale Earnhardt Jr. duel on the track during mid-race action. Stewart emerged as a strong contender to win at the site of his initial NASCAR Winston Cup Series victory, which came here last fall.

(Below) With the win apparently in hand, Stewart pits during the final caution for fresh tires and enough fuel to carry him to the checkers. Upon leaving his pit, however, a collision with Earnhardt Jr. forced him to return to pit road, spoiling his bid to become the season's 11th different winner.

recovering from his Daytona truck accident to post the fourth-fastest lap in the Power Team Chevrolet and grab the outside of the second row. Dale Earnhardt Jr. continued his qualifying success by claiming the inside of the third row, with Rudd delighting the Virginia fans with the sixth-fastest lap. Tony Stewart and Wally Dallenbach made up the fourth row ahead of Bobby Labonte and Bill Elliott. Martin and John Andretti just missed the top 10 to claim the sixth row.

Dale Jarrett, making his 400th career start, qualified 18th, while Jeff Burton and Chad Little, each making his 200th career start, qualified 29th and 26th, respectively. Matt Kenseth, who had threatened to win at California, was forced to use a provisional, as were Michael Waltrip, Kevin Lepage, Jerry Nadeau, Kyle Petty, Elliott Sadler and Mike Bliss. Rick Mast failed to get A.J. Foyt's Conseco Pontiac into the field, and Darrell Waltrip, out of provisionals, missed the race for the first time this season. Dave Marcis didn't make the field, nor did Ed Berrier, who was hoping to give Junie Donlavey's Ford a good run in its hometown.

When the green flag fell on Saturday evening's Pontiac Excitement 400, Richmond's usual throng of fans on hand to feel the thunder were hoping to see the string of different winners extended to 11. Mark Martin, however, was hoping to break the string and become the first two-time winner of the season, but his evening turned out to be a nightmare. His nephew, NASCAR Busch Series crew chief Christian Lovendahl, had been killed in an auto accident Friday evening after the Emerald Performance Group entry failed to make the field and returned to the Charlotte area. Lovendahl was the son of

Bobby Labonte gets out of shape after receiving a tap that sent him spinning down the frontstretch. The mishap dropped Labonte to a 26th-place finish and cut his lead in the standings to a mere three points over Ward Burton.

Mark's sister, Glenda White, and the popular star was struggling with the loss. Later in the event, Mark hit the wall after a right-front tire went down, sending him to 32nd place in the race results and costing him second place in the point standings.

For the longest time, it appeared the string would extend to 11 straight different winners. Tony Stewart, who had not led a lap in the first 10 races of the season, changed that quickly and appeared poised to emerge as the Richmond winner for a second straight time. Pole-sitter Wallace led early and often, but fell away from the point when he made a pit stop under yellow while nearly a dozen other lead-lap cars stayed out. With Wallace out of the way, Stewart made his move, and when the final caution sent the field to pit road with just over 30 laps to go, it appeared Stewart was on his way to victory.

As he was exiting pit road however, he and Dale Earnhardt Jr. came together, and Stewart immediately headed back to pit road with a flat left-rear tire. He returned to action at the tail end of the lead-lap cars and fought through the field to eighth in the remaining laps, but he could go no higher.

On the second lap after the final restart, "Junior" passed his father for the lead and then countered every move Terry Labonte

could make in the closing circuits. Labonte couldn't come up with the right move to get past the Budweiser Chevrolet, and as the cars flashed to the line, "Little E" became the first two-time winner of the season.

Jarrett fought to third place ahead of Rudd, who posted his second straight fourth-place finish, but failed to regain entry into The Winston. Wallace was fifth ahead of a steady Ward Burton, while Jeff Burton was seventh. Stewart claimed eighth place ahead of Bill Elliott, while Dale Earnhardt was 10th in the final rundown. Point-leader Bobby Labonte was collected in a tangle with Gordon and Jarrett and struggled to a 26th-place finish at Richmond.

Dale Earnhardt Jr. lights up his tires along the frontstretch shortly after becoming the season's first two-time winner.

PONTIAC EXCITEMENT 400 • final results

Geoffrey Bodine returned to action at Richmond for the first time since being sidelined due to an accident at Daytona. Bodine qualified fourth and finished the race on the lead lap in 13th place.

Fin. Pos.	Start Pos.	Car No.	Driver	Team		Fin. Pos.	Start Pos.	Car No.	Driver	Team
1	5	8	Dale Earnhardt Jr.	Budweiser Chevrolet		23	17	33	Joe Nemechek	Oakwood Homes Chevrolet
2	30	5	Terry Labonte	Kellogg's Chevrolet		24	42	21	Elliott Sadler	CITGO Ford
3	18	88	Dale Jarrett	Quality Care/Ford Credit Ford		25	23	10	Johnny Benson	Lycos.com Pontiac
4	6	28	Ricky Rudd	Texaco/Havoline Ford		26	9	18	Bobby Labonte	Interstate Batteries Pontiac
5	1	2	Rusty Wallace	Miller Lite Ford		27	35	32	Scott Pruett	Tide Ford
6	13	22	Ward Burton	Caterpillar Pontiac		28	41	44	Kyle Petty	Hot Wheels Pontiac
7	29	99	Jeff Burton	Exide Batteries Ford		29	21	40	Sterling Marlin	Coors Light Chevrolet
8	7	20	Tony Stewart	Home Depot Pontiac		30	40	25	Jerry Nadeau	MichaelHoligan.com Chevrolet
9	10	94	Bill Elliott	McDonald's Ford		31	24	4	Bobby Hamilton	Kodak Chevrolet
10	31	3	Dale Earnhardt	GM Goodwrench Service Chevrolet		32	11	6	Mark Martin	Valvoline/Cummins Ford
11	2	1	Steve Park	Pennzoil Chevrolet		33	3	31	Mike Skinner	Lowe's Chevrolet
12	34	36	Ken Schrader	M&M's Pontiac		34	32	93	Dave Blaney	Amoco Pontiac
13	4	60	Geoffrey Bodine	Power Team Chevrolet		35	27	77	Robert Pressley	Jasper Engines Ford
14	15	24	Jeff Gordon	DuPont Automotive Finishes Chevrolet		36	20	12	Jeremy Mayfield	Mobil 1 Ford
15	37	17	Matt Kenseth	DeWalt Tools Ford		37	36	13	Robby Gordon	Burger King Ford
16	8	75	Wally Dallenbach	TBS Dinner & A Movie Ford		38	28	11	Brett Bodine	Ralphs Supermarkets Ford
17	22	26	Jimmy Spencer	Big Kmart/Route 66 Ford		39	26	97	Chad Little	John Deere Ford
18	12	43	John Andretti	STP/Cheerios Pontiac		40	14	50	Ricky Craven	Midwest Transit Chevrolet
19	38	7	Michael Waltrip	Nations Rent Chevrolet		41	43	27	Mike Bliss	Pfizer/Viagra Pontiac
20	16	55	Kenny Wallace	Square D/Cooper Lighting Chevrolet		42	25	42	Kenny Irwin	BellSouth Chevrolet
21	39	16	Kevin Lepage	FamilyClick.com Ford		43	33	91	Todd Bodine	Little Joe's Auto Chevrolet
22	19	9	Stacy Compton	Kodiak/Cougar Ford						

THE WINSTON

(Left) Tony Stewart, last year's runner-up in The Winston, prepares to make another run for victory from his sixth-place starting spot.

(Right) An elated Dale Earnhardt Jr. claims victory in his first attempt at the sport's all-star event.

Over the course of the last 15 years, The Winston has built a reputation of being a no-holds-barred battle to the finish. And during those years, at times, the all-star race rivaled Independence Day for fireworks both on and off the track.

Perhaps it is the fact that The Winston is a non-points race and has no bearing on the final NASCAR Winston Cup Series point standings and the point-fund bonuses paid to the top drivers at the end of the season. Perhaps it is the fact that it pays a huge sum to the winner — this year $500,000. Perhaps it is the opportunity to prove you are the best among equals, because it is a winners-only race.

Perhaps it is all of that — and more. Whatever the reasons, though, the outcome of The Winston, more often than not, is hallmarked by brilliant driving, outstanding pit strategy and some bumping and shoving on the track. Usually, a little racing luck favors one driver over another in the closing laps of the race.

The format for this year's edition of The Winston featured a tweak or two, including a pair of chances to salvage a place in the main event for those drivers who had not already earned their way into the pack. The winner of the Winston Open would transfer into The Winston, and this year, a 16-lap No Bull Sprint offered another driver the chance to make it into the finale. Only the lead-lap cars at the end of the Winston Open would be eligible for the No Bull Sprint.

Bill Elliott claims the pole for The Winston after beating Mark Martin by a fraction of a second in the three-lap qualifying run. Elliott paced the field in the first two segments but fell to eighth in the final 10-lap sprint.

(Left) John Andretti's hopes for a good showing in The Winston were dashed quickly when a tap from behind resulted in this brush with the wall that sent him home without completing a lap.

(Below) Joe Nemechek, who started the final segment in fourth, fights to bring his Chevrolet under control after he tangled with Park in an incident that also collected Jeff Gordon and Tony Stewart. All four cars were through for the evening.

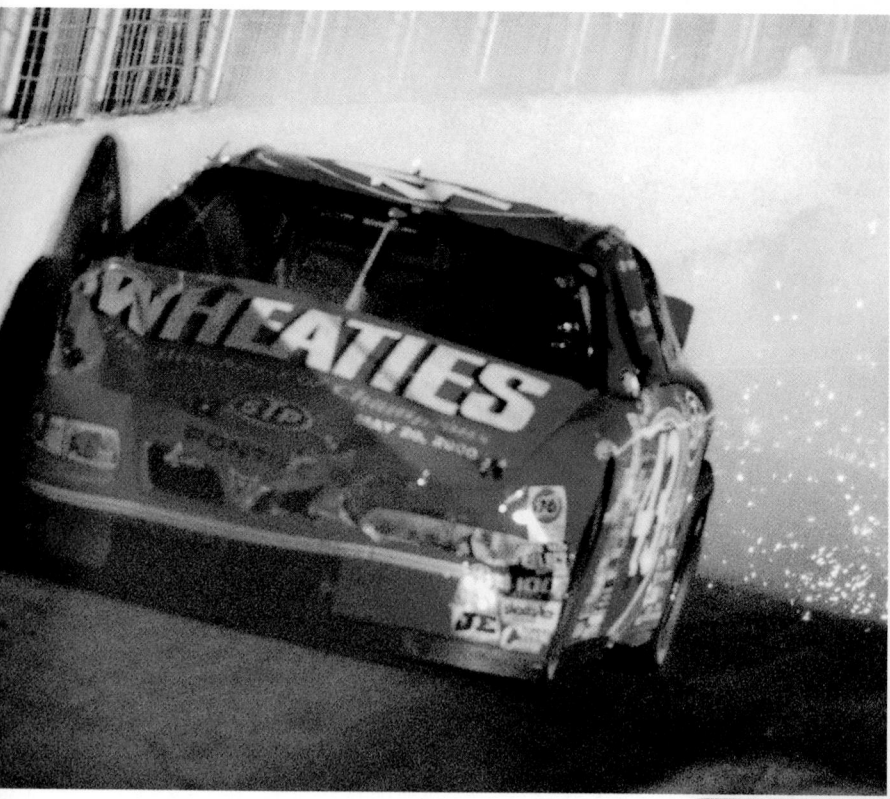

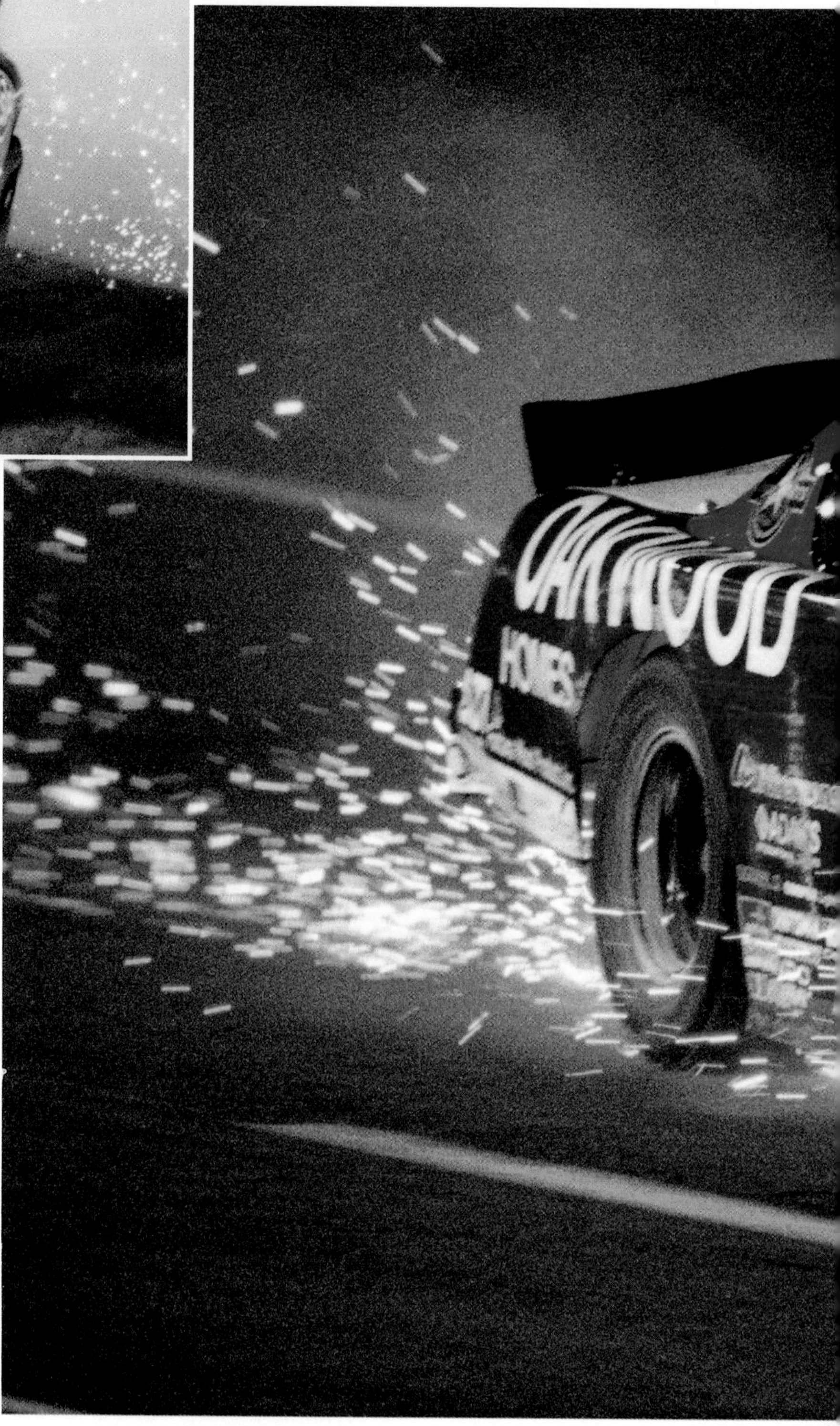

For Ricky Rudd, that meant two opportunities to try to fight his way back into The Winston. Jeremy Mayfield's California victory had bumped Rudd out of The Winston and into the Winston Open, and Rudd was determined to find a way back into the all-star event. He was one of just three drivers who had competed in all 15 previous runnings of The Winston, and he wanted to keep the record intact.

The mood in the garage area was somber as teams began practice for the weekend, and Kyle Petty's Hot Wheels Pontiac was missing from the field. During the "off" weekend between Richmond and The Winston, the sport lost Kyle's son Adam following an accident at New Hampshire in preparation for the NASCAR Busch Series event. The Petty family was devastated, Kyle withdrew his Hot Wheels entry for the race, and the entire racing community fought back tears for the family that had been the backbone of the sport since it began.

Bill Elliott emerged with the fastest cumulative time from the three-lap, two-tire pit stop qualifying session that determined the pole winner for The Winston, notching his first start from the inside of a front row since September 1997 at Richmond. His McDonald's Drive-Thru crew helped him beat Mark Martin's Valvoline Ford effort by just .022 second. Bobby Labonte claimed the inside of the second row for the start of the all-star race, nudging Rusty

Wallace to the fourth starting position. Dale Earnhardt Jr., the choice of Lowe's Motor Speedway president "Humpy" Wheeler to win The Winston, qualified fifth fastest with his Budweiser Chevrolet.

A pair of No Bull 25-lap qualifying races determined the starting grid for the Winston Open, with Jerry Nadeau and Jimmy Spencer emerging as the winners to gain the front-row positions. Spencer led the Open and appeared headed to The Winston, but with 11 laps left in the 30-lap event, Steve Park ripped his way past to put the yellow-and-black Pennzoil Chevrolet in victory lane — and into one of the final two starting slots in The Winston. In the 16-lap No Bull Sprint that followed, Nadeau found a way past Kevin Lepage with one lap to go and fought his way into the final starting spot for The Winston. Rudd struggled with handling problems and could not get the Texaco Ford dialed in enough to earn one of the transfer slots, and he watched his mark of 15 consecutive appearances in The Winston come to an end.

(Above) Steve Park rides high to avoid a spinning Mark Martin after the Valvoline Ford was tagged by Stewart near the end of the second segment.

(Right) Martin's hopes for a second win in The Winston ride back to the garage on a flatbed after the lap-55 incident that ended the race for the 1998 winner.

The Winston is divided into a pair of 30-lap segments, and then a final, 10-lap, green-flag shootout. Elliott controlled the field in the first 30 laps while the action ensued behind him. Park and Nadeau began clawing their way through the field, with Nadeau moving to sixth before the 30 laps were over. Park was even better, moving to fifth at the end of the first leg. Their runs were negated somewhat when the first 12 finishers of the first segment were inverted to start the second 30-lap portion, but they immediately began fighting their way back to the front.

After moving as high as third in the second segment, Earnhardt Jr. headed for pit road with a loose left-rear tire. He caught a break when a four-car accident occurred just as he was entering pit road, and he went straight through the pits to keep from loosing a lap. The accident involved his father, as well as Jeff Gordon, Park and Jeff Burton. "Little E" was able to pit under the caution flag, and later in the segment, he slipped up and slapped

He restarted 10th and, six laps later, rocketed past his father to take third place. Jarrett's Ford began trailing a thin plume of smoke — and Dale Jr. had the throttle wide open, moving past Nadeau to take second place and setting his sights on Jarrett.

Jarrett was helpless. Although the smoke didn't affect his Ford, he had nothing with which to battle the rookie driver and could only watch as the new tires on the Budweiser Chevrolet provided the needed advantage. Earnhardt Jr. swept past Jarrett and then rocketed under the flagstand to take the checkered flag. He became the first rookie to win The Winston, and he pocketed more than $516,000 for his efforts.

Jarrett finished second, while Earnhardt took his Chevrolet to third place, making it a Dale-Dale-Dale finish in the top three positions. Nadeau completed his sparkling weekend by taking fourth place ahead of Jeff Burton. Terry Labonte soldiered to sixth ahead of Rusty Wallace, while Elliott was forced to settle for eighth place after his outstanding performance. Bobby Labonte finished ninth ahead of Ward Burton in 10th.

the outside wall but was fortunate not to do any major damage to the red-and-black Chevrolet. Once again, Elliott showed the strength of his McDonald's Taurus, taking the field under the flag at the conclusion of the second leg of the race.

When the green flag dropped on the final 10-lap sprint, Dale Jarrett battled his way past Elliott for the point, and behind him things heated up immediately. Joe Nemechek and Park, battling for position, hit once on the backstretch, and on the next lap, the two cars came together again. Park's car went spinning, while Nemechek hit the outside wall and collected Tony Stewart and Gordon. During the caution, "Little E" came down pit road, taking on tires and gambling the new Goodyears would be enough to get him back through the field in the remaining laps.

THE WINSTON • final results

Dale Earnhardt's battered Chevrolet was good enough to take third place in the race, but a rough night on the track did not allow him to score his fourth all-star victory.

Segment 1 (30 Laps)		Segment 2 (30 Laps)		Segment 3 (10 Laps)					
				Finish	Start	Car No.	Driver	Team	
1	Bill Elliott	1	Bill Elliott	1	3	8	Dale Earnhardt Jr.	Budweiser Chevrolet	
2	Mark Martin	2	Dale Jarrett	2	2	88	Dale Jarrett	Quality Care/Ford Credit Ford	
3	Dale Earnhardt Jr.	3	Dale Earnhardt Jr.	3	10	3	Dale Earnhardt	GM Goodwrench Service Chevrolet	
4	Jeff Gordon	4	Joe Nemechek	4	7	25	Jerry Nadeau	MichaelHoligan.com Chevrolet	
5	Steve Park	5	Rusty Wallace	5	8	99	Jeff Burton	Exide Batteries Ford	
6	Jerry Nadeau	6	Steve Park	6	13	5	Terry Labonte	Kellogg's Chevrolet	
7	Rusty Wallace	7	Jerry Nadeau	7	5	2	Rusty Wallace	Miller Lite Ford	
8	Ward Burton	8	Jeff Burton	8	1	94	Bill Elliott	McDonald's Ford	
9	Bobby Labonte	9	Tony Stewart	9	11	18	Bobby Labonte	Interstate Batteries Pontiac	
10	Tony Stewart	10	Dale Earnhardt	10	15	22	Ward Burton	Caterpillar Pontiac	
11	Jeremy Mayfield	11	Bobby Labonte	11	14	66	Darrell Waltrip	Route 66/Big Kmart Ford	
12	Joe Nemechek	12	Jeff Gordon	12	16	42	Kenny Irwin	BellSouth Chevrolet	
13	Dale Earnhardt	13	Terry Labonte	13	6	1	Steve Park	Pennzoil Chevrolet	
14	Dale Jarrett	14	Darrell Waltrip	14	4	33	Joe Nemechek	Oakwood Homes Chevrolet	
15	Terry Labonte	15	Ward Burton	15	9	20	Tony Stewart	Home Depot Pontiac	
16	Jeff Burton	16	Kenny Irwin	16	12	24	Jeff Gordon	DuPont Automotive Finishes Chevrolet	
17	Darrell Waltrip	17	Mark Martin	17	17	6	Mark Martin	Valvoline/Cummins Ford	
18	Kenny Irwin	18	Jeremy Mayfield	18	18	12	Jeremy Mayfield	Mobil 1 Ford	
19	Michael Waltrip	19	Michael Waltrip	19	19	7	Michael Waltrip	Nations Rent Chevrolet	
20	John Andretti	20	John Andretti	20	20	43	John Andretti	STP/Cheerios Pontiac	

COCA-COLA 600

MAY 28, 2000 • LOWE'S MOTOR SPEEDWAY

(Left) The capacity crowd on hand at Lowe's Motor Speedway enjoys early-evening action in the Coca-Cola 600.

(Right) At the end of the night, a new name graced a NASCAR Winston Cup Series winner's circle for the first time — that of rookie driver Matt Kenseth.

Between Winston and Budweiser, Lowe's Motor Speedway was red to the core following Dale Earnhardt Jr.'s gutsy charge to become the first rookie driver to win the sport's all-star race. With no lifelines left, he had brilliantly answered the final question during LMS' annual presentation of "Who Wants To Be A Half-Millionaire."

The Memorial Day Weekend event at Charlotte always pays tribute to America's veterans, and this year, five cars carried special paint schemes recognizing the five branches of America's armed forces. Ricky Rudd carried the colors of the Marines on his Texaco Ford, while Dale Jarrett's Quality Care Ford was the Air Force car. Mike Skinner's Lowe's Chevrolet was bedecked in the colors of the Army, Jerry Nadeau's Michael Holigan Homes Chevrolet was the Coast Guard car, and Bobby Hamilton's Kodak Chevrolet honored the Navy.

Among the other cars with special paint schemes for the event was Dale Earnhardt's, with his GM Goodwrench Service Chevrolet arriving in the same Peter Max design it had carried in The Winston. One team not interested in changing anything was "Little E's" Budweiser crew. After winning The Winston, the team brought back the very same red-and-black Chevrolet for the Coca-Cola 600.

Jack Roush couldn't be happier in victory lane, especially while joining first-time winner Matt Kenseth, his youngest star and understudy to veteran Mark Martin.

The scoreboard shows:

9	20
10	55
11	26
12	2
13	4
14	24
15	4
16	3
17	43
18	1
19	6
20	28
4	12 17
42	13

Silence falls over fans and competitors prior to the command to start engines, while the huge throng salutes America's veterans at the Memorial Day Weekend classic.

NASCAR announced that Joe Nemechek would be fined $15,000 for "rough driving" after precipitating the crash in The Winston that included Steve Park, while John Andretti was struggling with injured ribs he suffered in his early-race accident in The Winston. Before the Coca-Cola 600 weekend was over, he would yield to Tim Fedewa, who drove the STP Pontiac in relief. Kyle Petty was again not at the track, with Steve Grissom nominated to drive the Hot Wheels Pontiac for the weekend.

Other news included the announcement of a new five-year extension of DuPont's sponsorship of Jeff Gordon, and Gordon's extension of his driving contract with Hendrick Motorsports until 2005. Ray Evernham finally ended the speculation surrounding his new Dodge team

by announcing his second driver in 2001 would be NASCAR Busch Series star Casey Atwood.

With The Winston in the history books, attention turned back to the point race, where Bobby Labonte held a meager three-point

Five cars carried special paint schemes as a tribute to the five branches of the U.S. armed forces. Among them was Dale Jarrett's Ford, which represented the Air Force.

margin over Ward Burton as teams prepared for the Coca-Cola 600. Despite his poor finish at Richmond, Mark Martin was just 30 points behind Ward and 33 behind Labonte after the first 11 races of the season. Roush Racing teammate Jeff Burton was fourth, 26 points behind Martin, while seven-time champion Earnhardt was fifth, 19 points behind the Exide Ford driver.

Defending NASCAR Winston Cup Series Champion Dale Jarrett was sixth, 53 behind Earnhardt, while Rusty Wallace held seventh place, 34 points behind Jarrett and 25 ahead of Rudd. Gordon held down ninth place in the standings, 11 behind Rudd and 43 ahead of Terry Labonte.

For the longest time during Bud Pole qualifying, it appeared that Jerry Nadeau would parlay his strong performance during The Winston weekend into the first NASCAR Winston Cup Series pole position of his career. He ripped off a lap in excess of 185 miles per hour and then watched as driver after driver failed to beat his speed.

Finally, with less than a handful of drivers left, Nadeau was forced to settle for the outside of the front row when Dale Jr. rolled to a new track record of just over 186 mph. It marked the first pole of Little E's NASCAR Winston Cup Series career, and it came in his 17th race.

(Left) Dale Earnhardt Jr. continued his fine performance during Race Weeks in Charlotte by notching the first Bud Pole of his NASCAR Winston Cup Series career. Alongside is Jerry Nadeau, who took the lead from Earnhardt Jr. on lap 50 and was clearly the fastest car on the track until engine problems sidelined his Chevrolet late in the race.

(Below) One look to the Eastern sky left little doubt that rain would become a factor in the event. The approaching deluge didn't last long, however, and the race resumed and ran its scheduled distance.

Matt Kenseth (17) sticks his Ford on the bottom of the turns to dispose of Ricky Rudd (28) and Jeff Burton (99). Kenseth spent the first three-quarters of the race battling through traffic on the track and adjusting his car in the pits until, on lap 375, he took the lead from Bobby Labonte and never looked back.

Bill Elliott and Jeremy Mayfield claimed the second row ahead of Mike Skinner and Kevin Lepage. Bobby Labonte and Dale Jarrett made up the fourth row, with Tony Stewart and Kenny Wallace right behind. ARCA driver Carl Long made the field in 35th place, while Terry Labonte, Chad Little, Johnny Benson, Stacy Compton, Elliott Sadler, Robby Gordon and Mike Bliss used provisionals.

Missing the field were Ted Musgrave, Ed Berrier, Dave Marcis, Steve Grissom in the Hot Wheels Pontiac and Darrell Waltrip, who was hoping to make the final Coca-Cola 600 start of his career. After qualifying was completed, Waltrip worked a deal with Long to start the race in his car and quickly moved his Big Kmart decals over to Long's Ford.

With the threat of rain in the offing, the Coca-Cola 600 field took the green flag Sunday, and it was obvious from the start that Dale Jr. was primed to make a run at his third point-race victory of the season. He ultimately led 175 of the 400 laps, and although the race was stopped for nearly an hour because of a rain shower, the Budweiser Chevrolet driver appeared ready to strike when the field restarted on lap 366 after the seventh caution period of the event. On that restart, Bobby Labonte held the point with Little E second, but neither driver would have anything for Matt Kenseth, who restarted the race in third place.

Crew chief Robby Reiser had made an air pressure adjustment in the right-rear tire, and when the green flew, Kenseth felt the DeWalt Tools Ford responded perfectly. The rookie fought past Earnhardt Jr. to take second place on lap 369, moved past

Terry Labonte (5) and Geoffrey Bodine (60), making his second start of the season, scream through the tri-oval side by side in their battle for position.

Fireworks light up the sky behind Lowe's Motor Speedway's victory lane while Matt Kenseth hoists his first big-league trophy. The win moved Kenseth up a spot to 13th in the driver standings and boosted his lead over Earnhardt Jr. in rookie points.

Labonte on lap 375 and eased away from the field. No one could challenge him, and with his half-second triumph, Kenseth became the first rookie in history to win the Coca-Cola 600. The popular victory made him just the fourth driver to make the Memorial Day classic his first NASCAR Winston Cup Series victory, putting him in the record books with David Pearson, Jeff Gordon and Bobby Labonte. The win came in his 18th career NASCAR Winston Cup Series start, and he wrote another page in the LMS record book by starting 21st en route to becoming the driver to win from the furthest back in the history of the race.

Bobby Labonte fought to second, adding to his point lead, while Earnhardt brought his Peter Max-designed Chevrolet to third place in the closing laps. Little E was forced to settle for fourth place ahead of Jarrett and Mayfield, while Skinner and Rusty Wallace finished seventh and eighth. Despite a spin early in the race, Park came home ninth while Gordon and Jeff Burton were 10th and 11th, the final drivers on the lead lap.

COCA-COLA 600 • final results

Mike Bliss (27) is sandwiched between Jimmy Spencer (26) and Chad Little (97) as the three drivers put on a show in front of the frontstretch grandstands.

Fin. Pos.	Start Pos.	Car No.	Driver	Team	Fin. Pos.	Start Pos.	Car No.	Driver	Team
1	21	17	Matt Kenseth	DeWalt Tools Ford	23	27	33	Joe Nemechek	Oakwood Homes Chevrolet
2	7	18	Bobby Labonte	Interstate Batteries Pontiac	24	33	42	Kenny Irwin	BellSouth Chevrolet
3	15	3	Dale Earnhardt	GM Goodwrench Service Chevrolet	25	11	26	Jimmy Spencer	Big Kmart/Route 66 Ford
4	1	8	Dale Earnhardt Jr.	Budweiser Chevrolet	26	24	77	Robert Pressley	Jasper Engines Ford
5	8	88	Dale Jarrett	Quality Care/Ford Credit Ford	27	10	55	Kenny Wallace	Square D/Cooper Lighting Chevrolet
6	4	12	Jeremy Mayfield	Mobil 1 Ford	28	32	75	Wally Dallenbach	RotoZip Tools Ford
7	5	31	Mike Skinner	Lowe's Chevrolet	29	29	60	Geoffrey Bodine	Power Team Chevrolet
8	16	2	Rusty Wallace	Mille Lite Ford	30	25	11	Brett Bodine	Ralphs Supermarkets Ford
9	18	1	Steve Park	Pennzoil Chevrolet	31	17	43	John Andretti	STP/Cheerios Pontiac
10	14	24	Jeff Gordon	DuPont Automotive Finishes Chevrolet	32	43	27	Mike Bliss	Pfizer/Viagra Pontiac
11	28	99	Jeff Burton	Exide Batteries Ford	33	40	9	Stacy Compton	Kodiak/Cougar Ford
12	19	6	Mark Martin	Valvoline/Cummins Ford	34	13	4	Bobby Hamilton	Kodak Chevrolet
13	31	22	Ward Burton	Caterpillar Pontiac	35	42	13	P.J. Jones	Burger King/Turtlewax Ford
14	9	20	Tony Stewart	Home Depot Pontiac	36	35	85	Darrell Waltrip	Route 66/Big Kmart Ford
15	6	16	Kevin Lepage	FamilyClick.com Ford	37	34	36	Ken Schrader	M&M's Pontiac
16	39	10	Johnny Benson	Lycos.com Pontiac	38	2	25	Jerry Nadeau	MichaelHoligan.com Chevrolet
17	20	28	Ricky Rudd	Texaco/Havoline Ford	39	23	14	Rick Mast	Conseco Pontiac
18	12	7	Michael Waltrip	Nations Rent Chevrolet	40	30	93	Dave Blaney	Amoco Pontiac
19	36	40	Sterling Marlin	Coors Light Chevrolet	41	26	32	Scott Pruett	Tide Ford
20	38	97	Chad Little	John Deere Ford	42	22	50	Ricky Craven	Midwest Transit Chevrolet
21	41	21	Elliott Sadler	CITGO Ford	43	3	94	Bill Elliott	McDonald's Ford
22	37	5	Terry Labonte	Kellogg's Chevrolet					

MBNA PLATINUM *400*

(Left) Tony Stewart gives the big "thumbs up" after a dominating performance at Dover made him the 12th winner of the season.

(Right) Dover's pit road is a very busy place with nearly the entire field pitting under caution early in the race.

After leading the point standings following the DieHard 500 at Talladega just four races ago, Mark Martin began to struggle and now found himself 81 points behind Bobby Labonte in the battle for this year's NASCAR Winston Cup Series title.

With plenty of racing left in the season, Martin knew he had time to return to a challenging position in the standings, but to do it, he and his Roush Racing teammates needed a good run at Dover's "Monster Mile." Martin found himself trailing Ward Burton by 27 points following the Coca-Cola 600, and worse, he was in a virtual tie with seven-time NASCAR Winston Cup Series Champion Dale Earnhardt.

Earnhardt's hard-fought third place at Charlotte moved him to just two points behind Martin, and suddenly, teams were beginning to believe they would have to deal with The Intimidator as a championship contender in the second half of the season. That realization sent shudders through many of the veteran teams. They knew full well what it would be like to have to contend with Earnhardt if he drew to less than 100 points of the leader. Jeff Burton fell to fifth place, 21 behind Earnhardt, while Dale Jarrett trailed the Exide Ford driver by 42 markers. Rusty Wallace remained seventh in the standings, 52 points behind Jarrett and now 39 ahead of Jeff Gordon, who had moved past Ricky Rudd into eighth place.

Tony Stewart was the beneficiary of a late-race caution that gave him a chance to make this stop for two new tires and enough fuel to carry him to the checkered flag.

(Left) Dale Jarrett ponders his car's setup while Brad Parrott (left) and crew chief Todd Parrott (right) review their notes. In Sunday's event, the Quality Care Ford did not lead, but a solid fourth-place finish was good enough to move Jarrett from sixth to fourth in the point standings.

(Below Left) Team owner Michael Kranefuss (left) confers with team member Buddy Cisco before the start of Sunday's MBNA Platinum 400. The team, coming off a strong sixth-place finish in the Coca-Cola 600, qualified fifth but lost an engine just past the halfway mark at Dover.

(Bottom) Gasman Dave Collins stands ready to perform his duties in the Mobil 1 pit for driver Jeremy Mayfield at Dover.

His efforts to make the field in his own Hot Wheels Pontiac failed during qualifying, and he was then enlisted to relief-drive for John Andretti, still recovering from his rib injuries suffered at Charlotte.

Missing from the garage area was Robby Gordon's team. Gordon had made the decision to step back slightly and regroup his efforts, concentrating on being totally prepared every time his team arrived at a track. He planned to run in seven of the next 11 races — primarily at the road courses and intermediate-sized tracks.

Dover's concrete surface was baking in the Delaware heat, and the combination of heat and a harder tire compound from Goodyear kept speeds from record levels during Bud Pole qualifying — but Rusty Wallace could have cared less. So what if he was 2.5 miles per hour slower than the track record he set here last September? He still had more than enough in his Miller Lite Ford to claim his fourth pole position of the season, although Bill Elliott made him work for it. Elliott missed the pole by one-hundredth of a second but claimed his fourth top-five and second straight top-three starting position. Kenny Wallace

Tony Stewart climbed to 10th place, two points ahead of Terry Labonte, while Mike Skinner, Matt Kenseth and Jeremy Mayfield all moved up a notch as Bill Elliott fell to 15th place.

Dover marked the return to the garage area of Kyle Petty, and Kyle planned to do double duty at the Monster Mile. He would pilot son Adam's entry in the NASCAR Busch Series event Saturday and drive his own Hot Wheels Pontiac in the Sunday NASCAR Winston Cup Series race. Kyle hoped his return to action would in some way alleviate the painful loss of Adam. He ran in the top five in the late going of the NASCAR Busch Series event but was forced to pit road for tires and fell out of contention for victory.

Jeremy Mayfield (12), Tony Stewart (20), Mike Skinner (31) and Dale Earnhardt Jr. (8) all took turns leading the race until Stewart took over for good with 64 laps remaining.

notched the third spot — right behind his older brother on t[...] — while Mark Martin was fourth fastest. Valvoline had announced it would be leaving the team as the primary sponsor at the conclusion of this year, and Mark was determined to claim several more victories in the red-white-and-blue Ford before the sponsorship ended.

Jeremy Mayfield nailed down the fifth-fastest lap, while Dale Earnhardt Jr. continued his outstanding qualifying efforts with sixth place. Rudd and Skinner made up the fourth row for the MBNA Platinum 400, while Bobby Labonte and Joe Nemechek beat Kenny Irwin and Wally Dallenbach for the final top-10 starting positions. Terry Labonte, Chad Little, Jimmy Spencer, Bobby Hamilton, Mike Bliss, Ed Berrier and Dave Marcis used provisionals to make the

The crews of Mark Martin, Mike Skinner (31) and Bobby Labonte (18) go head to head on pit road during one of 10 cautions during the race. Labonte took home a top-five finish with Skinner in the top 10, but Martin lost an engine before the three-quarter mark and was listed 36th in the final order.

(Right) Mike Skinner (31) tries to seize the lead from Dale Earnhardt Jr. (8) in the opening laps of the race, with Bobby Hamilton (4) and Jeremy Mayfield observing the action from behind. Skinner and Earnhardt Jr. saw a lot of each other this day: They started nose to tail, and they finished together with Skinner in ninth ahead of 10th-place Earnhardt Jr.

(Below) Jeff Gordon, heading for his transporter immediately after the race, evaluates his day for MRN Radio reporter Winston Kelley. A cut tire with 20 laps remaining proved costly and left the three-time Dover winner with a 34th-place finish.

field, while Kyle Petty and Carl Long, the ARCA driver who had helped Darrell Waltrip the previous week at Charlotte, failed to make the Dover race.

Chad Little's John Deere-sponsored team had a long and difficult walk to pit road prior to the start of the Sunday event after learning that crewmember Dave Rush, a fabricator in the shop and the team's catch-can man during races, had been fatally injured in a boating accident near his home in the Charlotte area Saturday night.

The battle at the front in the early going of the MBNA Platinum 400 was torrid, with pole-sitter Wallace yielding to Earnhardt Jr. on the 10th lap. Skinner and Mayfield also led, and on lap 107, Tony Stewart, who had started 16th, seized the lead from Mayfield and suddenly began to look as though he could be the 12th different winner in the first 13 races of the season.

Stewart began dominating the race, leading laps in huge chunks, and as the race wore on, he put car after car a lap behind. Despite his dominance, however, it appeared he would have to make a final green-flag pit stop for fuel with 15 or so laps remaining to complete the 400-lap distance.

Knowing he would have to stop, Stewart sprinted away from the field, trying to build as big a lead as possible in preparation for his dash to pit road. It all became moot, however, when Jeff Gordon cut a tire and whacked the wall on lap 382. The yellow came out and

Stewart headed for pit road. Gordon's yellow flag trapped Earnhardt, Nemechek and Rusty Wallace a lap down after they had made their green-flag stops for fuel. That left just five cars on the lead lap for the final sprint to the flag, and Stewart made the most of it. He held off a valiant effort from Coca-Cola 600 winner Kenseth and then eased to a 1.1-second victory over the DeWalt Tools driver.

Bobby Labonte came home third, increasing his point lead, while Jarrett was fourth and Rudd fifth. Earnhardt fought to sixth place, beating Nemechek, Ward Burton, Skinner and Dale Jr. Elliott, after crashing his primary car in Saturday practice, brought his backup Ford home in 12th place, while the Andretti/Petty combination resulted in a 13th-place finish for the STP Pontiac.

Tony Stewart takes the green flag on a restart in the closing laps ahead of Matt Kenseth, Bobby Labonte, Dale Jarrett and Ricky Rudd, the only cars remaining on the lead lap at the end of the event.

MBNA PLATINUM 400 • final results

Rusty Wallace, here in front of Dale Jarrett, jumped to the early lead from his fourth pole of the year, but he fell off the leader's pace early and was later caught in the pits during a late-race caution.

Fin. Pos.	Start Pos.	Car No.	Driver	Team
1	16	20	Tony Stewart	Home Depot Pontiac
2	26	17	Matt Kenseth	DeWalt Tools Ford
3	9	18	Bobby Labonte	Interstate Batteries Pontiac
4	18	88	Dale Jarrett	Quality Care/Ford Credit Ford
5	7	28	Ricky Rudd	Texaco/Havoline Ford
6	30	3	Dale Earnhardt	GM Goodwrench Service Chevrolet
7	10	33	Joe Nemechek	Oakwood Homes Chevrolet
8	23	22	Ward Burton	Caterpillar Pontiac
9	8	31	Mike Skinner	Lowe's Chevrolet
10	6	8	Dale Earnhardt Jr.	Budweiser Chevrolet
11	37	5	Terry Labonte	Kellogg's Chevrolet
12	2	94	Bill Elliott	McDonald's Ford
13	33	43	John Andretti	STP/Cheerios Pontiac
14	1	2	Rusty Wallace	Miller Lite Ford
15	34	10	Johnny Benson	Lycos.com Pontiac
16	32	21	Elliott Sadler	CITGO Ford
17	11	42	Kenny Irwin	BellSouth Chevrolet
18	3	55	Kenny Wallace	Square D/Cooper Lighting Chevrolet
19	17	1	Steve Park	Pennzoil Chevrolet
20	38	97	Chad Little	John Deere Ford
21	20	16	Kevin Lepage	FamilyClick.com Ford
22	39	26	Jimmy Spencer	Big Kmart/Route 66 Ford

Fin. Pos.	Start Pos.	Car No.	Driver	Team
23	31	36	Ken Schrader	M&M's Pontiac
24	12	75	Wally Dallenbach	TBS Dinner & A Movie Ford
25	27	93	Dave Blaney	Amoco Pontiac
26	24	77	Robert Pressley	Jasper Engines Ford
27	40	4	Bobby Hamilton	Kodak Chevrolet
28	13	11	Brett Bodine	Ralphs Supermarkets Ford
29	43	71	Dave Marcis	Realtree Camouflage Chevrolet
30	21	9	Stacy Compton	Kodiak/Cougar Ford
31	25	40	Sterling Marlin	Coors Light Chevrolet
32	19	24	Jeff Gordon	DuPont Automotive Finishes Chevrolet
33	35	66	Darrell Waltrip	Route 66/Big Kmart Ford
34	14	99	Jeff Burton	Exide Batteries Ford
35	41	27	Mike Bliss	Pfizer/Viagra Pontiac
36	4	6	Mark Martin	Valvoline/Cummins Ford
37	5	12	Jeremy Mayfield	Mobil 1 Ford
38	29	32	Scott Pruett	Tide Ford
39	15	7	Michael Waltrip	Nations Rent Chevrolet
40	22	60	Geoffrey Bodine	Power Team Chevrolet
41	42	90	Ed Berrier	Hills Bros. Coffee Ford
42	36	25	Jerry Nadeau	MichaelHoligan.com Chevrolet
43	28	14	Rick Mast	Conseco Pontiac

KMART *400*

(Left) Robert Pressley (77) leads the field on a restart to begin lap 185 with Jimmy Spencer on his left and eventual race-winner Tony Stewart right behind.

(Right) Tony Stewart is all smiles after grabbing his second winner's trophy in as many weeks and notching the fifth win of his young career.

Tony Stewart arrived in Michigan's lovely Irish Hills with a changed attitude. The first third of the season had not been kind to last year's NASCAR Winston Cup Series Rookie of the Year, and the Home Depot Pontiac driver is one of the most intensively competitive and outspoken personalities in the garage area.

He had come close to winning a couple of times during the season's earlier races — particularly at Richmond, until a bump on pit road from Dale Earnhardt Jr. resulted in a cut tire and a lost chance at victory. The pressure of the NASCAR Winston Cup Series season — coupled with the frustration of not winning yet this year — had resulted in Tony's much ballyhooed comments at Charlotte during The Winston weekend in which he complained about the loss of privacy all drivers encounter when they become successful.

At Dover, however, he held the winning cards and played them perfectly as he rolled to a powerful victory, the first of the season for the orange-and-white Home Depot team and the fourth of Stewart's brief NASCAR Winston Cup Series career. With the victory, Stewart also became the 12th different driver to win in the first 13 races of the season.

Bobby Labonte captured his first Bud Pole Award of the season with a blistering track-record run at just a fraction under 190 mph on the two-mile Michigan oval.

Winning again at the sport's highest level brought back the relaxed side of Stewart, once again laughing and joking with media members and fans. The Dover victory also helped him continue marching up through the point standings where he now stood ninth, just 37 markers behind eighth-place Ricky Rudd.

Bobby Labonte remained the point leader as teams unloaded for the first of two stops at the immaculate two-mile oval west of Detroit. His lead had increased over fellow Pontiac driver Ward Burton, who fell from 54 to 82 behind after the Dover event. Dale Earnhardt had closed on Ward with the Dover results, moving to third place, just 16 markers behind the Caterpillar Pontiac driver. Mark Martin continued to struggle, falling from third place to fifth, which allowed Dale Jarrett to move into fourth in the standings.

Jeff Burton and Rusty Wallace also fell a position to sixth and seventh place, respectively, while Jeff Gordon dropped from eighth to 10th, just 22 points ahead of Hendrick Motorsports teammate Terry Labonte.

(Above Left) Under the watchful eye of a NASCAR official, a crewmember dumps rainwater from the air cleaner of Mike Skinner's Lowe's Chevrolet in preparation to restart the event after a short, red-flag delay for rain.

(Left) Steve Park (center) and Dale Earnhardt Jr. (right) find protection from the rain under Jeff Gordon's umbrella while waiting out the rain delay.

(Below) Johnny Benson (10), Jimmy Spencer (26) and Joe Nemechek use the width of Michigan's racing groove to run in perfect three-wide formation. Spencer made great progress during the day's event by climbing through the field to a 15th-place finish after having to use a provisional to make the field.

(Left) Bobby Labonte and outside pole-winner Ricky Rudd bring the 43-car field toward the line in preparation for the initial green flag. Labonte and Rudd traded the lead four times before the first caution flag appeared on lap 19.

(Below) With rain clouds lurking overhead, the Quality Care crew swarms Dale Jarrett's Ford during a green-flag stop for four tires and fuel. Jarrett was a little off in qualifying but, with the help of his crew, was able to work his way to a fourth-place finish.

(Left) Geoffrey Bodine (60) and Robby Gordon (13) tangle in the first turn, while Rick Mast (14) escapes unscathed on the inside in an incident that brought out the final caution of the race. Bodine was finished for the day, but Gordon was able to complete the remaining laps under yellow.

(Below Left) Mike Skinner (31) gives Dave Blaney (93) a little push on the outside, trying to get the two of them past Kevin Lepage (16). Ricky Rudd (28) chooses to take the short way around on the low side.

season with a new lap record in very hot conditions at Michigan.

Ricky Rudd claimed the outside of the front row, while Jeff Gordon, Rusty Wallace and Joe Nemechek completed the top five. Dale Earnhardt Jr. and Jeff Burton were sixth and seventh fastest during qualifying, just ahead of Bill Elliott, Dale Earnhardt and John Andretti. Terry Labonte, Chad Little, Sterling Marlin, Jimmy Spencer, Bobby Hamilton, Brett Bodine and Ed Berrier used provisionals to make the starting lineup, leav-

Further down the point list, Jeremy Mayfield and the Mobil 1 team were delighted to welcome crew chief Peter Sospenzo back to the track. Sospenzo had been suspended for 30 days following the Talladega fuel incident, and the Kmart 400 marked the first time he was allowed to return to the track.

Media members had plenty to talk about in the few days between the Dover and Michigan events. Steve Park and Pennzoil had extended their contracts with Dale Earnhardt Inc., and Mayfield said he had signed an extension with his team, owned by Roger Penske and Michael Kranefuss. Joe Bessey said he was in search of another sponsor for the 2001 season to replace Power Team, and Barry Dodson, Eel River Racing's general manager, said it appeared that Pfizer and Viagra, the team's present sponsor, would leave at the end of the season to replace Valvoline as Mark Martin's primary sponsor beginning next year.

The Pontiacs arrived at Michigan sporting new, NASCAR-approved rear bumper covers, and it didn't take long for Ford and Chevrolet teams to start fussing — particularly when Bobby Labonte cranked off a lap at nearly 190 miles per hour during Bud Pole qualifying to gain the 19th pole of his career and the first of the 2000

ing Ricky Craven and Dave Marcis out of the field. Also missing the race was Darrell Waltrip, who had hoped to celebrate his final season with a strong run in the event carrying his car sponsor's name.

While Ricky Rudd and Rusty Wallace battled with Bobby Labonte at the front of the field in the early stages of the Kmart 400, Mayfield was working his way toward the front. The Kentuckian took over the point on lap 55 and then threatened to run off and leave the field, leading 85 of the next 99 laps, but storm clouds were gathering with each passing moment. The caution flew on lap 150 for rain, and Mayfield, among others, headed for pit road. But a tire violation during his stop sent him to the end of the longest line for the restart and ended his hopes for victory.

With the rain passing and track drying complete, the event restarted with Jarrett, Rudd, Bobby Labonte, Stewart, Earnhardt and Rusty Wallace battling for the lead. Mayfield fought his way from the back and got as high as sixth, but the engine in his Mobil 1 Ford expired on lap 177, bringing out a caution flag and sending the leaders to pit road.

Robert Pressley took just two tires, emerging from pit road as the race leader. On the restart, Stewart rocketed past Pressley to take the point, and although Jarrett and then Earnhardt made runs at the Home Depot Pontiac, Stewart had just enough to hold them off. Earnhardt appeared ready to make another run at Stewart in the final laps, but Robby Gordon and Geoffrey Bodine tangled in the first turn, bringing out the final yellow.

Trying to complete the race, cleanup crews hustled and the "one-to-go" was given on lap 193 — but then the clouds opened up again. This time there would be no track drying, and the results were declared official.

Stewart had become only the second driver of the season to win two events, and he became the first to win two straight. Earnhardt, by nipping Bobby Labonte at the line when the final yellow waved, was second, while Jarrett finished fourth. Pressley had a great race and finished fifth, with Ward Burton sixth and Wallace seventh. Elliott, John Andretti and Sterling Marlin completed the top 10 finishers.

Tony Stewart (20) and Dale Jarrett run together early in the race after starting 28th and 26th, respectively. Both drivers had cars with good race setups and were able to work their way up to the leaders by quarter distance in the event.

KMART 400 • final results

"War wagons" get more sophisticated all the time, and among the most innovative and high-tech of all is this gem fabricated by the Tide team at Cal Wells Racing.

Fin. Pos.	Start Pos.	Car No.	Driver	Team	Fin. Pos.	Start Pos.	Car No.	Driver	Team
1	28	20	Tony Stewart	Home Depot Pontiac	23	32	25	Jerry Nadeau	MichaelHoligan.com Chevrolet
2	9	3	Dale Earnhardt	GM Goodwrench Service Chevrolet	24	11	10	Johnny Benson	Lycos.com Pontiac
3	1	18	Bobby Labonte	Interstate Batteries Pontiac	25	17	93	Dave Blaney	Amoco Pontiac
4	26	88	Dale Jarrett	Quality Care/Ford Credit Ford	26	37	5	Terry Labonte	Kellogg's Chevrolet
5	31	77	Robert Pressley	Jasper Engines Ford	27	21	21	Elliott Sadler	CITGO Ford
6	13	22	Ward Burton	Caterpillar Pontiac	28	25	13	Robby Gordon	Burger King/Turtlewax Ford
7	4	2	Rusty Wallace	Miller Lite Ford	29	14	1	Steve Park	Pennzoil Chevrolet
8	8	94	Bill Elliott	McDonald's Ford	30	29	14	Rick Mast	Conseco Pontiac
9	10	43	John Andretti	STP/Cheerios Pontiac	31	34	55	Kenny Wallace	Square D/Cooper Lighting Chevrolet
10	39	40	Sterling Marlin	Coors Light Chevrolet	32	38	97	Chad Little	John Deere Ford
11	7	99	Jeff Burton	Exide Batteries Ford	33	43	90	Ed Berrier	Hills Brothers Coffee Ford
12	2	28	Ricky Rudd	Texaco/Havoline Ford	34	24	75	Wally Dallenbach	Redcell Batteries Ford
13	6	8	Dale Earnhardt Jr.	Budweiser Chevrolet	35	18	42	Kenny Irwin	BellSouth Chevrolet
14	3	24	Jeff Gordon	DuPont Automotive Finishes Chevrolet	36	42	11	Brett Bodine	Ralphs Supermarkets Ford
15	40	26	Jimmy Spencer	Big Kmart/Route 66 Ford	37	27	27	Mike Bliss	Pfizer/Viagra Pontiac
16	20	36	Ken Schrader	M&M's Pontiac	38	36	60	Geoffrey Bodine	Power Team Chevrolet
17	23	17	Matt Kenseth	DeWalt Tools Ford	39	35	44	Kyle Petty	Hot Wheels Pontiac
18	5	33	Joe Nemechek	Oakwood Homes Chevrolet	40	19	6	Mark Martin	Valvoline/Cummins Ford
19	16	32	Scott Pruett	Tide Ford	41	22	12	Jeremy Mayfield	Mobil 1 Ford
20	30	31	Mike Skinner	Lowe's Chevrolet	42	33	9	Stacy Compton	Kodiak/Cougar Ford
21	12	16	Kevin Lepage	FamilyClick.com/TV Guide Ford	43	41	4	Bobby Hamilton	Kodak Chevrolet
22	15	7	Michael Waltrip	Nations Rent Chevrolet					

POCONO 500

JUNE 19, 2000 • POCONO RACEWAY

(Left) The Mobil 1 team greets Jeremy Mayfield on pit road after a thrilling, bump-and-run finish that gave Mayfield the win.

(Right) Mayfield celebrates his second win of the 2000 season, the third of his NASCAR Winston Cup Series career, at the site of his initial win two years before.

Mark Martin and Tony Stewart arrived at Pocono Raceway at opposite ends of the spectrum. Martin, with five consecutive finishes outside of the top 10, had plummeted from the top of the NASCAR Winston Cup Series point ladder all the way to ninth place following the Michigan event.

Stewart, on the other hand, came to Drs. Rose and Joe Mattioli's triangular superspeedway with great momentum. His Michigan victory was his second straight — making him the first driver of the season to score back-to-back triumphs — and the Home Depot Pontiac driver now found himself in seventh place, up two positions from the previous week. Could he make it three in a row and gain even more ground on point-leader Bobby Labonte and the others in front of him in the standings?

Some in the garage area felt Martin's free fall had cost him any chance at winning the elusive NASCAR Winston Cup Series title in his final season with Valvoline sponsorship. And, according to those same folks, Stewart's victories would not be enough to propel him into the championship battle. Neither Martin nor Stewart bought into such thinking, however. There was more than half the season remaining on the schedule and anything could happen to Labonte that might drop him back to within reach of many in the championship quest.

Rusty Wallace grabbed his fifth Bud Pole of the year at Pocono and led more than half the laps in the race. But a call for four tires when others took just two cost him the track position he needed to win.

In an on-track battle of rookie contenders, Ed Berrier (90) looks for the favorable inside position on Stacy Compton (9), with Mike Bliss keeping pace on the far outside. Later in the race, Bliss' accident in the first turn brought out the caution that set the stage for the exciting finish.

Labonte's consistency had been the Interstate Batteries team's hallmark this season. Taking a page from Dale Jarrett's championship-winning book from the previous season, Labonte and the green-and-black-clad team had done the best they could do in each race. Although more than one victory had eluded them to this point, they had put together the kinds of finishes that bring championships. As far as Bobby and his team were concerned, there was no better place to be this weekend than in the lovely Pocono Mountains. Labonte swept both events here last year, and he was hoping to make it three in a row.

His point lead was now 98 over Dale Earnhardt, who had moved into the runner-up slot in the standings. Earnhardt held a

four-point lead over Ward Burton, while Jarrett was just 59 points behind the Caterpillar Pontiac driver. Jeff Burton moved back into fifth place, 87 markers behind Jarrett, while Rusty Wallace also moved up a notch, trailing the Exide Ford driver by 13 points.

Jeff Gordon takes advantage of a little spare time due to the weekend's changing weather to sign autographs for some of his many fans. Once the race began, Gordon struggled with an ill-handling car but still was able to score his 10th top-10 Pocono finish in 15 career starts.

track record by more than one mile per hour and claimed his fifth Bud Pole of the year, marking the first time in his career he has won more than four poles in a single season.

His lap was almost a tenth of a second faster than the time turned by John Andretti, who would start next to Rusty on the front row. Ricky Rudd notched his 10th top-10 starting position of the season by claiming the inside of the second row next to Dale Jarrett in fourth. Gordon and Martin claimed the third row, while Mike Skinner and Jeff Burton made up the fourth row. Stewart was on his game, qualifying ninth fastest, with Joe Nemechek grabbing the final top-10 starting position.

Darrell Waltrip was the fastest driver in second-round qualifying, but his lap was just a smidgen too slow to knock

(Above) Tires played a big part in Earnhardt's day. Here, Earnhardt gets new right sides in the opening laps after cutting a tire. In the closing laps, a quick, two-tire stop under caution put him out front for the restart and nearly gave him the win.

(Right) Rookie Scott Pruett (left) and veteran John Andretti greet some fans with a wave and a smile on their way to the starting grid for the Pocono 500. Andretti's strong qualifying effort placed him on the outside of the front row for the start of the race.

(Below) Pruett's day didn't begin quite as well as Andretti's did, with the Tide Ford having trouble before the cool, damp Monday-morning start. Doug Yates (black pants with headset) who builds engines for the Tide team, helps push the car back to the pits where it eventually fired.

Ricky Rudd remained in eighth place, 11 points behind Stewart, while Jeff Gordon found himself 66 points behind Martin. Matt Kenseth and Terry Labonte traded positions after the Michigan race, with Kenseth now in 11th, 66 points behind Gordon. Mike Skinner, Bill Elliott and Dale Earnhardt Jr. completed the top 15.

Pocono's 2.5-mile track is unique. It incorporates three turns of varying radii connected by three straightaways of varying lengths. Setting up a chassis to turn fast laps on the triangular track requires a combination of brute power and handling finesse to accommodate the different degrees of banking in the three corners. And when Bud Pole qualifying was completed, Rusty Wallace and his Miller Lite team had done the best job of setting up their car for the challenging layout. Rusty broke the

Michael Waltrip (7) and Ken Schrader (36) battle side by side through Pocono's third turn — a flat sweeper that allows two-wide racing onto the long frontstretch. Waltrip was optimistic after qualifying 12th for the race, but his day ended early when his engine failed after just 35 laps, bringing out the second of five yellow flags during the event.

Mike Bliss out of 36th place on the qualifying list. It meant that Waltrip would join Dwayne Leik and Bill Baird as those who would not compete in the event. Chad Little, Kenny Irwin, Stacy Compton, Geoffrey Bodine, Scott Pruett, Ed Berrier and Dave Marcis all used provisionals to make the field.

Teams arrived early Sunday morning to prepare their mounts and push them through the inspection line, but they could have stayed in their motel beds. Rain showers, mist and fog blanketed the race-track, and after a delay while officials evaluated the forecast, the event was postponed until 10 a.m. the next day. The change of schedule put a crimp in the travel plans of all the teams, who needed to go back to their shops, change cars and restock transporters before the long trip to Northern California for the upcoming race at Sears Point.

When the field took the green flag on Monday, Wallace immediately took command of the event, looking for his second victory of the season. He put the blue-and-white Taurus in the wind and led

seemingly at will for the first three-quarters of the race. But in the closing laps, Stewart seized the lead and established the orange-and-white Home Depot Pontiac as the car to beat. He built a solid lead and, with just 17 laps remaining, appeared headed for his third straight victory.

Then the fifth caution flag of the event flew, erasing his lead, and Stewart headed for pit road. His crew elected to give him just two

Dale Jarrett's Quality Care Ford fronts Jimmy Spencer, Sterling Marlin, Jeff Gordon and Matt Kenseth. Although the defending Series champion was not able to lead a lap, he stayed among the leaders and finished second, his fifth consecutive top-five finish.

The Galaxy Motorsports crew had a busy day after an early-race incident damaged the Ford driven by Wally Dallenbach. But with repairs — and plenty of tape — the team was able to keep Dallenbach in the race.

tires to put him back onto the track with the lead, but when the jack dropped, Tony stalled the Pontiac briefly. It was just enough time to drop him to fourth in the lineup for the restart. Earnhardt and Jeremy Mayfield had also taken two tires and emerged from the pits in first and second, respectively. Jarrett and Martin sandwiched Stewart on the restart, and none of those three drivers could make a bid for victory in the closing laps.

Instead, it was Earnhardt at the point, bringing tens of thousands of fans to their feet every time the driver of the black Chevrolet crossed the start/finish line, clicking another lap off the total. Mayfield fought gamely in second, closing to a car-length or two at times, but it appeared as though there was not enough in the Mobil 1 Ford to beat the GM Goodwrench Chevrolet.

The two drivers took the white flag and Earnhardt held sway through turns one and two. Diving into the third turn, Mayfield drove his Ford deeper than usual and moved up to Earnhardt's bumper. The slightest bit of contact resulted, with Earnhardt forced

to lift and gather up his machine. Mayfield immediately darted for the opening, emerged from the turn with the lead and flat-footed it to the checkered flag.

Jarrett and Rudd also managed to squeeze by Earnhardt, who recovered for fourth place. Martin stopped his decline through the point standings with a fifth-place finish, beating Stewart, while Jeff Burton and Jeff Gordon claimed seventh and eighth. Mike Skinner was ninth, while Rusty Wallace took 10th after taking four tires on the last pit stop and starting the final sprint to the flag in 14th place.

POCONO 500 • final results

Jeremy Mayfield leads Rusty Wallace, Ricky Rudd and Tony Stewart through the third turn. Mayfield led only two laps in the second half of the race, one of those ending with the checkered flag.

Fin. Pos.	Start Pos.	Car No.	Driver	Team		Fin. Pos.	Start Pos.	Car No.	Driver	Team
1	22	12	Jeremy Mayfield	Mobil 1 Ford		23	24	55	Kenny Wallace	Square D/Cooper Lighting Chevrolet
2	4	88	Dale Jarrett	Quality Care/Ford Credit Ford		24	40	60	Geoffrey Bodine	Power Team Chevrolet
3	3	28	Ricky Rudd	Texaco/Havoline Ford		25	38	42	Kenny Irwin	BellSouth Chevrolet
4	16	3	Dale Earnhardt	GM Goodwrench Service Chevrolet		26	18	16	Kevin Lepage	FamilyClick.com/TV Guide Ford
5	6	6	Mark Martin	Valvoline/Cummins Ford		27	32	22	Ward Burton	Caterpillar Pontiac
6	9	20	Tony Stewart	Home Depot Pontiac		28	42	90	Ed Berrier	Hills Brothers Coffee Ford
7	8	99	Jeff Burton	Exide Batteries Ford		29	43	71	Dave Marcis	Realtree Chevrolet
8	5	24	Jeff Gordon	DuPont Automotive Finishes Chevrolet		30	35	93	Dave Blaney	Amoco Pontiac
9	7	31	Mike Skinner	Lowe's Chevrolet		31	41	32	Scott Pruett	Tide Ford
10	1	2	Rusty Wallace	Miller Lite Ford		32	20	11	Brett Bodine	Ralphs Supermarkets Ford
11	28	77	Robert Pressley	Jasper Engines Ford		33	36	27	Mike Bliss	Pfizer/Viagra Pontiac
12	14	5	Terry Labonte	Kellogg's Chevrolet		34	21	10	Johnny Benson	Lycos.com Pontiac
13	11	18	Bobby Labonte	Interstate Batteries Pontiac		35	13	14	Rick Mast	Conseco Pontiac
14	29	17	Matt Kenseth	DeWalt Tools Ford		36	34	26	Jimmy Spencer	Big Kmart/Route 66 Ford
15	27	1	Steve Park	Pennzoil Chevrolet		37	39	9	Stacy Compton	Kodiak/Cougar Ford
16	30	21	Elliott Sadler	CITGO Ford		38	25	94	Bill Elliott	McDonald's Ford
17	37	97	Chad Little	John Deere Ford		39	17	75	Wally Dallenbach	TBS Dinner & A Movie Ford
18	19	36	Ken Schrader	M&M's Pontiac		40	33	4	Bobby Hamilton	Kodak Chevrolet
19	15	8	Dale Earnhardt Jr.	Budweiser Chevrolet		41	23	44	Kyle Petty	Hot Wheels Pontiac
20	26	25	Jerry Nadeau	MichaelHoligan.com Chevrolet		42	10	33	Joe Nemechek	Oakwood Homes Chevrolet
21	2	43	John Andretti	STP/Cheerios Pontiac		43	12	7	Michael Waltrip	Nations Rent Chevrolet
22	31	40	Sterling Marlin	Coors Light Chevrolet						

SAVE MART/KRAGEN *350*

(Left) The Richard Petty-owned Pontiac arrived at Sears Point with the same paint scheme Petty used in his first appearance with STP sponsorship back in 1972.

(Right) Jeff Gordon slings his Chevrolet around the winding road course ahead of Tony Stewart. A trip to Sears Point was just what Gordon and the DuPont team needed.

During the season-ending race at Texas World Speedway in 1971, a rotund company president paid a visit to Richard Petty and the Petty Enterprises team. Petty knew the face; he had seen the man kissing and hugging Mario Andretti in victory lane at Indianapolis. In the short span of a few weeks following that 1971 meeting in the Texas garage, Petty and Andy Granatelli came to terms on a sponsorship package, and the Petty Enterprises team arrived for the 1972 opener at Riverside International Raceway with its familiar Petty Blue Dodge, which now also carried the famed red logo of STP.

Richard won that race in the new color combination, beginning a primary sponsorship relationship that was to last for nearly three decades. The Petty Enterprises/STP relationship was the beginning of what we now know as a way of life in motorsports — but times change and costs escalate. Cheerios and other General Mills products would take over primary billing on the "43" beginning with the next event at Daytona. Now, however, it seemed most appropriate that STP would take its final bows as the team's primary sponsor in California, the same state where it had made its debut in the dusty desert near Los Angeles more than 28 years earlier.

Richard Petty was hoping to send his longtime sponsor out with a win. Instead, an accident in the early going sent the STP Pontiac home with a last-place finish.

Goodwrench Service team had worked its way back into the position of contender, and week after week, Earnhardt had been driving the black Monte Carlo with the zest that carried him to seven titles in the past. There was no reason to doubt he was back in the mix for the championship.

Defending NASCAR Winston Cup Series Champion Dale Jarrett was also in the middle of the battle, now just 58 points behind Earnhardt. Ward Burton had slipped to fourth place, while the remainder of the top 10 — Jeff Burton, Rusty Wallace, Tony Stewart, Ricky Rudd, Mark Martin and Jeff Gordon — all remained in the same positions they

(Above) The Home Depot team looks anxiously for driver Tony Stewart to enter pit road, while John Andretti stands by, ready to take the driving duties in relief.

(Right) With the driver change nearly complete, Andretti prepares to re-enter the race. Once on the track, Andretti did an outstanding job working his way back into the pack and brought the Home Depot Pontiac home with a 10th-place finish.

The topography was considerably different — the golden hills of Northern California's wine country versus the baked barrens of Riverside — but the Petty Enterprises team brought its STP Pontiac painted in the same color scheme Richard's Dodge carried in his first year of STP sponsorship. Petty won that Riverside race back in 1972, benefiting from a broken valve spring in Bobby Allison's engine, and John Andretti hoped he could find a way to send the STP colors out in style with a victory at Sears Point Raceway.

While Andretti and his team were working at finding the right qualifying package for the STP Pontiac, Dale Earnhardt wore a tight smile on his face. He had gained 41 points on Bobby Labonte at Pocono and now was only 57 markers behind in the point battle. His consistent finishes and steady progression through the standings had finally put the seven-time NASCAR Winston Cup Series champion within striking distance of Labonte — and Earnhardt's steely-blues took on an even greater gleam than usual. His GM

held prior to the event at Pocono.

One of the biggest surprises during practice was the speed turned by Kyle Petty's Hot Wheels Pontiac. Kyle would be the first to tell you he is not as good a road racer as some of the others in the NASCAR Winston Cup Series garage, but he also was quick to point out that the engine program at Petty Enterprises had improved over the past month. He rocketed around the Sears Point turns during Bud Pole qualifying, bouncing from curb to curb in his effort, and when he was finished, his lap was the second fastest of the session, giving him his first top-10 qualifying effort of the season. It wasn't good enough for the pole — Rusty Wallace claimed his sixth of the season — but it did finally bring a smile to Kyle's beleaguered face. Point leader Bobby Labonte was third fastest with his Joe Gibbs

Racing teammate Tony Stewart alongside. That made three Pontiacs in the top four starting positions, while Jeff Gordon unlimbered his road-course Monte Carlo and grabbed the inside of the third row. Sterling Marlin was a surprising sixth fastest, while Mark Martin and Bill Elliott made up the fourth row ahead of Scott Pruett and Ricky Rudd.

Ward Burton, Matt Kenseth, Jeremy Mayfield, Chad Little, Robert Pressley, Kenny Irwin and Dave Blaney used provisionals to make the field, leaving Rick Mast, Geoffrey Bodine and R.K. Smith, in Dave Marcis' Real Tree Chevrolet, out in the cold.

With five consecutive road-course victories in his pocket and racing at the track located less than an hour from where he was born in Vallejo, Calif., there was little reason to overlook Gordon in the early odds-making for Sunday's event. Yet many did, thinking the

(Above) Sterling Marlin muscles his Chevrolet in front of (in order) Ward Burton, Ricky Rudd, Mark Martin and Robby Gordon. Marlin eclipsed his previous best on a road course (sixth) with an outstanding run to a second-place finish.

(Left) Kyle Petty leads Brett Bodine (11) and a tightly packed string of competitors through the Esses. Petty had his best qualifying effort in some time and started the race from the outside of the front row next to pole-winner Rusty Wallace.

(Above Left) Dale Earnhardt, the 1995 winner of this event, puts the pressure on Bobby Labonte (18). Although Earnhardt's qualifying effort put him 29th on the starting grid, he hunted down point leader Labonte and kept him in sight, finishing two spots behind him in sixth. (Above Right) Mike Skinner (31) chases Steve Park's Pennzoil Chevrolet behind Bobby Labonte and Scott Pruett.

problems of rebuilding during the fiery forge of weekly competition was too much for the DuPont team. With a new crew chief, a new over-the-wall pit crew and several new faces within the team, the Hendrick Motorsports effort had been quietly working its way into a position where it could contend on a weekly basis. Gordon knew the car he had was a proven winner, and he felt he merely needed to find the right track position during the race to be able to battle for the victory.

The chance finally came when he took the lead for the first time on lap 46 and then began to reel off the laps, leaving the field behind by a tenth of a second at a time. Caution flags erased his lead and juggled the running order, and on the final restart, Gordon found himself behind Kenny Wallace, Mike Skinner, Ward Burton and Bobby Hamilton. Gordon carved his way to the front, chopped

Matt Kenseth (17), Jerry Nadeau (25) and Dave Blaney go spinning through turn 11. Although they sustained some sheet metal damage, all three drivers kept going, with Nadeau fighting all the way back to an eighth-place finish.

Jeff Gordon (24) slips past Kenny Wallace on lap 86 to take the lead for the last time. Starting fifth on the final restart and with a fast and proven DuPont Chevrolet, Gordon began a 13-lap charge to the front to score his third consecutive Sears Point victory, his sixth straight on a road course.

down Kenny Wallace's lead and, on lap 86, moved past the Square D Chevrolet to take the point for the final time.

His biggest concern at that point was whether or not he had enough fuel to make the distance. He would have to go 42 laps on his final load of gas, which he was able to do as he eased his way to a four-second victory over Sterling Marlin. Mark Martin came home third ahead of Bobby Labonte, with Rudd and Earnhardt right behind. Dale Jarrett claimed seventh ahead of Jerry Nadeau and Robby Gordon, while Tony Stewart was credited with 10th place.

Ironically, Stewart's finish came in the capable hands of John Andretti. The Petty Enterprises hopes of giving STP a great going-away present ended when Andretti was involved in an accident early in the race. John was pressed into service driving the Home Depot Pontiac when Stewart needed relief, and although he was wrapped in a foam pad to help him fit into Stewart's seat, John could not comfortably reach the pedals properly. He still managed to give Stewart and the orange-clad team another top 10, beating Joe Nemechek to the finish line.

SAVE MART/KRAGEN 350 • final results

Brian Simo made his NASCAR Winston Cup Series debut at Sears Point driving for Junie Donlavey. Simo qualified the car with the 34th-fastest time and held his own in the race until a mechanical problem dropped him off the pace.

Fin. Pos.	Start Pos.	Car No.	Driver	Team
1	5	24	Jeff Gordon	DuPont Automotive Finishes Chevrolet
2	6	40	Sterling Marlin	Coors Light Chevrolet
3	7	6	Mark Martin	Valvoline/Cummins Ford
4	3	18	Bobby Labonte	Interstate Batteries Pontiac
5	10	28	Ricky Rudd	Texaco/Havoline Ford
6	29	3	Dale Earnhardt	GM Goodwrench Service Chevrolet
7	18	88	Dale Jarrett	Quality Care/Ford Credit Ford
8	20	25	Jerry Nadeau	MichaelHoligan.com Chevrolet
9	11	13	Robby Gordon	Menards/CD-2 Ford
10	4	20	Tony Stewart	Home Depot Pontiac
11	19	33	Joe Nemechek	Oakwood Homes Chevrolet
12	28	7	Michael Waltrip	Nations Rent Chevrolet
13	17	55	Kenny Wallace	Square D/Cooper Lighting Chevrolet
14	14	4	Bobby Hamilton	Kodak Chevrolet
15	21	36	Ken Schrader	M&M's Pontiac
16	30	99	Jeff Burton	Exide Batteries Ford
17	15	1	Steve Park	Pennzoil Chevrolet
18	35	10	Johnny Benson	Lycos.com Pontiac
19	2	44	Kyle Petty	Hot Wheels Pontiac
20	13	31	Mike Skinner	Lowe's Chevrolet
21	37	22	Ward Burton	Caterpillar Pontiac
22	27	27	Mike Bliss	Pfizer/Viagra Pontiac

Fin. Pos.	Start Pos.	Car No.	Driver	Team
23	42	42	Kenny Irwin	BellSouth Chevrolet
24	31	8	Dale Earnhardt Jr.	Budweiser Chevrolet
25	40	97	Chad Little	John Deere Ford
26	1	2	Rusty Wallace	Miller Lite Ford
27	25	5	Terry Labonte	Kellogg's Chevrolet
28	33	66	Darrell Waltrip	Route 66/Big Kmart Ford
29	43	93	Dave Blaney	Amoco Pontiac
30	22	11	Brett Bodine	Ralphs Supermarkets Ford
31	36	9	Stacy Compton	Kodiak/Cougar Ford
32	38	17	Matt Kenseth	DeWalt Tools Ford
33	39	12	Jeremy Mayfield	Mobil 1 Ford
34	12	26	Jimmy Spencer	Big Kmart/Route 66 Ford
35	8	94	Bill Elliott	McDonald's Ford
36	34	90	Brian Simo	Hills Brothers Coffee Ford
37	41	77	Robert Pressley	Jasper Engines Ford
38	32	21	Elliott Sadler	CITGO Ford
39	9	32	Scott Pruett	Tide Ford
40	26	75	Wally Dallenbach	TBS Dinner & A Movie Ford
41	24	16	Kevin Lepage	FamilyClick.com/TV Guide Ford
42	23	23	Boris Said	Federated Auto Parts Ford
43	16	43	John Andretti	STP/Cheerios Pontiac

PEPSI *400*

JULY 1, 2000 • DAYTONA INTERNATIONAL SPEEDWAY

NASCAR 2000

(Left) Jeff Burton stands with a very happy Jack Roush who, after more than 12 years as a car owner, finally captured a NASCAR Winston Cup Series win at Daytona.

(Right) The starting field for the Pepsi 400 lines up behind Dale Jarrett and Ricky Rudd, just as it did in the season-opening Daytona 500.

Since its beginning, the Pepsi 400 — then known as the Firecracker 250 and later as the Firecracker 400 — has been a family-oriented weekend during the middle of the NASCAR Winston Cup Series season. It is always held during the Independence Day weekend, and the beach beckons families while crewmembers and drivers work at the track. In the past, many crewmembers arrived a day or two early and stayed a day or two after the event, stretching the weekend as much as they could to give them a chance to enjoy the sun and surf with their families.

This year, the Pepsi 400 was the centerpiece of an even more memorable moment for one of NASCAR's families. Ernie Irvan, whose home burned to the ground several months earlier, was the honored guest at a surprise party at Daytona. A black drape was lifted to reveal replicas of the 15 NASCAR Winston Cup Series trophies he won in his abbreviated career. The originals, along with other memorabilia that marked his tenure as a racer, were destroyed in the fire.

NASCAR representatives, the fine folks at R.J. Reynolds and track representatives were all responsible for helping Irvan replace the trophies and winner's circle photographs that were destroyed in the blaze. Irvan could barely find words to express his appreciation for the replacement of what he thought was completely lost.

Vying to break a winless streak dating back to September 1998 at Martinsville, Ricky Rudd prepares to unleash his Texaco Ford on the high banks at Daytona.

career NASCAR Winston Cup Series start and the first race for Brad Parrott as the new crew chief for Scott Pruett and the Tide Ford team. After serving as older brother Todd's assistant at Robert Yates Racing for the last four years, and after turning down several other crew chief opportunities during that span, Brad had decided to take the job with Pruett.

Point leader Bobby Labonte's Pontiac carried a new paint scheme for the Pepsi 400, headlining the upcoming Major League Baseball All-Star game in Atlanta, and the Cheerios colors appeared on John Andretti's Petty Enterprises Pontiac for the first time. Mark Martin's five-year deal with Pfizer, beginning in 2001, was announced, and for the first time, Martin talked about retiring from competition at the conclusion of that five-year contract. Almost as an aside during the Roush Racing announcement of the Pfizer sponsorship deal, it was revealed that Chad Little would not return to drive the John Deere-sponsored Fords for Roush in 2001.

(Above) Crew chief Jimmy Makar (left) and driver Bobby Labonte create a photo op to display their special colors commemorating Major League Baseball's year 2000 All-Star game.

(Right) Pole-winner Dale Jarrett wears a confident smile as he prepares to go to work at Daytona, knowing that, as defending champion of this event and having won the Daytona 500 earlier in the season, his chances of picking up his second win of the year had to be good.

(Below Right) Jerry Nadeau (25) makes a move up the middle in the early going between fourth-place starter Dave Blaney (93) and Ward Burton (22), who qualified sixth. Trailing the action is Ed Berrier (90), who had a strong qualifying run in Junie Donlavey's Ford, alongside Elliott Sadler, who started in 10th.

While Irvan was brimming with excitement, Johnny Benson and the Tyler Jet team were on the other end of the emotional spectrum. A dispute with sponsor Lycos.com was brought to light as Benson and his fellow crewmembers stripped the decals from the team's Pontiac in the garage area, reverting to the simple white Benson had driven in the season-opening Daytona 500.

The Pepsi 400 weekend also marked Rusty Wallace's 500th

In the cooler night air at Daytona, drivers didn't mind racing three-wide — always an exciting site on the famous superspeedway. Above on the left, Jimmy Spencer splits the Chevrolet of Michael Waltrip (7) and the Ford Wally Dallenbach (75). On the right, Dallenbach gets an "aero push" from Ricky Craven on the high side, while Matt Kenseth (17) tries to sneak between Dallenbach and Robert Pressley (77).

Labonte's solid fourth-place performance at Sears Point — where he had simply hoped to emerge with a run that would keep him in the hunt for the title — allowed him to pad his point lead. He was now 67 markers ahead of Dale Earnhardt, while Dale Jarrett trailed the GM Goodwrench Service Chevrolet driver by 62 points. Ward and Jeff Burton held onto fourth and fifth places, while Ricky Rudd closed to within four points of the Exide Ford driver in their battle for fifth place.

Martin, who seemed to have ended his bad racing luck, was now seventh in the standings, just seven points behind Rudd and eight ahead of streaking Tony Stewart. Rusty Wallace, who struggled at Sears Point after spinning away a good finish, fell from seventh

With the capacity crowd on their feet and in front of a national prime-time audience on CBS, Jarrett streaks under the green flag with 42 hungry drivers in fast pursuit — NASCAR Winston Cup Series' version of Saturday night at the races.

Scott Pruett shows a steady hand and a level head in only his second Daytona start, holding the center line between Jimmy Spencer (26) and Ed Berrier (90) up front, with Michael Waltrip (7) and Robert Pressley (77) at the rear.

to ninth in the standings and now trailed Stewart by 26. Jeff Gordon's second victory of the season moved him to just 30 points behind Wallace.

Jarrett, with nine top-five finishes to his credit, came to Daytona looking for a three-peat. He won last year's running of the Pepsi 400, and the last time the Quality Care team was at The Beach, Jarrett notched his only victory thus far this season, claiming his third career Daytona 500. Although the Taurus that won the Daytona 500 was in the Daytona USA attraction outside the fourth turn, Jarrett felt his chances were good with the red-white-and-blue Ford built by his Robert Yates team. He proved it in qualifying, claiming his third Bud Pole of the season and the 10th of his career. Teammate Rudd made it a Yates front row for the second time in as many tries at Daytona by finishing his run just a tick slower than Jarrett.

Bill Elliott's Drive-Thru crew finished his new Taurus just 15 hours before the opening of practice, and Elliott rewarded his team for their hard work by putting the Ford on the inside of the second row, while Dave Blaney drove the fastest Pontiac to the fourth starting position. Martin and Ward Burton made up the third row, with Stewart and Jerry Nadeau seventh and eighth fastest during the first qualifying session. Jeff Burton and Elliott Sadler beat Ed Berrier and Rusty Wallace for the final top-10 starting positions.

The second of five cautions occurred with this incident on lap 82 with Terry Labonte (5) out of shape through the tri-oval. Labonte's Monte Carlo also tagged Michael Waltrip's Chevrolet (7), with neither car able to return to action in the event.

Terry Labonte, Jeremy Mayfield, Sterling Marlin, Joe Nemechek, Michael Waltrip, Bobby Hamilton and Geoffrey Bodine used provisionals to make the field, sending Brett Bodine, Dave Marcis and Robby Gordon home for the final race to be televised by CBS.

With the lights blazing and a huge throng on hand, Jarrett led the field under the green flag and immediately set sail. Johnny Benson's white and unsponsored Pontiac was a clear contender, as was Elliott's new Ford, and as the race wound on, Jeff Burton and others emerged from the field as potential winners. Jarrett had a problem with a lug nut during the third caution period, sending him backward to 27th place on the restart and forcing the defending race champion to fight his way back through the field.

Elliott's bid for victory ended when he was clipped by Mike Skinner, sending the Ford into the wall on lap 114. Jeff Burton took just two tires and emerged at the front on lap 121, while Jarrett continued to work his way toward the leaders. Jarrett captured second place with 15 laps to go, and many expected the powerful Ford to easily dispatch Burton.

The Exide Ford driver had other ideas, however, and blocked every move Jarrett threw at him. Lap after lap, Jarrett tried to find a way past Burton, and the drama was heightened when the final caution flag flew on lap 155 when Blaney and Jimmy Spencer tangled. The green flag flew with four laps left, and Jarrett again tried everything he knew of to pass Burton. But Burton had every answer.

He flashed under the checkered flag with a car-length to spare and claimed the first NASCAR Winston Cup Series point-race victory for Roush Racing at Daytona since Jack Roush began fielding cars in 1988. Rusty Wallace fought his way to third place ahead of Martin, while Rudd and Stewart finished fifth and sixth. Ward Burton claimed seventh ahead of Richard Childress Racing teammates Earnhardt and Skinner, with Gordon claiming 10th.

The celebration begins with Jeff Burton and his No. 99 Exide Ford. Burton could see it coming — he finished third here a year ago, was second to Jarrett in February, and now had finally made it to Daytona's coveted victory lane.

PEPSI 400 • final results

This thermostat, set to 240 degrees Fahrenheit, controls the electric heater that preheats the motor oil in Kenny Wallace's Square D Chevrolet prior to starting the engine — an essential step in preparing the car for competition.

Fin. Pos.	Start Pos.	Car No.	Driver	Team	Fin. Pos.	Start Pos.	Car No.	Driver	Team
1	9	99	Jeff Burton	Exide Batteries Ford	23	14	36	Ken Schrader	M&M's Pontiac
2	1	88	Dale Jarrett	Quality Care/Ford Credit Ford	24	4	93	Dave Blaney	Amoco Pontiac
3	12	2	Rusty Wallace	Miller Lite Ford	25	39	40	Sterling Marlin	Coors Light Chevrolet
4	5	6	Mark Martin	Valvoline/Cummins Ford	26	11	90	Ed Berrier	Hills Brothers Coffee Ford
5	2	28	Ricky Rudd	Texaco/Havoline Ford	27	33	66	Darrell Waltrip	Route 66/Big Kmart Ford
6	7	20	Tony Stewart	Home Depot Pontiac	28	24	27	Mike Bliss	Pfizer/Viagra Pontiac
7	6	22	Ward Burton	Caterpillar Pontiac	29	32	50	Ricky Craven	Midwest Transit Chevrolet
8	18	3	Dale Earnhardt	GM Goodwrench Service Chevrolet	30	16	44	Kyle Petty	Hot Wheels Pontiac
9	15	31	Mike Skinner	Lowe's Chevrolet	31	25	14	Rick Mast	Conseco Pontiac
10	34	24	Jeff Gordon	DuPont Automotive Finishes Chevrolet	32	17	26	Jimmy Spencer	Big Kmart/Route 66 Ford
11	40	33	Joe Nemechek	Oakwood Homes Chevrolet	33	27	1	Steve Park	Pennzoil Pontiac
12	21	18	Bobby Labonte	Interstate Batteries Pontiac	34	43	60	Geoffrey Bodine	Power Team Chevrolet
13	20	10	Johnny Benson	Tyler Jet Motorsports Pontiac	35	31	8	Dale Earnhardt Jr.	Budweiser Chevrolet
14	29	43	John Andretti	Cheerios Pontiac	36	42	4	Bobby Hamilton	Kodak Chevrolet
15	8	25	Jerry Nadeau	MichaelHoligan.com Chevrolet	37	30	16	Kevin Lepage	FamilyClick.com/TV Guide Ford
16	19	97	Chad Little	John Deere Ford	38	3	94	Bill Elliott	McDonald's Ford
17	23	77	Robert Pressley	Jasper Engines Ford	39	13	9	Stacy Compton	Kodiak/Cougar Ford
18	10	21	Elliott Sadler	CITGO Ford	40	36	32	Scott Pruett	Tide Ford
19	26	55	Kenny Wallace	Square D/Cooper Lighting Chevrolet	41	37	5	Terry Labonte	Kellogg's Chevrolet
20	22	17	Matt Kenseth	DeWalt Tools Ford	42	41	7	Michael Waltrip	Nations Rent Chevrolet
21	35	75	Wally Dallenbach	WCW Ford	43	38	12	Jeremy Mayfield	Mobil 1 Ford
22	28	42	Kenny Irwin	BellSouth Chevrolet					

THATLOOK.COM *300*

(Left) The Pontiacs of Ward Burton and Tony Stewart (20) lean on each other through the turns in a tight battle at New Hampshire International Speedway.

(Right) Ricky Craven thrills the fans at his home track, taking a solid, early lead in the thatlook.com 300.

Jeff Burton's Beach party was history, but the young Virginian was still glowing from posting his first career restrictor-plate victory when teams arrived at Bob and Gary Bahre's New Hampshire International Speedway for the 18th event of the year.

Competitors now were entering the second half of the season with Bobby Labonte maintaining his lead at the top of the NASCAR Winston Cup Series point ladder. But the Pepsi 400 results had helped close the gap, and the Interstate Batteries Pontiac driver was beginning to feel the heavy breathing of his closest competitors. Bobby finished 12th at Daytona, while Dale Earnhardt posted an eighth place and gained 15 markers in the process. The seven-time champion was just 52 points behind Labonte, and many in the garage area were beginning to believe that Earnhardt just might have the right combination to claim a record eighth title.

Dale Jarrett's fighting second place at Daytona allowed him to gain 53 points on Labonte, and he was now just 24 behind Earnhardt and 76 behind the leader. Ward Burton finished seventh at Daytona and was fourth in the standings, 104 behind Jarrett, while Jeff Burton's win — his second of the year — pushed him to just 33 behind his brother and allowed him to open up a 29-point margin over sixth-place Ricky Rudd.

Determined to continue his record string of 654 consecutive starts, Terry Labonte came to New Hampshire ready to compete despite a broken bone in his leg.

The tightly bunched field hugs the inside groove through New Hampshire's 12-degree banked turns in the 11th NASCAR Winston Cup Series event held at the 1.058-mile oval.

(Left) Rusty Wallace leads the pack of 43 thundering cars under the initial green flag and into the first turn. The pole was Wallace's seventh of the season, coming in the 18th event of the year.

(Below Left) Fifth-place starter Ricky Craven (50) slips inside front-row starter John Andretti (43) to take the lead on the third lap of the race. Craven then set sail and led the next 63 laps.

(Bottom Left) Tony Stewart's covered Pontiac sits at the front of the line of cars on pit road during a short, red-flag delay for rain near the midpoint of the race.

the Texan planned to continue his Iron Man streak of 654 consecutive starts in NASCAR Winston Cup Series competition that dated back to 1979.

Kyle Petty, still struggling with the loss of son Adam at this track just two months earlier, decided not to compete and named Steve Grissom to drive the Hot Wheels Pontiac at New Hampshire. Richard Petty made the trip and asked to meet with the media prior to the beginning of practice on Friday to answer questions regarding Petty Enterprises, Kyle and Adam. He had barely concluded the media briefing as the first practice session began, when suddenly engines fell silent.

Only a few minutes into the session, driver Kenny Irwin crashed at nearly the exact spot where Adam had. Emergency workers did all they could, but after being transported to a nearby hospital, the sport lost the 1998 NASCAR Winston Cup Series Rookie of the Year and a member of its close-knit family.

Later that afternoon, gloom shrouded the Bud Pole qualifying session as Rusty Wallace claimed his seventh Bud Pole of the season, the 33rd of his career. There was no joy in his accomplishment, however, and it was very difficult for every competitor to be focused on the task at hand. Sabco Racing driver Sterling Marlin chose not to participate in the session at all.

John Andretti qualified on the outside of the front row, with Martin and Jeff Burton side by side in the second row. Ricky Craven had a superb run to the fifth-fastest lap, while Stewart and Ken Schrader were sixth and seventh fastest. Gordon qualified eighth on the grid, while Jerry Nadeau sparkled in front of his New England fans, beating Jarrett for the inside of the fifth row. Marlin ultimately used a provisional to make the race, as did Johnny Benson, Michael Waltrip, Wally Dallenbach, Stacy Compton and Ed Berrier. Grissom also used a provisional to put the Hot Wheels Pontiac into the field in his substitute role, making Dave Marcis the only driver who failed to make the race.

In the early going of the thatlook.com 300, Craven had the throng of fans on their feet as he rolled to the point and ultimately led for 63 laps in front of his home crowd. When Craven faltered, Geoffrey Bodine put the Power Team Chevrolet at the point, underscoring that he was completely recovered from his accident at Daytona in February.

As the race ground on, Stewart, Nadeau, Martin, Earnhardt and Joe Nemechek began to establish themselves as the most likely con-

Mark Martin held seventh, a mere two points behind Rudd after finishing fourth at Daytona, while Tony Stewart's sixth place put him 13 points behind Martin. Rusty Wallace's third place at The Beach left him ninth, just 16 behind Stewart, while Jeff Gordon's 10th place in the Pepsi 400 dropped him to 61 behind the Miller Lite Ford driver and 334 out of first place in the standings.

Terry Labonte arrived at New Hampshire on crutches after an accident at Daytona left him with a broken bone in his right leg, but

John Andretti and Jeremy Mayfield (12) pursue Tony Stewart (20) in the first half of the event. Stewart took the point for the last time on lap 219 and led the final 55 circuits on the way to victory, making him the first three-time winner of the season.

After green-flag stops, Stewart took the lead for the final time on lap 219 — but it appeared he would still have to stop one last time for a "splash-and-go" in the waning laps if the race were to go the full distance. Anticipating having to make a stop, the Home Depot Pontiac driver rocketed away from the field, doing all he could to build his lead. His margin grew to nearly eight seconds over Nemechek until, on lap 268, the rain began falling again. It brought out the red flag for the

tenders for victory. With rain in the offing, all were trying to get to the point and remain there. Stewart seized the lead for the first time on lap 86 and held it for 40 circuits until the yellow flew as a shower dropped water on the track. Eight laps later, the red flag was displayed causing a rain delay of nearly an hour. After the track was dried, the green flag flew again, but lingering gray skies meant the race might not make the full distance and every lap became important to those in contention for victory.

second time at nearly 5 p.m., and after almost an hour of waiting for the weather to clear, NASCAR officials declared the results official.

Stewart had won his second rain-shortened event of the season and became the first driver this year to win three times. Nemechek was left with second place, while Martin fought to third ahead of a career-best fourth place by Nadeau. Gordon finished fifth ahead of Earnhardt and Jarrett, with Jeremy Mayfield eighth, point-leader Labonte ninth and Ricky Rudd rounding out the top 10.

THATLOOK.COM 300 • final results

Scott Pruett's Tide Ford goes through one of several technical inspections that take place during every race weekend. Inspections remain a critical component in maintaining the best competition possible for the benefit of the teams and, most important, the fans.

Fin. Pos.	Start Pos.	Car No.	Driver	Team	Fin. Pos.	Start Pos.	Car No.	Driver	Team
1	6	20	Tony Stewart	Home Depot Pontiac	23	7	36	Ken Schrader	M&M's Pontiac
2	30	33	Joe Nemechek	Oakwood Homes Chevrolet	24	15	94	Bill Elliott	McDonald's Ford
3	3	6	Mark Martin	Valvoline/Cummins Ford	25	37	40	Sterling Marlin	Coors Light Chevrolet
4	9	25	Jerry Nadeau	MichaelHoligan.com Chevrolet	26	19	55	Kenny Wallace	Square D/Cooper Lighting Chevrolet
5	8	24	Jeff Gordon	DuPont Automotive Finishes Chevrolet	27	41	75	Wally Dallenbach	America Online Ford
6	24	3	Dale Earnhardt	GM Goodwrench Service Chevrolet	28	23	1	Steve Park	Pennzoil Chevrolet
7	10	88	Dale Jarrett	Quality Care/Ford Credit Ford	29	42	9	Stacy Compton	Kodiak/Cougar Ford
8	16	12	Jeremy Mayfield	Mobil 1 Ford	30	35	32	Scott Pruett	Tide Ford
9	20	18	Bobby Labonte	Interstate Batteries Pontiac	31	28	16	Kevin Lepage	FamilyClick.com/TV Guide Ford
10	14	28	Ricky Rudd	Texaco/Havoline Ford	32	25	27	Mike Bliss	Pfizer/Viagra Pontiac
11	4	99	Jeff Burton	Exide Batteries Ford	33	27	66	Darrell Waltrip	Route 66/Big Kmart Ford
12	11	14	Rick Mast	Conseco Pontiac	34	29	93	Dave Blaney	Amoco Pontiac
13	17	60	Geoffrey Bodine	Power Team Chevrolet	35	39	7	Michael Waltrip	Nations Rent Chevrolet
14	38	10	Johnny Benson	Tyler Jet Motorsports Pontiac	36	40	44	Steve Grissom	Hot Wheels Pontiac
15	1	2	Rusty Wallace	Miller Lite Ford	37	43	90	Ed Berrier	Hills Brothers Coffee Ford
16	33	21	Elliott Sadler	CITGO Ford	38	21	77	Robert Pressley	Jasper Engines Ford
17	5	50	Ricky Craven	Midwest Transit Chevrolet	39	31	31	Mike Skinner	Lowe's Chevrolet
18	12	22	Ward Burton	Caterpillar Pontiac	40	2	43	John Andretti	Cheerios Pontiac
19	22	17	Matt Kenseth	DeWalt Tools Ford	41	18	26	Jimmy Spencer	Big Kmart/Route 66 Ford
20	13	11	Brett Bodine	Ralphs Supermarkets Ford	42	34	97	Chad Little	John Deere Ford
21	26	8	Dale Earnhardt Jr.	Budweiser Chevrolet	43	32	5	Terry Labonte	Kellogg's Chevrolet
22	36	4	Bobby Hamilton	Kodak Chevrolet					

PENNSYLVANIA *500*

(Left) Rich Bickle climbs aboard the Kellogg's Chevrolet in relief of the ailing Terry Labonte during the first caution of the race on lap 26. They were able to make the switch without losing a lap.

(Right) Rusty Wallace acknowledges the enthusiastic crowd in Pocono's winner's circle following an unexpected victory, his second win of the year.

The chase had really begun at Rockingham in February, when Dale Earnhardt chopped and hacked Bobby Labonte's lead to miniscule proportions in the closing laps of the Dura Lube/Kmart 400. Earnhardt failed to find a way to pass Labonte, but his determined charge underscored his team's return to the highest level of competitiveness.

The seven-time champion then won at Atlanta and put together a string of seven top-five and 15 top-10 finishes in the first 18 races of the season. Finally, after his sixth-place finish at New Hampshire, Earnhardt had fought to within 45 points of the Interstate Batteries Pontiac driver in their battle for the top position on the point ladder. The gleam was back in Earnhardt's steely-blues, and the confidence was back in his step. He was right where he wanted to be: on Labonte's bumper and in position to use his intimidation factor when needed in hopes of forcing a mistake that would vault him past Labonte in the point standings.

At the same time, Dale Jarrett's defense of his title was taking shape. D.J. fought to seventh place at the rain-shortened New Hampshire event and now found himself just 23 points behind Earnhardt and 68 behind Labonte in what had become a three-way battle for the championship.

Rich Bickle monitors the action within the Kellogg's team, ready to take the wheel from Terry Labonte at the event's first caution.

was named as Morgan-McClure's new crew chief for Bobby Hamilton's Kodak Chevrolet, and Jim Smith bought out Jim Mattei's interests in Michael Waltrip's Nations Rent Chevrolet. MB2 Motorsports acquired Johnny Benson's Tyler Jet team, and Ted Musgrave was named to drive the BellSouth Chevrolet for the next two races. When the BellSouth team arrived at Pocono, the number had been changed from "42" to "01," and the paint scheme had been changed to blue and silver. Kyle Petty made the decision to drive the

(Left) Second in points at Pocono, Dale Earnhardt had been applying the pressure on point-leader Bobby Labonte both on and off the track, and he didn't mind giving Labonte a subtle reminder as to who was coming up from behind.

(Below) On the track, Bobby Labonte keeps his Pontiac among the lead group and out of trouble. Having swept both Pocono events in 1999, Labonte used experience and confidence to come away with a solid finish and pad his lead in the standings.

(Bottom) Tony Stewart awaits a signal from the NASCAR official before leading the starting field off pit road. Stewart grabbed his first Bud Pole of the year but had a disappointing day, finishing a lap off the pace in 26th place.

After finishing 18th at New Hampshire, Ward Burton's challenge had fallen away and the Virginian now found himself 214 points behind the leader. But even more important, he was in a virtual dogfight with three other drivers for the fourth slot on the ladder. Tony Stewart's third victory of the season vaulted him to fifth, up three places in the standings, and he trailed Ward by just a single point. Mark Martin found himself just two points behind the Home Depot Pontiac driver and three behind Ward, while Jeff Burton was only four points behind Mark and just seven behind Ward.

Ricky Rudd dropped to eighth in the standings but was just 37 points behind Ward, while Rusty Wallace was 42 points behind the "Star Car" driver. Jeff Gordon remained in 10th, 29 behind Rusty, and the battle was truly on. Just over 100 points separated fourth place from 10th.

Since the teams visited Pocono Raceway five weeks earlier, much had occurred within the sport. Danny Gill

Steve Park's Pennzoil crew provides four tires, fuel and a left-side chassis adjustment during a pit stop under caution on lap 149.

Hot Wheels Pontiac until the Bristol race in August and said that Steve Grissom then would drive the car for the remainder of the season, while Kyle would compete in NASCAR Busch Series events in Adam Petty's Sprint-sponsored entries. Kyle planned to return to the NASCAR Winston Cup Series in 2001 with the Sprint-sponsored team.

A battered Terry Labonte arrived at Pocono still the worse for wear after having his broken leg jostled in an early-race accident at New Hampshire. The Kellogg's team had enlisted the services of Rich Bickle for the weekend, and Terry planned to drive the Chevrolet until the first caution in the race to keep his string of consecutive starts alive and gather important NASCAR Winston Cup Series points. Bickle then would drive the car for the remainder of the Pennsylvania 500. Stacy Compton broke two bones in his left wrist in a testing accident at Indianapolis and wore a half-cast for the Pocono event.

The BellSouth Chevrolet arrived at Pocono with a new number and Ted Musgrave behind the wheel for team owner Felix Sabates. Musgrave was workman-like in his first outing with the car, bringing home a 16th-place finish for the team.

Someone finally found an answer to Rusty Wallace's Bud Pole qualifying runs that had earned the Miller Lite driver seven poles in the first 18 races of the season. Stewart beat Wallace by seven-hundredths of a second to claim an entry into the 2001 Bud Shootout

and nail down the third pole of his brief career. It was the second pole of the season for a Pontiac driver and put the orange-and-white Home Depot entry in the top starting spot for the first time since the August Bristol event last year. Martin and Jeremy Mayfield, eyeing a sweep of the Pocono races this year, made up the second row ahead of Hendrick Motorsports teammates Gordon and Nadeau. Bill Elliott and Jeff Burton beat Johnny Benson and Steve Park for the seventh and eighth starting positions.

Ward Burton and Bobby Hamilton, along with Stacy Compton, Mike Bliss, Darrell Waltrip, Ed Berrier and Dave Marcis used provisionals, while Geoffrey Bodine and Carl Long failed to make the field. For Bodine, it was a bitter disappointment after leading the race at New Hampshire and posting a 13th-place finish.

top five. Mark Martin's Valvoline Ford lost its engine after just 25 laps, followed by Sterling Marlin, John Andretti, Kyle Petty and Hamilton, all with engine failures as well. While others struggled with mechanical problems, Earnhardt picked his way to second place. Then, on lap 146, Earnhardt's worst fears were realized. He cut a tire and was forced to pit road, but not before suffering significant body damage due to the tire's rubber casing flapping around under the right-front fender. He would eventually finish 25th — a huge blow after working his way to a challenging position in the point standings.

In the late stages of the race, Mayfield appeared to have positioned himself to claim two straight Pocono victories. He took over the point from Wallace on lap 182 and built a small lead, but Wallace

Jeremy Mayfield (12) and Kevin Lepage engage in a minor dispute over real estate coming off the third turn. Mayfield, trying for the Pocono sweep in 2000, looked to have things well in hand until a cut tire derailed his effort about a mile from the finish line.

When the field rolled out onto the triangular superspeedway, a pair of cars dropped to the tail end of the field. Terry Labonte's Chevrolet, which Bickle had qualified 22nd, fell backwards in anticipation of a driver exchange at the first caution flag, and Dale Earnhardt Jr. went to the rear because a practice accident on Saturday forced him to go to his backup Budweiser Chevrolet.

It didn't take long for the hopes of several contenders to go by the wayside. Rudd cut a tire and whacked the wall while running in the

and Jeff Burton teamed up and began to run Mayfield down. As the laps clicked away, fans stood and cheered the fabulous racing that was taking place at the front of the field.

Despite their best efforts, neither Wallace nor Burton appeared to have enough to push Mayfield from the point, and as the three drivers took the white flag for the final lap, Mayfield looked like the easy winner. Heading into the second turn, however, Mayfield felt a tire going down, and he had no options. He went into the corner a bit high and checked up slightly, opening the hole underneath that Wallace dove for. Rusty took the point and held off a determined Burton to claim his 51st career NASCAR Winston Cup Series victory.

As the Mobil 1 Ford limped to the finish, Jeff Gordon and Dale Jarrett flashed under Mayfield to claim third and fourth places. Matt Kenseth had a fine fifth-place finish ahead of Bobby Labonte, while Skinner claimed seventh place and Rick Mast eighth in A.J. Foyt's Pontiac. Jimmy Spencer also moved past Mayfield to grab ninth place, and in the span of a half lap, Mayfield went from a sure winner to a 10th-place finish.

(Above Right) Jeremy Mayfield (12) and Rusty Wallace (2) drag race down Pocono's long frontstretch in their battle for the lead. Mayfield wrested the point from Wallace on lap 182 and held on to a slight lead over the next 17 laps.

(Right) When the checkered flag fell, Mayfield was nowhere in sight. Here, Wallace captures the victory with Jeff Burton hot on his heels in second. Seven other drivers passed Mayfield as he limped back to the flag to take a 10th-place finish.

PENNSYLVANIA 500 • final results

Sixth place in the Pennsylvania 500 was good enough for Bobby Labonte to extend his lead by eight more points to 53. Now, however, Dale Jarrett held second place as Earnhardt's 25th-place finish dropped him to third in the standings, 107 behind the Interstate Batteries Pontiac.

Fin. Pos.	Start Pos.	Car No.	Driver	Team	Fin. Pos.	Start Pos.	Car No.	Driver	Team
1	2	2	Rusty Wallace	Miller Lite Ford	23	23	16	Kevin Lepage	FamilyClick.com/TV Guide Ford
2	8	99	Jeff Burton	Exide Batteries Ford	24	40	27	Mike Bliss	Pfizer/Viagra Pontiac
3	5	24	Jeff Gordon	DuPont Automotive Finishes Chevrolet	25	25	3	Dale Earnhardt	GM Goodwrench Service Chevrolet
4	11	88	Dale Jarrett	Quality Care/Ford Credit Ford	26	1	20	Tony Stewart	Home Depot Pontiac
5	24	17	Matt Kenseth	DeWalt Tools Ford	27	6	25	Jerry Nadeau	MichaelHoligan.com Chevrolet
6	13	18	Bobby Labonte	Interstate Batteries Pontiac	28	37	22	Ward Burton	Caterpillar Pontiac
7	17	31	Mike Skinner	Lowe's Chevrolet	29	36	21	Elliott Sadler	CITGO Ford
8	35	14	Rick Mast	Conseco Pontiac	30	19	11	Brett Bodine	Ralphs Supermarkets Ford
9	28	26	Jimmy Spencer	Big Kmart/Route 66 Ford	31	31	75	Wally Dallenbach	America Online Ford
10	4	12	Jeremy Mayfield	Mobil 1 Ford	32	7	94	Bill Elliott	McDonald's Ford
11	22	5	Terry Labonte	Kellogg's Chevrolet	33	42	90	Ed Berrier	Hills Brothers Coffee Ford
12	9	10	Johnny Benson	MB2 Motorsports Pontiac	34	16	33	Joe Nemechek	Oakwood Homes Chevrolet
13	15	8	Dale Earnhardt Jr.	Budweiser Chevrolet	35	39	9	Stacy Compton	Kodiak/Cougar Ford
14	20	77	Robert Pressley	Jasper Engines Ford	36	33	32	Scott Pruett	Tide Ford
15	10	1	Steve Park	Pennzoil Chevrolet	37	43	71	Dave Marcis	Realtree Chevrolet
16	26	01	Ted Musgrave	BellSouth Chevrolet	38	14	28	Ricky Rudd	Texaco/Havoline Ford
17	21	7	Michael Waltrip	Nations Rent Chevrolet	39	38	4	Bobby Hamilton	Kodak Chevrolet
18	18	93	Dave Blaney	Amoco Pontiac	40	32	44	Kyle Petty	Hot Wheels Pontiac
19	29	36	Ken Schrader	M&M's Pontiac	41	12	43	John Andretti	Cheerios Pontiac
20	30	97	Chad Little	John Deere Ford	42	34	40	Sterling Marlin	Coors Light Chevrolet
21	27	55	Kenny Wallace	Square D/Cooper Lighting Chevrolet	43	3	6	Mark Martin	Valvoline/Cummins Ford
22	41	66	Darrell Waltrip	Route 66/Big Kmart Ford					

BRICKYARD *400*

(Left) Pole-winner Ricky Rudd (28) leads the field under the green flag followed by Darrell Waltrip (66), Bobby Labonte (18), Dale Earnhardt Jr. (8) and Dale Jarrett (88) to begin the seventh running of the Brickyard 400.

(Right) Bobby Labonte got a real lift — both in the points and in the wallet — with his popular victory at Indianapolis.

Bobby Labonte and Dale Jarrett, sitting first and second in the point standings, found themselves at the top of another heap when they arrived at Indianapolis for the seventh running of the Brickyard 400.

Jarrett's Brickyard win in 1999 moved him into select company with Jeff Gordon as the only two drivers able to snare the coveted silver brick trophy twice. And with Jarrett's pair of victories coming in the last four Brickyard events, Jarrett found himself in a favorite's role at The Brickyard.

Although Bobby Labonte had yet to triumph at the 2.5-mile oval, he finished second, third and second in his last three appearances at the famed Speedway, causing many to rate the Interstate Batteries Pontiac driver as a co-favorite in this year's event.

Labonte's sixth place at Pocono combined with Jarrett's fourth place, reduced the Texan's point lead over Jarrett to 53, and Dale had every hope that he would be able to close the gap even more as the season headed toward its final third. The Quality Care Ford driver moved back to second place in the point standings following Pocono and was now even more determined than ever to successfully defend the NASCAR Winston Cup Series title he had claimed at the conclusion of the 1999 season.

Team owner Felix Sabates used the media-rich Brickyard atmosphere to announce that Chip Ganassi had purchased a majority share in Sabco Racing.

Dale Earnhardt's 25th place at Pocono cost him dearly, dropping him from second, 45 points behind Labonte, to third where he now faced a 107-point deficit. As far as Earnhardt was concerned, there was no better place to begin closing that gap than at Indianapolis where he had claimed victory in 1995.

Jeff Burton jumped from seventh to fourth place in the standings following his runner-up finish at Pocono, while Rusty Wallace's victory moved him from ninth to fifth on the point ladder. Tony Stewart fell one slot to sixth, and Ward Burton plummeted

---

(Left) The field of 43 cars rumbles past the starting line and into the first turn led by 1997 Brickyard 400 winner Ricky Rudd. Following closely in second is Darrell Waltrip, who added a highlight to his final season as a driver by capturing the outside of the front row during qualifying.

(Below) Steve Park and Jerry Nadeau started together in 22nd and 23rd, respectively. Nadeau had an outstanding run to fourth place, duplicating his career-best finish that came at New Hampshire two races ago.

from fourth to seventh. Jeff Gordon climbed two rungs to eighth after his third place at the triangular track, while Mark Martin found himself mired in ninth, down three positions after his engine problems at Pocono. Ricky Rudd fell from eighth to 10th, while Mike Skinner, Matt Kenseth, Terry Labonte, Dale Earnhardt Jr. and Jeremy Mayfield remained 11th through 15th, respectively.

In the days between races at Pocono and The Brickyard, Felix Sabates announced he had sold a majority interest in his Sabco Racing team to Chip Ganassi. And Johnny Benson got some good news when Atlanta-based Aaron's Rents stepped in to sponsor his team for the remainder of the year,

(Above) Jeff Burton (99) looks for passing room on the inside of Wally Dallenbach (75) and Geoffrey Bodine while charging through the pack from his 33rd-place start. Burton eventually worked his way to a sixth-place finish, while Bodine came home in 12th.

(Right) Kenny Wallace brings his Chevrolet to a stop on pit road while his Square D crew charges into action during the race's first caution on lap 17.

assuring Benson of a ride for the rest of the season. Jeff Gordon's DuPont Chevrolet carried a special paint scheme for the weekend devoted to the comic strip "Peanuts" in tribute to artist George Schultz. But Hendrick Motorsports teammate Terry Labonte was not having such a light-hearted time. Labonte found himself suffering from bouts of dizziness as a lingering effect of his Pepsi 400 accident at Daytona and was forced to end his record string of 655 consecutive NASCAR Winston Cup Series starts that dated back to 1979. Todd Bodine was nominated to drive the Kellogg's Chevrolet, leaving Earnhardt with the longest active string of consecutive starts at 633.

Many expected the horsepower from the vaunted Robert Yates engine shop to enable Jarrett to claim the Bud Pole Award following the first round of qualifying at Indianapolis. The Yates horsepower did its job, but the driver was Jarrett's teammate, Ricky Rudd, who claimed his second pole of the season and the first of his career at The Brickyard. The biggest surprise in qualifying, however, came from Darrell Waltrip, who rocketed to the outside of the front row in his finest qualifying performance of the last five seasons. After a year of nightmarish starts and finishes, Darrell was beside himself after

Kevin Lepage, Ted Musgrave, Dave Blaney and Stacy Compton used provisionals to make the field, leaving David Keith, Rich Bickle, Dave Marcis, Robby Gordon, Steve Grissom and Bill Baird out of the event.

During a Friday practice session, Joe Nemechek lost the engine in his Chevrolet and Mayfield ended up in the oil that had spilled on the track. He slid hard into the third-turn wall and, after a trip to the hospital, car owner Michael Kranefuss decided to have Mayfield sit out the race. Kyle Petty, whose Hot Wheels Pontiac had not made the field, filled in for Mayfield in the Mobil 1 Ford.

The Brickyard 400 had barely taken the green flag when Mark Martin's difficult season continued. Tagged by Skinner, Martin whacked the first-turn wall backwards, ending his hopes for a sweep of the weekend's events. He already had won Friday's IROC race, while Earnhardt finished second to claim his fourth IROC title, and Martin had high hopes for a Saturday victory to go with the IROC win. His day was over, however, and in

(Left) Jeff Gordon's paint scheme honoring the "Peanuts" comic strip and its creator, the late Charles Schulz, did not prove lucky. Gordon, the Brickyard 400 champion in 1994 and '98, was collected in Mark Martin's early-race accident and finished two laps down in 33rd.

(Below) Rusty Wallace's Miller Lite crew works with great precision and blinding speed to keep their driver out front on the track. With their help, Wallace paced the field for most of the day, leading 110 of the event's 160 laps.

his qualifying run and jumped into younger brother Michael's arms for a huge fraternal bear hug. He then proceeded to revive the "Icky Shuffle" he last performed when he finally won the Daytona 500 in 1989.

Bobby Labonte and Jeremy Mayfield qualified third and fourth fastest ahead of Jarrett and "Little E," with Bill Elliott and "Big E" making up the fourth row. Mike Skinner and Rusty Wallace claimed the fifth row, beating Scott Pruett and Mark Martin for the final top-10 slots.

Rudd's track record, set in the first round of qualifying, didn't last long. Brett Bodine erased Rudd's mark with a lap at 181.072 mph during the second round of qualifying, marking the first time in the history of the Brickyard 400 that the second-round fastest qualifier was quicker than the pole-sitter. Matt Kenseth, Ken Schrader, Chad Little,

Interstate Batteries team principals (from left) Joe Gibbs, Jimmy Makar and Bobby Labonte pay homage to the storied Brickyard with the traditional kiss of the bricks that remain part of the track at the start/finish line.

the blue-and-white Ford, then dove to the inside and completed the pass. Once in front, he eased away from Wallace. Rusty gave the chase everything he had, but it wasn't enough and Labonte continued to move away, winning by just over four seconds.

Wallace was frustrated. He had bobbled just the slightest bit after battling Labonte for more than 100 laps. It was the difference between sweet victory and bitter defeat.

the same accident, Jeff Gordon saw his chance for a third Brickyard 400 victory evaporate. He collided with Rick Mast in the aftermath of Martin's accident and eventually finished 33rd.

The battle at the front sorted itself into a two-car duel, with Rusty Wallace holding the point and Bobby Labonte stalking just a few feet off the rear bumper of the Miller Lite Ford. For more than 100 laps, Labonte chased and nibbled at Wallace, and for the longest time, it appeared that Rusty had the measure of the green-and-black Pontiac.

Then, just 14 laps from the end, Bobby saw his opportunity. Wallace went into the third turn just a touch wide. Bobby nudged

After three years of finishing second and third, Bobby Labonte had finally won at The Brickyard and, in the process, increased his point lead. It was only the second victory of the season for Labonte, but it came in one of the most important races of the year. Bill Elliott fought to a very strong third-place finish ahead of outstanding performances from Jerry Nadeau, Tony Stewart and Jeff Burton. Jarrett was seventh, Earnhardt eighth and Skinner ninth, while Scott Pruett claimed the first top-10 finish of his young NASCAR Winston Cup Series career.

BRICKYARD 400 • final results

At lap 120, Robert Pressley takes tires and fuel under green along Indy's massive pit road. With only two caution periods in the event, both of them before the 50-lap mark, teams had to make the most of pit strategy and quick stops under green to remain competitive in the 160-lap event.

Fin. Pos.	Start Pos.	Car No.	Driver	Team	Fin. Pos.	Start Pos.	Car No.	Driver	Team
1	3	18	Bobby Labonte	Interstate Batteries Pontiac	23	42	93	Dave Blaney	Amoco Pontiac
2	10	2	Rusty Wallace	Miller Lite Ford	24	41	01	Ted Musgrave	BellSouth Chevrolet
3	7	94	Bill Elliott	McDonald's Ford	25	13	10	Johnny Benson	Aaron's Pontiac
4	23	25	Jerry Nadeau	MichaelHoligan.com Chevrolet	26	37	17	Matt Kenseth	DeWalt Tools Ford
5	18	20	Tony Stewart	Home Depot Pontiac	27	19	77	Robert Pressley	Jasper Engines Ford
6	33	99	Jeff Burton	Exide Batteries Ford	28	16	22	Ward Burton	Caterpillar Pontiac
7	5	88	Dale Jarrett	Quality Care/Ford Credit Ford	29	17	55	Kenny Wallace	Square D/Cooper Lighting Chevrolet
8	8	3	Dale Earnhardt	GM Goodwrench Service Chevrolet	30	20	40	Sterling Marlin	Coors Light Chevrolet
9	9	31	Mike Skinner	Lowe's Chevrolet	31	34	27	Mike Bliss	Pfizer/Viagra Pontiac
10	11	32	Scott Pruett	Tide Ford	32	4	12	Kyle Petty	Mobil 1 Ford
11	2	66	Darrell Waltrip	Route 66/Big Kmart Ford	33	29	24	Jeff Gordon	DuPont Automotive Finishes Chevrolet
12	27	60	Geoffrey Bodine	Power Team Chevrolet	34	28	21	Elliott Sadler	CITGO Ford
13	6	8	Dale Earnhardt Jr.	Budweiser Chevrolet	35	31	75	Wally Dallenbach	Rotozip Ford
14	36	90	Hut Stricklin	Hills Brothers Coffee Ford	36	40	16	Kevin Lepage	FamilyClick.com/TV Guide Ford
15	25	5	Todd Bodine	Kellogg's Chevrolet	37	43	9	Stacy Compton	Kodiak/Cougar Ford
16	22	1	Steve Park	Pennzoil Chevrolet	38	24	14	Rick Mast	Conseco Pontiac
17	21	26	Jimmy Spencer	Big Kmart/Route 66 Ford	39	26	11	Brett Bodine	Ralphs Supermarkets Ford
18	35	33	Joe Nemechek	Oakwood Homes Chevrolet	40	32	4	Bobby Hamilton	Kodak Chevrolet
19	39	97	Chad Little	John Deere Ford	41	30	50	Ricky Craven	Midwest Transit Chevrolet
20	14	7	Michael Waltrip	Nations Rent Chevrolet	42	15	43	John Andretti	Cheerios Pontiac
21	1	28	Ricky Rudd	Texaco/Havoline Ford	43	12	6	Mark Martin	Valvoline/Cummins Ford
22	38	36	Ken Schrader	M&M's Pontiac					

GLOBAL CROSSING @ THE GLEN

(Left) Jeff Gordon (24) and Tony Stewart rip through the Esses in the opening laps, banging fenders and rubbing sheet metal in their tussle for position.

(Right) Steve Park flashes a winner's smile for those on hand in victory lane at Watkins Glen. His initial NASCAR Winston Cup Series win came in his 77th career start.

For more than 100 laps, Bobby Labonte stalked Rusty Wallace at Indianapolis before finding the opening he needed to post the Brickyard 400 victory. Wallace fought with everything available to him in his Miller Lite Ford, but in the end, Labonte's relentless pursuit won out. The brilliant duel between two of the sport's best drivers ended with Wallace frustrated and Labonte kissing the strip of bricks at the famed oval's start/finish line.

With the Brickyard 400 in the record book, the scene shifted to another of this country's most famous racetracks. The locale was different — the metropolitan area of Indianapolis had given way to the Finger Lakes region of Upstate New York with some of the most scenic vistas of the year. There is something simply majestic about glacier-carved, deep and narrow lakes nestled between hills covered with vineyards. Sited above the village of Watkins Glen is the home of road racing in America, the teardrop-shaped road course that has played a major part on the world's road-racing stage since the day the trains were stopped to allow the running of the first Watkins Glen Grand Prix in 1948.

Obviously, much has changed at The Glen since those early days. The facilities have changed considerably, but the spirit of competition and the eagerness to win at The Glen remains as fierce as it was

Bill Elliott slings his McDonald's Ford around the Watkins Glen circuit. Elliott, who took 13th place in this event, captured his first NASCAR Winston Cup Series win at Riverside in 1983, the only road-course victory of his career.

when the likes of Jimmy Clark, Graham Hill, Jackie Stewart and other international heroes claimed the laurel victory wreaths.

Jeff Gordon brought his string of six straight road-racing victories to The Glen, while Mark Martin, winner of three consecutive Glen events in 1993-94-95, hoped to get his season back on track after consecutive last-place finishes at Pocono and Indianapolis. Terry Labonte, long one of the NASCAR Winston Cup Series' best road racers, chose to sit out the Glen event, still nursing the dizziness that forced him to miss the Brickyard 400. Ron Hornaday was set to drive the Kellogg's Chevrolet. P.J. Jones was selected to drive the BellSouth Chevrolet for the road-course event, while Tom Hubert was nominated to drive Jeremy Mayfield's Ford while Mayfield recovered from his Indianapolis injury.

(Above) Ricky Rudd, whose quick feet and smooth driving style brought him two career victories at The Glen, fights off a challenge from Dale Earnhardt, whose career-best here is third, which he accomplished three separate times.

(Right) The starting field, lined up largely according to owner points, snakes its way into turn 11 and approaches the frontstretch where the green flag waits to begin the Global Crossing @ The Glen.

With Friday's qualifying session rained out, reporters found Mike Skinner, John Andretti and Kenny Wallace in the garage area. All were part of the "Silly Season" rumor mill, with each driver the subject of team switches for the upcoming season. Skinner flatly said he would remain with the Richard Childress-owned team he drives for, despite the fact that crew chief Larry McReynolds had announced he would leave the team at the end of the season to become an analyst for Fox television broadcasts next season. Andretti said he was set to return to Petty Enterprises, while Wallace said he had a year remaining on his contract with Andy Petree Racing and sponsor Square D. Wallace said he had no plans to leave his current team.

Todd Bodine (above left), from nearby Chemung, N.Y., joined the field with support from his home state. Bodine's day was much different than that of Robby Gordon (above right), who started the race from the 42nd position and raced to a fourth-place finish. Bodine started behind Gordon in last place and advanced only one spot in the finishing order due to a clutch failure early the event.

The Bud Pole qualifying session began on Saturday morning, but before all the cars could turn laps, rain once more interrupted the session. Unfortunately for some competitors, the rainout meant that they would miss the event. The first 35 cars in the field were determined by current car-owner points, and Darrell Waltrip moved into the field in the 36th starting position by using a Past Champion's Provisional. The remainder of the field was determined by the order in which the teams had drawn for positions in the qualifying order, which ensured starting positions for Mike Bliss, Kyle Petty, Rick Mast, Ron Fellows, Stacy Compton, Robby Gordon and Todd Bodine. It also meant that Brett Bodine, Scott Pruett, Boris Said, Brian Simo and R.K. Smith (in Dave Marcis' Chevrolet) were left out of the event.

By Sunday, the threat of rain was gone. Under overcast conditions the field greeted the green flag for the Global Crossing @ The Glen. Bobby Labonte and Dale Jarrett shared the front row for the start, with Dale Earnhardt and Jeff Burton in the second row ahead of Rusty Wallace and Tony Stewart. Ward Burton and Jeff Gordon were in the fourth row ahead of Ricky Rudd and Mark Martin, and it didn't take long for the huge throng of spectators to get a taste of the action.

On the second lap, Gordon arrowed up alongside Stewart and the two got together after exiting the first turn. They raced into the Esses side by side, pushing and shoving, with neither driver wanting to yield. Gordon eventually whacked the guardrail with the

right side of his DuPont Chevrolet and was forced to pit road for repairs, losing a lap in the process. Although he ultimately regained the lead lap, his hopes of a seventh straight road-course victory were over.

One by one, contenders fell by the wayside. Ron Fellows charged to 16th after starting 40th, but engine woes ended his day. Jerry Nadeau raced to the front before losing third gear. Rusty Wallace found the sandpit between turns 10 and 11 and lost the edge in his Miller Lite Ford. Rick Rudd was forced to pit road to have his carburetor replaced, and Ward Burton fell from a challenging position in the late going when he was forced to return to pit road after a stop because he had just four lug nuts on the left-rear tire.

Jeff Burton (99) and Mark Martin (6) chase Steve Park, but to no avail. Park was flawless over the final 27 laps and put his Pennzoil Chevrolet in victory lane for the first time.

There was no shortage of celebration for Park's first win, and when his crew showered him with accolades in victory lane, Park took the opportunity to shower them with some ice-cold Gatorade.

A Long Island native, Park listened to crew chief Paul Andrews in his ear and put together the best drive of his brief NASCAR Winston Cup Series career. Andrews, who guided Alan Kulwicki to his first victory in 1988 and then did the same for Jeremy Mayfield in 1998, kept Park cool under Martin's charge and eased him to his first career NASCAR Winston Cup Series win.

The victory made Park the 13th different winner this season and came just 10 days before his 33rd birthday. The Glen win also made him the third first-time winner of the season, moving him alongside Dale Earnhardt Jr. and Matt Kenseth. He led more than half the race and became the third active driver to claim his first career victory at a road course, joining Ricky Rudd and Bill Elliott, both of whom scored their first career NASCAR Winston Cup Series wins at Riverside, Calif., in 1983.

At the front of the field, Jeff Burton, Bobby Labonte and Mark Martin were having solid runs, but the surprise of the afternoon was Steve Park. Few had given him a chance of winning, but in the end, Park had everything right with his Pennzoil Chevrolet. He took the lead from Martin on lap 31 and held the point for 53 of the remaining 60 laps with both Jeff Burton and Martin giving chase. Burton was trying his best to catch the yellow-and-black Chevrolet, but he was unable to do so and eventually yielded second place to his Roush Racing teammate. Although Martin was able to close to just car-lengths, he couldn't find a way past Park.

Martin and Burton finished second and third, respectively, ahead of Robby Gordon's strong fourth-place finish. Point-leader Bobby Labonte had a solid run to fifth ahead of Stewart, who fought back from his early-race incident with Gordon to finish sixth. Dale Jarrett was seventh ahead of Joe Nemechek, Wally Dallenbach and Matt Kenseth.

GLOBAL CROSSING @ THE GLEN • final results

Jeff Burton flies through the Esses ahead of Bobby Labonte in their personal battle for championship points. The two drivers swapped the lead over the first 30 laps, but in the end, Burton chipped away at Labonte's point lead by finishing third, two spots ahead of Labonte.

Fin. Pos.	Start Pos.	Car No.	Driver	Team
1	18	1	Steve Park	Pennzoil Chevrolet
2	10	6	Mark Martin	Valvoline/Cummins Ford
3	4	99	Jeff Burton	Exide Batteries Ford
4	42	13	Robby Gordon	Sony/Team Menard Ford
5	1	18	Bobby Labonte	Interstate Batteries Pontiac
6	6	20	Tony Stewart	Home Depot Pontiac
7	2	88	Dale Jarrett	Quality Care/Ford Credit Ford
8	21	33	Joe Nemechek	Oakwood Homes Chevrolet
9	35	75	Wally Dallenbach	Redcell Batteries Ford
10	12	17	Matt Kenseth	DeWalt Tools Ford
11	9	28	Ricky Rudd	Texaco/Havoline Ford
12	22	97	Chad Little	John Deere Ford
13	17	94	Bill Elliott	McDonald's Ford
14	30	55	Kenny Wallace	Square D/Cooper Lighting Chevrolet
15	13	5	Ron Hornaday	Kellogg's Chevrolet
16	31	4	Bobby Hamilton	Kodak Chevrolet
17	27	7	Michael Waltrip	Nations Rent Chevrolet
18	19	36	Ken Schrader	M&M's Pontiac
19	39	14	Rick Mast	Conseco Pontiac
20	36	66	Darrell Waltrip	Route 66/Big Kmart Ford
21	29	01	P.J. Jones	BellSouth Chevrolet
22	7	22	Ward Burton	Caterpillar Pontiac

Fin. Pos.	Start Pos.	Car No.	Driver	Team
23	8	24	Jeff Gordon	DuPont Automotive Finishes Chevrolet
24	34	60	Geoffrey Bodine	Power Team Chevrolet
25	3	3	Dale Earnhardt	GM Goodwrench Service Chevrolet
26	23	77	Robert Pressley	Jasper Engines Ford
27	15	10	Johnny Benson	Aaron's Pontiac
28	32	21	Elliott Sadler	CITGO Ford
29	41	9	Stacy Compton	Kodiak/Cougar Ford
30	20	40	Sterling Marlin	Coors Light Chevrolet
31	24	26	Jimmy Spencer	Big Kmart/Route 66 Ford
32	28	16	Kevin Lepage	FamilyClick.com/TV Guide Ford
33	16	12	Tom Hubert	Mobil 1 Ford
34	5	2	Rusty Wallace	Miller Lite Ford
35	33	93	Dave Blaney	Amoco Pontiac
36	11	31	Mike Skinner	Lowe's Chevrolet
37	26	43	John Andretti	Cheerios Pontiac
38	25	25	Jerry Nadeau	MichaelHoligan.com Chevrolet
39	37	27	Mike Bliss	Pfizer/Viagra Pontiac
40	14	8	Dale Earnhardt Jr.	Budweiser Chevrolet
41	38	44	Kyle Petty	Hot Wheels Pontiac
42	43	34	Todd Bodine	I Love NY Chevrolet
43	40	87	Ron Fellows	Bully Hill Vineyards Chevrolet

PEPSI 400 PRESENTED BY MEIJER

(Left) Michigan's top finishers race across the line, with event winner Rusty Wallace dispatching of second-place Ricky Rudd (28), third-place Bobby Labonte (18) and Dale Jarrett (88), who finished fourth.

(Right) Johnny Benson recently received word that Valvoline would become sponsor and part owner of his car next year, and he responded to the news with a strong, fifth-place finish.

People in the NASCAR Winston Cup Series garage area were quickly becoming believers.
For the longest time, despite solid and well-judged runs during the spring and summer, some thought Labonte's front-running challenge for his first career NASCAR Winston Cup Series title would eventually falter.

Instead, Labonte and the Jimmy Makar-led crew fought on a race-to-race basis, seeking — and finding — the best possible finish in each event. The team was competitive at every type of track, and Labonte coolly dueled with Rusty Wallace at Indianapolis before finding an opening and emerging victorious. At The Glen, Labonte once again battled for the best finish he could gain and came home with a rock-solid fifth place.

He arrived at the two-mile Michigan Speedway with a 101-point margin over defending NASCAR Winston Cup Series Champion Dale Jarrett, and, although far too early to begin planning his championship acceptance speech, Labonte and the entire green-and-black-clad crew were clearly the odds-on favorites to win the title. As defending race champions at Michigan, the team confidently went about its business from the opening of practice.

NASCAR Craftsman Truck Series standout Andy Houston made his NASCAR Winston Cup Series debut at Michigan driving for Cal Wells and was impressive until engine failure sidelined his effort.

Michigan was a family affair of sorts for the Earnhardts. Dale Jr. (above left) became the first to exceed 190 mph in a stock car at Michigan and set a new track record in qualifying. Kerry Earnhardt (above center) tied Stricklin as the fastest second-round qualifier in his NASCAR Winston Cup Series debut. Andy Houston (above right) extended the family's presence even further: He's nephew to Dale's wife, Teresa. Here, he gets a few pointers on signing autographs from the seven-time champ.

Jarrett finished seventh at The Glen, but still lost points to Labonte in the last two races. It was time for his Quality Care team to mount its challenge, and as far as Jarrett was concerned, this was a fine place to begin. He knew the way to victory lane at Michigan, having won three times before in the Irish Hills.

After spinning and whacking the styrofoam blocks at The Glen, Dale Earnhardt struggled to a 25th-place finish and now found himself 217 points behind Labonte. In fact, Earnhardt had more to be concerned with than just catching Labonte, with Jeff Burton using his third place at The Glen to move within four points of The Intimidator.

Tony Stewart climbed to fifth place, swapping positions with Rusty Wallace after the Glen results were tallied, while Ward Burton's 28th place at Indy and 22nd place at Watkins Glen dropped him to just three points ahead of Ricky Rudd in their battle for seventh place on the point ladder. Mark Martin's second place the

The top five drivers in the point standings enjoy a relaxing few minutes prior to going to work at Michigan. Entering the race, (from left) Jeff Burton sat fourth in points, Tony Stewart was in fifth, and Bobby Labonte remained ahead of Dale Jarrett in second and Dale Earnhardt in third.

Tony Stewart (20) takes the inside on Dale Earnhardt Jr. (8) with Jeff Gordon eyeing the fight from behind. Stewart was on his way to the front after qualifying in 19th, but shortly after this photo was taken, he got loose and spun in the second turn, taking Gordon with him into the wall.

previous week moved him to just 12 points behind Rudd, while Jeff Gordon fell from eighth in points to 10th after his altercation with Stewart at Watkins Glen.

After missing two races, Terry Labonte returned to the wheel of the Kellogg's Chevrolet, and Hendrick Motorsports used the occasion to announce a three-year extension of Kellogg's sponsorship of the team. In other team-related news, Valvoline announced it would sponsor Johnny Benson and the MB2 team next year, but the announcement carried an interesting twist. The company would also become partners in the team with MB2 principals Tom Beard, Nelson Bowers and Read Morton, with Valvoline owning 50 percent of the organization.

The massive crowd on hand was treated to a beautiful day in Michigan's Irish Hills, in terms of both weather and racing. The 200-lap event featured 21 lead changes among eight different drivers.

An early-race caution brings nearly everyone down pit road for tires, fuel and needed chassis adjustments. Eight cautions during the race allowed most pit stops to take place under the yellow, but the final caution on lap 179 proved pivotal by putting Rusty Wallace in position to take the win.

"Little E" stole the headlines, however, when he rocketed to a new track record for stock cars at Michigan and became the first driver to exceed 190 miles per hour on the two-mile oval. His lap at 191.149 mph was more than a mile per hour faster than the one turned by Jarrett, who beat Rick Mast for the other slot on the front row to start the Pepsi 400 presented by Meijer. Ricky Rudd lined up on the rear bumper of his Robert Yates Racing teammate with the fourth-fastest lap, while Bobby Labonte and Jeremy Mayfield claimed the third row. Mark Martin and Jerry Nadeau were seventh and eighth fastest, while Ward Burton and Rusty Wallace grabbed the final top-10 starting positions from Scott Pruett and Ken Schrader.

Hut Stricklin and Kerry Earnhardt, driving a Dave Marcis-owned Chevrolet, turned identical laps during the second round of qualifying, and Stricklin was given the 26th starting position because car owner Junie Donlavey was one position ahead of Marcis in the car-owner point standings. Kerry Earnhardt's first career start

made the family the first in the modern era of the sport to have a father race against two sons in a NASCAR Winston Cup Series race.

The elder Earnhardt was forced to use a provisional to make the field, as were Robert Pressley, Jimmy Spencer, Ted Musgrave, Bobby Hamilton, Brett Bodine and Robby Gordon. That left Geoffrey Bodine, Darrell Waltrip, Stacy Compton, Kyle Petty, David Keith and Carl Long out of the field for Sunday's event.

Time after time this season, Rusty Wallace appeared poised to win until something happened in the closing laps of the race. There was Indy, of course, where Bobby Labonte's relentless stalking cost

Tight packs of cars racing three and four wide are not uncommon at Michigan. Here, Ricky Craven (50) holds the low line with Steve Park (1) chasing Scott Pruett (32) in the middle groove, while Mike Skinner (31), Jeff Gordon (24) and Wally Dallenbach (75) work the high side.

Wallace the Brickyard win. Earlier in the season, he dominated Martinsville but made a costly decision to pit for tires while others stayed on the track, and he could only work his way back to eighth. At the spring Richmond race, he took four tires in the late going while "Little E" took two and went on to win. In the first Pocono race, he again took four tires while others took two, and he fell down the list after leading more than half the race.

This time it was the Pepsi 400 at Michigan, and when the green dropped, Wallace flew away from the field. He led more than half the race and it appeared that a strategic call in the closing laps of the event would cost him the chance to post his third victory of the season.

He pitted under the green flag with 30 laps remaining and took four tires and fuel. That set the stage, and when Bobby Labonte and

Ricky Rudd pitted just five laps later, each took just two tires. They returned to the track well ahead of Wallace, and, despite the fact Rusty had four new tires on his Miller Lite Ford, it appeared he would be unable to make up the difference on the leaders.

Then, finally, Lady Luck smiled on him. Robby Gordon spun with 21 laps to go, and Rudd saw his two-second advantage disappear. Worse, he knew that he was a sitting duck for the restart with Wallace on four fresher Goodyears while the Texaco Ford had just the pair of new tires.

When the green flag dropped, Rudd was proven correct. Wallace dispatched Labonte, and then, a lap later, he rocketed past Rudd. Wallace moved away from the battle between Rudd, Labonte and Jarrett for second place and eased to the 52nd victory of his career. Rudd and Labonte were able to fend off Jarrett, while Johnny Benson had a great run in his home state to claim fifth. Earnhardt battled all the way from 37th to grab sixth place ahead of Jimmy Spencer and Matt Kenseth. Ward Burton beat younger brother Jeff for ninth place, while Mark Martin just missed 10th place behind his Roush Racing teammate.

Jeff Gordon and Tony Stewart, who had tangled at Watkins Glen, ironically were involved again. Early in the event, Stewart collided with "Little E" and slid, collecting Gordon on the way to the wall. Stewart finished 41st, while Gordon was 36th.

After the final restart, Rusty Wallace used his four fresh tires to work past Bobby Labonte (18) before setting his sites on Ricky Rudd. Both Rudd and Labonte had taken just two tires on their last stops, trading fresh rubber for improved track position.

PEPSI 400 PRESENTED BY MEIJER • final results

Rusty Wallace celebrates his fifth career win at Michigan — his third of the 2000 season and the 52nd of his career. The victory also moved Wallace into the top five in the championship point standings.

Fin. Pos.	Start Pos.	Car No.	Driver	Team
1	10	2	Rusty Wallace	Miller Lite Ford
2	4	28	Ricky Rudd	Texaco/Havoline Ford
3	5	18	Bobby Labonte	Interstate Batteries Pontiac
4	2	88	Dale Jarrett	Quality Care/Ford Credit Ford
5	23	10	Johnny Benson	Aaron's Pontiac
6	37	3	Dale Earnhardt	GM Goodwrench Service Chevrolet
7	39	26	Jimmy Spencer	Big Kmart/Route 66 Ford
8	28	17	Matt Kenseth	DeWalt Tools Ford
9	9	22	Ward Burton	Caterpillar Pontiac
10	24	99	Jeff Burton	Exide Batteries Ford
11	7	6	Mark Martin	Valvoline/Cummins Ford
12	8	25	Jerry Nadeau	MichaelHoligan.com Chevrolet
13	6	12	Jeremy Mayfield	Mobil 1 Ford
14	41	4	Bobby Hamilton	Kodak Chevrolet
15	21	40	Sterling Marlin	Coors Light Chevrolet
16	14	31	Mike Skinner	Lowe's Chevrolet
17	11	32	Scott Pruett	Tide Ford
18	30	16	Kevin Lepage	FamilyClick.com/TV Guide Ford
19	12	36	Ken Schrader	M&M's Pontiac
20	33	5	Terry Labonte	Kellogg's Chevrolet
21	18	7	Michael Waltrip	Nations Rent Chevrolet
22	36	97	Chad Little	John Deere Ford
23	25	33	Joe Nemechek	Oakwood Homes Chevrolet
24	22	93	Dave Blaney	Amoco Pontiac
25	20	75	Wally Dallenbach	TBS Dinner & A Movie Ford
26	40	01	Ted Musgrave	BellSouth Chevrolet
27	29	43	John Andretti	Cheerios Pontiac
28	31	27	Mike Bliss	Pfizer/Viagra Pontiac
29	3	14	Rick Mast	Conseco Pontiac
30	34	55	Kenny Wallace	Square D/Cooper Lighting Chevrolet
31	1	8	Dale Earnhardt Jr.	Budweiser Chevrolet
32	38	77	Robert Pressley	Jasper Engines Ford
33	15	1	Steve Park	Pennzoil Chevrolet
34	43	13	Robby Gordon	Turtlewax/Team Menard Ford
35	35	96	Andy Houston	Ronald McDonald House Charities Ford
36	16	24	Jeff Gordon	DuPont Automotive Finishes Chevrolet
37	13	50	Ricky Craven	Midwest Transit Chevrolet
38	17	94	Bill Elliott	McDonald's Ford
39	26	90	Hut Stricklin	Hills Brothers Coffee Ford
40	32	21	Elliott Sadler	CITGO Ford
41	19	20	Tony Stewart *	Home Depot Pontiac
42	42	11	Brett Bodine	Ralphs Supermarkets Ford
43	27	71	Kerry Earnhardt	Realtree Chevrolet

GORACING.COM 500

(Left) Rookie of the year contender Matt Kenseth (17) dices with Roush Racing driver Kevin Lepage at Bristol. They finished 39th and 18th, respectively.

(Right) Rusty Wallace's Miller Lite crew played its part in Wallace's winning both the pole for the race and the event itself. It was his 53rd career victory.

With his third victory of the season in his pocket, Rusty Wallace refused to concede he was out of the point race. He was more than 350 points behind leader Bobby Labonte, but with 12 races remaining in the season, the 1989 NASCAR Winston Cup Series champion knew the title was far from locked up for any driver.

Certainly, the Miller Lite Ford driver admitted he needed to find more consistency in the final third of the season, and he also needed a little help from Labonte in the form of some poor racing luck to aid in closing the gap.

But through his superb career, Rusty has always been one who never gives up until the final lap of the season's last race is completed. He would compete — and drive his heart out every lap for the rest of the year — in hopes of claiming his second career NASCAR Winston Cup Series crown.

Bobby Labonte's third place at Michigan helped him gain another 10 points on Dale Jarrett, with Jarrett finishing fourth and failing to lead a lap. Labonte's lead was now 111 over the defending NASCAR Winston Cup Series champion, and with Dale Earnhardt finishing sixth at Michigan, Labonte's cushion over the seven-time champion was now 237 points. Jeff Burton held fourth place 15

David Green filled in for an injured Bill Elliott and finished 36th in his first NASCAR Winston Cup Series start of the year.

points behind Earnhardt, while Wallace moved back into fifth place just 100 points behind Burton and 115 out of third.

Tony Stewart's 41st-place finish at Michigan cost him his temporary hold on fifth place, and, coupled with Ricky Rudd's runner-up finish at Michigan, Stewart now was just two points ahead of the Texaco Ford driver. Ward Burton held eighth place, 36 behind Stewart and 23 ahead of Mark Martin, while Jeff Gordon remained 10th in the standings despite his accident at Michigan that ended his day with a 36th-place finish. Gordon was now a distant 604 points down to leader Bobby Labonte.

Two drivers found themselves on the sidelines as practice opened for the goracing.com 500 at Bristol Motor Speedway. Bill Elliott had tripped over a garden hose while carrying a bag of fertilizer at his home, and the resulting fall broke the bottom half of his left kneecap. Following surgery to pin the bones back together again, Elliott turned his McDonald's Ford over to David Green for the 500-lapper at Thunder Valley. And in another non-track accident, Stacy Compton broke his collarbone while playing racquetball during the week, and Bobby Hillin was tapped to fill in with the Melling Racing Ford.

(Left) The start of the late August 500-lap run at Bristol Motor Speedway saw Bud Pole winner Rusty Wallace fight for the early lead with Jeff Gordon, in the DuPont Chevrolet. Gordon had an uncharacteristically bad night and finished 23rd.

(Below) The top stars of NASCAR racing again played to a standing-room-only crowd at the east Tennessee high-banked oval. It seems that every time seats are added at Bristol, they're almost immediately snapped up.

(Bottom) Darrell Waltrip, who "owned" BMS during his heyday in the 1980s, made a ceremonial lap around the track before the race. The goracing.com 500 was Waltrip's last appearance at the Bristol track as a driver because of his retirement at the end of the 2000 NASCAR Winston Cup Series season.

Carrying a special paint scheme that featured Harley-Davidson motorcycles, Wallace was ready and raring to go when the green flag dropped on Bud Pole qualifying Friday evening. And when the session was complete, Wallace had claimed his eighth pole of the season and nailed down the seventh pole of his 34 career races at Bristol. As it turned out, he needed every bit of speed he could squeeze from his run, with Jeff Gordon grabbing the outside of the front row just .008 of a mile per hour slower.

Steve Park continued to impress by claiming the inside of the second row, while Mike Skinner beat Jerry Nadeau for the fourth-

Wallace's 2000 sweep of Bristol (he also won the spring race) came only after he managed to hold off Tony Stewart's Home Depot Pontiac during the final laps. The two cars were separated by one-half second at the finish.

(Right) Brett Bodine (11) makes tracks away from the damaged Amoco Pontiac of Dave Blaney, who, after running just 49 laps, was the first driver out of the race.

(Below) Defending NASCAR Winston Cup Series champion Dale Jarrett (88) and Ward Burton also experienced Bristol's wrath. Both, however, continued and took the checkered flag.

fastest lap. Stewart qualified sixth fastest ahead of Mark Martin and Sterling Marlin, while Robert Pressley and Kevin Lepage beat Elliott Sadler and Dale Earnhardt Jr. for the fifth-row starting slots.

With Ricky Rudd, Chad Little, Jimmy Spencer, Ted Musgrave, Wally Dallenbach, Rick Mast and Dave Marcis using provisionals to make the field, Mike Bliss, Hut Stricklin, Carl Long and Ricky Craven found themselves forced to sit out the race.

The August night race at Bristol is one of the most spectacular shows of the season, and it has become one of the hardest tickets to obtain in the world of sports. The visual — and visceral — scene of 43 cars rocketing around the high-banked half-mile bowl, and the

Wallace's love affair with the half-mile Bristol oval continued in victory lane as fireworks added to the festivities. The St. Louis native won his first NASCAR Winston Cup Series race here in 1986 and his 50th in March.

sound and fury of the unleashed power created by the sport's master engine builders is one that remains with the beholder for days after the event is completed.

Wallace's love affair with Bristol began when he notched the first victory of his storied career at the track in 1986, and that romance took on an added chapter this Saturday night under the full moon.

He led the first portion of the race, worked with his crew on the handling of his Ford during the middle stages of the event and, in the final 50 laps, avoided two accidents that threatened to collect him. He rolled to a hard-fought victory over Tony Stewart at the end, notching his second straight win, his fourth of the season and the 53rd of his career. The victory gave him a sweep of the Bristol events this season and left him gushing with pride and compliments for the crew that had prepared his Miller Lite Ford and then worked their magic throughout the event on pit road.

Wallace was just a half-second ahead of Stewart at the end, with Mark Martin coming home in third place. Dale Earnhardt was fourth ahead of Steve Park, while Jeff Burton finished sixth. Elliott Sadler had a great run in the Wood Brothers' CITGO Ford to claim seventh, while Sterling Marlin and Dale Jarrett beat Ricky Rudd for 10th place.

Point leader Bobby Labonte struggled with leg cramps in the middle of the race and also lost a lap when he spun between turns three and four on lap 320. Later, his Interstate Batteries Pontiac was slightly damaged when it was clipped by Skinner's spinning Chevrolet. He ultimately finished 15th, allowing Jarrett, Earnhardt, Burton and Wallace to gain points in the process.

GORACING.COM 500 • final results

Jeff Burton (99) was "all charged up" at Bristol, driving all the way from his 35th-place starting spot to a sixth-place finish and taking the award presented by his sponsor for advancing the most positions in the event.

Fin. Pos.	Start Pos.	Car No.	Driver	Team	Fin. Pos.	Start Pos.	Car No.	Driver	Team
1	1	2	Rusty Wallace	Miller Lite Ford	23	2	24	Jeff Gordon	DuPont Automotive Finishes Chevrolet
2	6	20	Tony Stewart	Home Depot Pontiac	24	39	26	Jimmy Spencer	Big Kmart/Route 66 Ford
3	7	6	Mark Martin	Valvoline/Cummins Ford	25	36	60	Geoffrey Bodine	Power Team Chevrolet
4	17	3	Dale Earnhardt	GM Goodwrench Service Chevrolet	26	24	55	Kenny Wallace	Square D/Cooper Lighting Chevrolet
5	3	1	Steve Park	Pennzoil Chevrolet	27	34	33	Joe Nemechek	Oakwood Homes Chevrolet
6	35	99	Jeff Burton	Exide Batteries Ford	28	14	11	Brett Bodine	Ralphs Supermarkets Ford
7	11	21	Elliott Sadler	CITGO Ford	29	42	14	Rick Mast	Conseco Pontiac
8	8	40	Sterling Marlin	Coors Light Chevrolet	30	38	97	Chad Little	John Deere Ford
9	31	88	Dale Jarrett	Quality Care/Ford Credit Ford	31	43	71	Dave Marcis	Realtree Chevrolet
10	37	28	Ricky Rudd	Texaco/Havoline Ford	32	5	25	Jerry Nadeau	MichaelHoligan.com Chevrolet
11	16	22	Ward Burton	Caterpillar Pontiac	33	41	75	Wally Dallenbach	World Championship Wrestling Ford
12	15	36	Ken Schrader	M&M's Pontiac	34	20	4	Bobby Hamilton	Kodak Chevrolet
13	29	10	Johnny Benson	Aaron's Pontiac	35	18	12	Jeremy Mayfield	Mobil 1 Ford
14	4	31	Mike Skinner	Lowe's Chevrolet	36	26	94	David Green	McDonald's Ford
15	32	18	Bobby Labonte	Interstate Batteries Pontiac	37	9	77	Robert Pressley	Jasper Engines Ford
16	23	5	Terry Labonte	Kellogg's Chevrolet	38	33	32	Scott Pruett	Tide Ford
17	40	01	Ted Musgrave	BellSouth Chevrolet	39	22	17	Matt Kenseth	DeWalt Tools Ford
18	10	16	Kevin Lepage	FamilyClick.com/TV Guide Ford	40	21	9	Bobby Hillin	Kodiak/Cougar Ford
19	19	7	Michael Waltrip	Nations Rent Chevrolet	41	13	13	Robby Gordon	Turtlewax/Team Menard Ford
20	28	43	John Andretti	Cheerios Pontiac	42	27	66	Darrell Waltrip	Route 66/Big Kmart Ford
21	12	8	Dale Earnhardt Jr.	Budweiser Chevrolet	43	30	93	Dave Blaney	Amoco Pontiac
22	25	44	Kyle Petty	Hot Wheels Pontiac					

PEPSI SOUTHERN 500

(Left) Jeremy Mayfield notched the pole and got the Pepsi Southern 500 off to an exciting start. He led over 100 laps, but a meeting with the wall ended any chance of victory for the Mobil 1 Ford driver.

(Right) Good fortune, in the form of Mother Nature, smiled on Bobby Labonte in his quest for the NASCAR Winston Cup Series championship. Labonte made a late-race pit stop, got back onto the track in first place and cinched the win after the event was red-flagged because of rain.

W ith back-to-back victories at Michigan and Bristol and three wins in his last five outings, Rusty Wallace arrived at Darlington Raceway with two goals in mind. The first was to continue a charge he hoped would pull him back into the championship battle, and the second was to score a victory at what he considers one of the most important races in a driver's career.

Darlington is difficult at best. In the past, the tricky egg-shaped oval carried the nickname "The Lady in Black," derived from the black sealer used to cover the sandblasted asphalt racing surface. The nickname was changed to "The Track Too Tough to Tame" in the 1990s and has more than lived up to that name. The pioneer superspeedway in NASCAR racing, Darlington has rewarded — and frustrated — drivers since the first Southern 500 was won by Johnny Mantz 50 years ago. In that race, drivers used dog collars to hold the doors shut, rope to hold themselves in the driver's seats and four-spoke lug wrenches to change the street tires they occasionally borrowed from family sedans of spectators parked in the infield.

Bizarre? Yes. But through the years, the Southern 500 has had enough strange and quirky occurrences to build the tradition that one simply never knows what will happen on any given Sunday at Darlington.

Team owner Rick Hendrick, looking fit, was on hand at Darlington. Of his three drivers, Jeff Gordon posted the best finish — fourth.

(Left) The two Dales — Earnhardt and Jarrett — went into the Pepsi Southern 500 nipping at Labonte's heels in the point race. The spread didn't change that much after the event's conclusion.

(Middle) The DeWalt crew hustles to find the problem with Matt Kenseth's Ford. The rookie of the year candidate finished 33rd.

(Bottom) Steve Park (1) ducks under Ted Musgrave. They finished 10th and 13th, respectively.

Wallace has challenged for a Darlington victory time after time during his career, but a trophy from the track has eluded him over and over. With "Lite-ning," the chassis he drove to victory earlier this year at Pocono, Wallace felt he was ready to finally score a Darlington win and claim victory in the Pepsi Southern 500 — an event many drivers feel is a career's crowning achievement.

With his Bristol victory, Rusty moved to within 290 points of leader Bobby Labonte, and despite being fifth in the standings, he knew if he continued to run well and if Labonte had a little poor racing luck, he could climb right back into the championship battle.

After finishing 15th at Bristol, Labonte did indeed look vulnerable as the stretch run to the championship heated up. He was just 91 points ahead of defending NASCAR Winston Cup Series champion Dale Jarrett, while Dale Earnhardt continued to close the gap by finishing fourth at Bristol and cutting Labonte's lead over him to 195. Jeff Burton was 25 points behind Earnhardt, while Tony Stewart occupied sixth place in the standings after finishing second in Thunder Valley. Ricky Rudd held seventh ahead of Mark Martin and Ward Burton, while Jeff Gordon was 10th, well clear of the 11th-place battle between Mike Skinner and Matt Kenseth. Steve Park and Johnny Benson were 13th and 14th, with Dale Earnhardt Jr. ahead of Ken Schrader for the final position in the top 15.

Labonte looked even more vulnerable Friday morning after he made contact with the third-turn wall during practice. The impact damaged his primary car, and his team was forced to switch to the backup. In Bud Pole qualifying, Labonte could do no better than 38th, while Jeremy Mayfield put another layer to his up-

Pump it up! Dale Jarrett's jackman puts everything he has into his work while the catch-can man hands off an empty gas can.

and-down season by notching the pole. Johnny Benson continued his impressive performances with the Aaron's Rent Pontiac, grabbing the outside of the front row, while Ward Burton and Skinner claimed the second row. Martin and Earnhardt were the fifth and sixth fastest in the qualifying session, with Scott Pruett and Ken Schrader beating Jarrett and Gordon for the fourth row.

Forced to use a provisional, Bobby Labonte lined up 37th to start the race with older brother Terry beside him. Steve Park, David Green, substituting for the second week for Bill Elliott, and Robert Pressley also used provisionals, as did Wally Dallenbach. Darrell Waltrip, making his final start at Darlington, used a provisional to start his 800th career NASCAR Winston Cup Series race. That left Stacy Compton as the only driver to not make the Pepsi Southern 500 field.

Rain marred three events at Darlington over the last four years, and when the field rumbled under the green flag to start the Pepsi Southern 500, there was considerable doubt whether the event would be able to go the distance. Jeremy Mayfield dominated the

early going, and after just 37 laps, he had built a lead of more than four seconds. The red flag fell on the field when the first rain shower of the afternoon hit, erasing Mayfield's lead and causing to a two-hour stoppage of the race.

When the event restarted, Mayfield again set sail, leading 104 of the race's first 117 laps. On lap 118, however, the Mobil 1 Ford found

Jeff Burton (99) scoots past Bobby Labonte while chasing after the win. Luck, however, was on Labonte's side, and Burton finished second.

(Top) Jeremy Mayfield (12), here running with Steve Grissom, was strong early in the race, but rain was just one circumstance that worked against him.

(Right) Mike Bliss (27) mixes it up with fellow rookie Matt Kenseth on the frontstretch. The incident brought out the race's eighth caution flag.

(Bottom) When Dale Earnhardt went into the lead on lap 175, the move brought the crowd to its feet.

itself in the outside wall after trying to lap Dave Marcis, and with the incident went Mayfield's hopes for victory.

The event then turned into a crew chief's nightmare with rain threatening to halt the race on several occasions, causing teams to make various decisions regarding their strategies both on the track and along pit road.

But the race continued and when NASCAR officials threw a yellow flag on lap 320 after Jerry Nadeau lost the engine in his Chevrolet, all the lead-lap cars headed for pit road — and there lay the tale of victory.

Bobby Labonte's Interstate Batteries team turned the fastest stop, sending the point leader back to the track in first place, and before the event could be restarted, the clouds opened and Darlington was deluged. Already after 7 p.m., there was no hope of getting the track dried in time to finish the remaining laps, and NASCAR dropped the checkered flag with Labonte following the pace car across the line for his third victory of the season.

Labonte's win came, in large part, courtesy of a late-race pit stop, and the reigning world championship pit crew proved their mettle by putting Labonte at the front of the field.

Jeff Burton finished second ahead of Dale Earnhardt, while Jeff Gordon and Dale Jarrett were fourth and fifth. Ward Burton fell to sixth place after his pit stop, with Kevin Lepage seventh, Ricky Rudd eighth and Tony Stewart ninth. Steve Park claimed 10th place. Rusty Wallace's hopes for a Southern 500 victory and a third straight NASCAR Winston Cup Series triumph ended with a 30th-place finish, while Darrell Waltrip had electrical problems and was listed 42nd in his final Darlington appearance.

PEPSI SOUTHERN 500 • final results

It was another successful weekend for team owner Joe Gibbs, who picked up his sixth win of the season, three with Tony Stewart and three with Bobby Labonte.

Fin. Pos.	Start Pos.	Car No.	Driver	Team	Fin. Pos.	Start Pos.	Car No.	Driver	Team
1	37	18	Bobby Labonte	Interstate Batteries Pontiac	23	28	71	Dave Marcis	Realtree Chevrolet
2	35	99	Jeff Burton	Exide Batteries Ford	24	7	32	Scott Pruett	Tide Ford
3	6	3	Dale Earnhardt	GM Goodwrench Service Chevrolet	25	40	94	David Green	McDonald's Ford
4	10	24	Jeff Gordon	DuPont Automotive Finishes Chevrolet	26	36	44	Steve Grissom	Hot Wheels Pontiac
5	9	88	Dale Jarrett	Quality Care/Ford Credit Ford	27	18	11	Brett Bodine	Ralphs Supermarkets Ford
6	3	22	Ward Burton	Caterpillar Pontiac	28	20	27	Mike Bliss	Pfizer/Viagra Pontiac
7	30	16	Kevin Lepage	FamilyClick.com/TV Guide Ford	29	15	25	Jerry Nadeau	MichaelHoligan.com Chevrolet
8	17	28	Ricky Rudd	Texaco/Havoline Ford	30	16	2	Rusty Wallace	Miller Lite Ford
9	29	20	Tony Stewart	Home Depot Pontiac	31	25	33	Joe Nemechek	Oakwood Homes Chevrolet
10	39	1	Steve Park	Pennzoil Chevrolet	32	12	26	Jimmy Spencer	Big Kmart/Route 66 Ford
11	13	8	Dale Earnhardt Jr.	Budweiser Chevrolet	33	24	17	Matt Kenseth	DeWalt Tools Ford
12	31	14	Rick Mast	Conseco Pontiac	34	32	90	Hut Stricklin	Hills Brothers Coffee Ford
13	27	01	Ted Musgrave	BellSouth Chevrolet	35	14	55	Kenny Wallace	Square D/Cooper Lighting Chevrolet
14	5	6	Mark Martin	Valvoline/Cummins Ford	36	41	77	Robert Pressley	Jasper Engines Ford
15	38	5	Terry Labonte	Kellogg's Chevrolet	37	34	43	John Andretti	Cheerios Pontiac
16	8	36	Ken Schrader	M&M's Pontiac	38	2	10	Johnny Benson	Aaron's Pontiac
17	33	40	Sterling Marlin	Coors Light Chevrolet	39	23	60	Geoffrey Bodine	Power Team Chevrolet
18	21	21	Elliott Sadler	CITGO Ford	40	11	7	Michael Waltrip	Nations Rent Chevrolet
19	42	75	Wally Dallenbach	World Championship Wrestling Ford	41	1	12	Jeremy Mayfield	Mobil 1 Ford
20	22	93	Dave Blaney	Amoco Pontiac	42	43	66	Darrell Waltrip	Route 66/Big Kmart Ford
21	26	97	Chad Little	John Deere Ford	43	4	31	Mike Skinner	Lowe's Chevrolet
22	19	4	Bobby Hamilton	Kodak Chevrolet					

CHEVROLET MONTE CARLO *400*

SEPTEMBER 9, 2000 • RICHMOND INTERNATIONAL RACEWAY

NASCAR 2000

(Left) While Tony Stewart's crew goes to work on the No. 20 Home Depot Pontiac, Jeff "Flash" Gordon lives up to his nickname while heading toward his stall.

(Right) Twenty-five races into the season, Ricky Rudd's year could be described as one of hard work and extreme effort. Here, he unwinds after finishing ninth on the lead lap.

The driver is the one who gets the headlines. But an important component of NASCAR Winston Cup Series racing is the team behind the driver. Bobby Labonte's Pepsi Southern 500 victory — the first win of his career at the storied track — came via his team's brilliant pit stop that moved him into the lead. The performance of the Interstate Batteries crew put Labonte in position to claim his third win of the season when the deluge hit the track just a few minutes later.

Labonte's victory also allowed him to boost his point lead over the other contenders, and, although Labonte was quick to point out there was much racing left in the season and that anything could happen to dash his hopes of winning the title, he knew he had made it through a minefield at Darlington.

Dale Earnhardt finished third in the Pepsi Southern 500, with Jeff Burton second and Dale Jarrett fifth. Jarrett now trailed Labonte by 111 points, with Earnhardt 94 markers behind the defending NASCAR Winston Cup Series champion. Burton held fourth, just 20 points behind Earnhardt in the furious battle to catch the point leader. Rusty Wallace, who entered Darlington with the hope of further closing the point gap between himself and Labonte, finished 30th and now trailed by 397 points. His hopes of a second career title had all but ended for this year.

Is Casey Atwood NASCAR's next "wunderkind?" The young charger made his NASCAR Winston Cup Series debut at Richmond.

Tony Stewart, who fought back to finish ninth at Darlington after a flat tire cost him a lap, closed on Wallace for fifth place and now trailed the Miller Lite driver by just 43 points, while Ricky Rudd trailed the Home Depot Pontiac driver by 39. Ward Burton moved to within 20 points of Rudd, while Mark Martin dropped to ninth place, 17 points behind the Caterpillar Pontiac driver. Jeff Gordon remained mired in 10th place in the standings despite finishing fourth in the Pepsi Southern 500.

Jarrett, hoping against hope to successfully defend his title, knew the going would be difficult in the remaining 10 races. Having fought with Labonte and crew chief Jimmy Makar to win the title last year, Jarrett was fully aware of the consistency with which Labonte's team could perform. Although he

(Left) "Okay, Mark, here's the deal." Crew chief Jimmy Fennig discusses pre-race strategy with his driver. Their plan worked well, as Martin scored a third-place finish in the event.

(Below) While the drivers obviously had other things to think about, sunset at Richmond International Raceway is an impressive sight.

felt the Quality Care team still had the opportunity to come from behind and claim the title, Jarrett also knew that he and his team needed to start leading laps and winning races. Top-five finishes at this point of the season would not erase the deficit.

Richmond's night race would be the place to begin, Jarrett knew. Robert Yates' cars and motors had performed well at the three-quarter mile "mini-superspeedway" in the past, and Jarrett hoped that tradition would hold forth. The Chevrolet Monte Carlo 400 also was a Winston No Bull 5

(Above) Ray Evernham keeps a close eye on his charge — driver Casey Atwood. Ray's heading up Dodge's re-entry into the NASCAR Winston Cup Series in 2001, with Atwood slated to compete for rookie honors in one of Evernham's new Intrepids.

event, and Jarrett was one of the five drivers eligible to claim the $1 million bonus if he could win the race.

Jarrett, however, could manage a lap only good enough for the 18th starting position in Bud Pole qualifying, and he wondered if this race would be another where he would lose points to Labonte. Bobby qualified on the outside of the front row, while Jeff Burton thrilled his home-state fans by grabbing just the second pole in his NASCAR Winston Cup Series career. His fast lap ended a string of 134 races since his last pole in August 1996 at Michigan.

Jerry Nadeau and Rick Mast continued their strong qualifying runs of late by claiming the second row, with Rusty Wallace and

Casey Atwood (19) seems to be sending a "Motorola message" as he zips by Stacy Compton. Atwood started the Chevrolet Monte Carlo 400 35th and finished a creditable 19th in his first major-league NASCAR event. Compton, also scheduled to make the switch to Dodge in 2001, brought the Kodiak/Cougar Ford home in the 24th spot.

Ward Burton right behind. Bill Elliott, back behind the wheel after missing two races while recovering from his broken kneecap, turned the seventh-fastest lap, while Johnny Benson continued to sizzle, grabbing the outside of the fourth row ahead of Ken Schrader and

Mark Martin. Casey Atwood, making his NASCAR Winston Cup Series debut behind the wheel of a Motorola Ford fielded by Ray Evernham, claimed the 35th starting spot, while Terry Labonte, Sterling Marlin, Chad Little, Michael Waltrip, Ted Musgrave, Steve Grissom and Scott Pruett used provisionals to make the field. Darrell Waltrip failed to qualify, as did Dave Marcis, Robby Gordon and Mike Bliss.

While pole sitter Jeff Burton set the early pace in the race, a game of bumper-tag took place behind him. Michael Waltrip and Wally Dallenbach tangled first, and then it was Geoffrey Bodine and John Andretti's turn. Teammates Kenny Wallace and Joe Nemechek got into it, and then Brett Bodine and Jimmy Spencer continued their Darlington contretemps. With all of that going on, Rusty Wallace took over the point and appeared headed for yet

Bobby Labonte's crew worked hard to keep him in the hunt, but he ended up with a 15th-place finish, one lap down. He still left Richmond with a healthy lead in NASCAR Winston Cup Series points.

Jeff Gordon's crew kept him in the hunt all evening with solid pit stops like this one. On the final caution, however, Gordon elected to stay on the track — a decision that ultimately brought him the win.

another victory until his Miller Lite Ford lost a cylinder, and later, the entire engine.

Wallace's engine failure brought out the sixth caution flag of the evening, and when the cars lined up for the restart, Steve Park was at the point. Some 40 laps later, the seventh yellow of the evening brought the leaders to the pits for new tires and fuel. Bobby Labonte surfaced in second place, but he was forced to return to pit road three times under the yellow flag to make repairs to a leak in his power steering.

The determining yellow flag of the race — brought out for debris on the track from Atwood's blown tire — occurred on lap 377. Jeff Burton, Gordon and Park stayed on the track, while Earnhardt and Martin gambled that four fresh tires would allow them to run down the leaders in the final 30 laps. On the drop of the green flag, Gordon fought his way past Burton to take the point. Earnhardt and Martin used their fresh tires to battle their way toward the front, but Gordon was on cruise control. Earnhardt eventually made it to second place and began his run at Gordon, but he had abused his tires trying to get past Park for second and had nothing left to mount a final charge. Unchallenged, Gordon sailed to his third win of the year, while Earnhardt nailed down second place, the best finish of those drivers eligible to win the Winston No Bull 5.

Martin finished third ahead of Park, while Jeff Burton faded to fifth. Tony Stewart was sixth ahead of Johnny Benson and Ward Burton, while Ricky Rudd and Jerry Nadeau claimed the final top-10 positions. After running in the top 10 throughout the evening, Elliott was forced to settle for 12th place at the end, and Jarrett's Ford, which suffered damage when it ran over a brake rotor on the track, came home a disappointing 31st.

After crew chief Jimmy Makar was forced to cut the power steering belt on the Interstate Batteries Pontiac, Bobby Labonte clawed his way up from the back of the pack and was able to salvage a 15th-place finish at Richmond.

CHEVROLET MONTE CARLO 400 • final results

Jeff Gordon shared yet another victory with his boss man, Rick Hendrick. The win was the 96th of Hendrick's career as a car owner.

Fin. Pos.	Start Pos.	Car No.	Driver	Team	Fin. Pos.	Start Pos.	Car No.	Driver	Team
1	13	24	Jeff Gordon	DuPont Automotive Finishes Chevrolet	23	34	75	Wally Dallenbach	RotoZip Tools Ford
2	22	3	Dale Earnhardt	GM Goodwrench Service Chevrolet	24	28	9	Stacy Compton	Kodiak/Cougar Ford
3	10	6	Mark Martin	Valvoline/Cummins Ford	25	37	5	Terry Labonte	Kellogg's Chevrolet
4	12	1	Steve Park	Pennzoil Chevrolet	26	25	50	Ricky Craven	Midwest Transit Chevrolet
5	1	99	Jeff Burton	Exide Batteries Ford	27	42	44	Steve Grissom	Hot Wheels Pontiac
6	14	20	Tony Stewart	Home Depot Pontiac	28	4	14	Rick Mast	Conseco Pontiac
7	8	10	Johnny Benson	Aaron's Pontiac	29	39	97	Chad Little	John Deere Ford
8	6	22	Ward Burton	Caterpillar Pontiac	30	30	31	Mike Skinner	Lowe's Chevrolet
9	26	28	Ricky Rudd	Texaco/Havoline Ford	31	17	88	Dale Jarrett	Quality Care/Ford Credit Ford
10	3	25	Jerry Nadeau	MichaelHoligan.com Chevrolet	32	20	17	Matt Kenseth	DeWalt Tools Ford
11	27	43	John Andretti	Cheerios Pontiac	33	19	26	Jimmy Spencer	Big Kmart/Route 66 Ford
12	7	94	Bill Elliott	McDonald's Ford	34	5	2	Rusty Wallace	Miller Lite Ford
13	31	8	Dale Earnhardt Jr.	Budweiser Chevrolet	35	21	11	Brett Bodine	Ralphs Supermarkets Ford
14	11	55	Kenny Wallace	Square D/Cooper Lighting Chevrolet	36	32	90	Hut Stricklin	Hills Brothers Coffee Ford
15	2	18	Bobby Labonte	Interstate Batteries Pontiac	37	36	77	Robert Pressley	Jasper Engines Ford
16	43	32	Scott Pruett	Tide Ford	38	33	4	Bobby Hamilton	Kodak Chevrolet
17	9	36	Ken Schrader	M&M's Pontiac	39	18	12	Jeremy Mayfield	Mobil 1 Ford
18	23	93	Dave Blaney	Amoco Pontiac	40	29	33	Joe Nemechek	Oakwood Homes Chevrolet
19	35	19	Casey Atwood	Motorola Ford	41	24	60	Geoffrey Bodine	Power Team Chevrolet
20	38	40	Sterling Marlin	Coors Light Chevrolet	42	16	21	Elliott Sadler	CITGO/Virginia Tech Ford
21	41	01	Ted Musgrave	BellSouth Chevrolet	43	40	7	Michael Waltrip	Nations Rent Chevrolet
22	15	16	Kevin Lepage	FamilyClick.com/TV Guide Ford					

DURA LUBE 300 SPONSORED BY KMART

SEPTEMBER 17, 2000 • NEW HAMPSHIRE INTERNATIONAL SPEEDWAY

NASCAR 2000

(Left) Jeff Burton (99) kept the pressure on himself — and everybody else — en route to leading every lap in the Dura Lube 300 at New Hampshire. At the end, he was able to ease up a little, as the event ended under caution. Bobby Labonte (18) and Ricky Rudd finished second and third.

(Right) Even a guy who leads every lap can pick up an occasional "donut!"

Imagine trying to build and test engines for the Daytona 500 in four days. A difficult task at best. Yet, that was the task faced by engine builders for all of the NASCAR Winston Cup Series teams after NASCAR announced at Richmond that one-inch restrictor plates would be used for the following weekend's race at New Hampshire International Speedway.

Not only would the engines have to be built, but teams would also have to scramble for test dates at tracks like The Milwaukee Mile in the days prior to the opening of practice at New Hampshire. It meant a thrash seldom seen in the sport, with private planes zipping around the country to obtain parts and pieces for the new motors, and even more planes delivering the hastily prepared engines in time for test sessions.

Engine builders were divided into teams working 16-20 hours a day to build and dyno the engines. In some cases, the dyno rooms ran around the clock. For some teams, it was even more frantic because engine suppliers did not have time to build enough motors for all of their clients. More than one team brought every transmission and gear combination available from their shops to New Hampshire, hoping to find the right setup to be competitive on the track. Most team transporters arrived at New

Bill Elliott found a little valuable pre-race quiet time with his wife, Cindy, and son Chase.

Richmond, Bobby Labonte arrived at New Hampshire with his largest point lead of the year. Dale Earnhardt moved into second place in the standings after Richmond, but the seven-time titlist found himself trailing by 158 points. Jarrett fell to third place, six points behind Earnhardt, after he finished 31st at Richmond. Jeff Burton was still fourth in the point standings, just 19 points behind Jarrett. Tony Stewart's sixth place coupled with Rusty Wallace's 34th at Richmond moved the Home Depot Pontiac driver into fifth in the standings. Rudd

(Above) Beep! Beep! Scott Pruett, in the "Tide ride," appears to be waiting for Robert Pressley (left) and Terry Labonte to "open it up" and give him a shot at getting by. Unfortunately, Pruett's run didn't last much longer, as an accident sidelined him one-third of the way through the event.

(Right) Pit road is a flurry of activity during one of seven cautions during the 300-mile event. For the serious race watcher, half the excitement of the sport is found here, where the competitors really do prove they're athletes.

Hampshire without motors in the cars, and once the engines were completed, they were flown to the track to be installed in the waiting chassis.

When the rain-delayed practice for the Dura Lube 300 presented by Kmart finally did begin, teams were ready, and when the speed charts were posted at the end of the first session, eyebrows raised. Both Ricky Rudd and Dale Jarrett were buried at the bottom of the list, and many wondered if the pair — with the vaunted Robert Yates power plants — had missed the boat. Not so, Rudd said later. The team made the decision to spend the session working on race setups rather than on qualifying. His words were validated after the Bud Pole qualifying session, with Jarrett fourth fastest and the Texaco Ford easily in the field in 19th place.

Despite problems with his power steering and the resulting 15th-place finish at

While Dale Earnhardt Jr., in the Budweiser Chevrolet, leads a pack of cars around the New Hampshire mile, his DEI teammate, Steve Park, attempts to get his Pennzoil Chevrolet to go around on the outside. Both were involved in accidents and didn't get to finish the race.

remained in seventh, while Mark Martin's move up to eighth place dropped Ward Burton one spot to ninth. Richmond winner Jeff Gordon remained 10th in the championship point standings as teams prepared for the 26th race of the season.

While engine builders were working around the clock, "Silly Season" was heating up. After announcing just two weeks before that he would remain with Andy Petree Racing, Kenny Wallace made the decision to leave the "55" team and move to Eel River Racing in 2001. That opened up the Square D car, and Bobby Hamilton immediately became a candidate when it was announced that he and Larry McClure jointly made the decision that Hamilton would leave the Kodak Chevrolets at the end of the season. Michael Waltrip also joined in when it was learned that he would leave the Nations Rent team to become the driver for a new NAPA-sponsored team from Dale Earnhardt Inc., joining Earnhardt Jr. and Steve Park in the DEI stable beginning next season.

With John Deere leaving Roush Racing and Kurt Busch named to drive the car for the remaining events this year, Chad Little found

himself without a ride. And Monday morning after the Richmond race, Geoffrey Bodine was told in a phone call from team owner Joe Bessey that Bodine would no longer be driving the Power Team entries this year. Bessey would try to put the car into the field himself for the remainder of the season.

Bobby Labonte responded to his growing point lead by capturing his second pole position of the season, while Jeff Burton claimed the

Is Jeff Gordon (24) trying to intimidate "The Intimidator" or is the guy in the black No. 3 Chevrolet attempting to unnerve Gordon?

Although Burton did keep the No. 99 Exide Ford out front all the way through the Dura Lube 300 sponsored by Kmart, the action was tight and close for much of the day. It seems that the latest restrictor-plate rule actually helped keep things competitive.

outside of the front row. Clearly, the restrictor plates worked, with Labonte's pole speed nearly five miles per hour slower than Rusty Wallace's record set in July. Sterling Marlin was third fastest, while Wallace slotted into the grid behind fourth-place Jarrett. Park was sixth fastest in the qualifying session, with Elliott Sadler and Jerry Nadeau claiming the fourth row. Ken Schrader and Mike Bliss beat Ted Musgrave and Ricky Craven for the final top-10 positions. Gordon, after being penalized 100 points and $25,000 for the magnesium manifold used on his winning engine at Richmond, qualified 18th. Hendrick Motorsports immediately filed an appeal, saying the part supplied by General Motors was legal. The team's appeal of the penalty, however, was denied.

Dale Earnhardt was the first driver to use a provisional to start the race, with Matt Kenseth, Robert Pressley, Dave Blaney, Wally Dallenbach, Hut Stricklin and Joe Bessey also joining the field via the provisionals. That left Dave Marcis and Steve Grissom as the only drivers who failed to make the field.

Michael Waltrip (7) does his best to outrun hard-charging Jimmy Spencer, while Rick Mast (14) holds his position on the inside. Spencer bested the trio by finishing in 15th, the first car one-lap down, while Mast got caught up in an accident with only a handful of laps remaining.

Crew chief Frankie Stoddard (left) lets everyone know that the New Hampshire event was his team's third win of the year. Jeff Burton (right) signals that he's the first driver to lead every lap of a race since Cale Yarborough did it 22 years ago, while team owner Jack Roush just enjoys the whole scene.

With shortened practice sessions because of the weather, not many teams knew what to expect when the green flag flew over the field to start the Dura Lube 300. No one — not even Jeff Burton's Exide team — expected one driver to lead every lap and become the first driver since 1978 to lead an entire NASCAR Winston Cup Series race.

But that's what happened. Burton immediately jumped in front of pole sitter Bobby Labonte and went on to lead the first 200 laps easily. After some bumping and grinding, Burton was able to keep Earnhardt a lap down in the final 50 laps, and then fought off determined charges from both Bobby Labonte and Ricky Rudd to post his third victory of the season.

It was an incredibly dominating performance, and afterward, Burton credited car owner Jack Roush and crew chief Frankie Stoddard with the work done in the few days since the restrictor-plate announcement. Burton was one of the drivers who tested at Milwaukee, and he said the team came to New Hampshire totally prepared, despite the short preparation time after the Richmond race.

Bobby Labonte finished second, with Rudd third, Jarrett fourth and Rusty Wallace fifth. Jeff Gordon, John Andretti and Mark Martin followed them across the finish line, with Joe Nemechek and Ken Schrader claiming the final top-10 positions. Earnhardt's 12th-place finish caused him to fall from the runner-up position in the point standings all the way to fourth.

DURA LUBE 300 SPONSORED BY KMART • final results

Eric Wilson, the tire specialist and jackman on Ken Schrader's team, keeps an eye on his driver, who posted a 10th-place finish in the M&M's Pontiac, only his second top 10 of the year.

Fin. Pos.	Start Pos.	Car No.	Driver	Team	Fin. Pos.	Start Pos.	Car No.	Driver	Team
1	2	99	Jeff Burton	Exide Batteries Ford	23	16	20	Tony Stewart	Home Depot Pontiac
2	1	18	Bobby Labonte	Interstate Batteries Pontiac	24	23	31	Mike Skinner	Lowe's Chevrolet
3	19	28	Ricky Rudd	Texaco/Havoline Ford	25	34	5	Terry Labonte	Kellogg's Chevrolet
4	4	88	Dale Jarrett	Quality Care/Ford Credit Ford	26	40	93	Dave Blaney	Amoco Pontiac
5	5	2	Rusty Wallace	Miller Lite Ford	27	42	60	Joe Bessey	Power Team Chevrolet
6	18	24	Jeff Gordon	DuPont Automotive Finishes Chevrolet	28	43	90	Hut Stricklin	Hills Brothers Coffee Ford
7	31	43	John Andretti	Cheerios Pontiac	29	36	66	Darrell Waltrip	Route 66/Big Kmart Ford
8	15	6	Mark Martin	Valvoline/Cummins Ford	30	28	22	Ward Burton	Caterpillar Pontiac
9	30	33	Joe Nemechek	Oakwood Homes Chevrolet	31	20	8	Dale Earnhardt Jr.	Budweiser Chevrolet
10	9	36	Ken Schrader	M&M's Pontiac	32	26	14	Rick Mast	Conseco Pontiac
11	27	10	Johnny Benson	Aaron's Pontiac	33	35	97	Chad Little	John Deere Ford
12	37	3	Dale Earnhardt	GM Goodwrench Service Chevrolet	34	6	1	Steve Park	Pennzoil Chevrolet
13	7	21	Elliott Sadler	CITGO/Virginia Tech Ford	35	14	4	Bobby Hamilton	Kodak Chevrolet
14	11	01	Ted Musgrave	BellSouth Chevrolet	36	12	50	Ricky Craven	Midwest Transit Chevrolet
15	29	26	Jimmy Spencer	Big Kmart/Route 66 Ford	37	21	94	Bill Elliott	McDonald's Ford
16	24	9	Stacy Compton	Kodiak/Cougar Ford	38	32	16	Kevin Lepage	FamilyClick.com/TV Guide Ford
17	38	17	Matt Kenseth	DeWalt Tools Ford	39	41	75	Wally Dallenbach	RotoZip/Red Cell Ford
18	39	77	Robert Pressley	Jasper Engines Ford	40	17	12	Jeremy Mayfield	Mobil 1 Ford
19	10	27	Mike Bliss	Pfizer/Viagra Pontiac	41	33	32	Scott Pruett	Tide Ford
20	13	7	Michael Waltrip	Nations Rent Chevrolet	42	22	11	Brett Bodine	Ralphs Supermarkets Ford
21	8	25	Jerry Nadeau	MichaelHoligan.com Chevrolet	43	25	55	Kenny Wallace	Square D/Cooper Lighting Chevrolet
22	3	40	Sterling Marlin	Coors Light Chevrolet					

MBNA.COM *400*

(Left) Jeremy Mayfield put the No. 12 Mobil 1 Ford on the pole at Dover and led the MBNA.com 400 six times. Hence, it was hard to believe that even after his car suffered a blown engine, he finished the race as far back as 35th place.

(Right) Tony Stewart celebrates his fourth victory of the 2000 season.

C ale Yarborough turned the trick twice — in 1973 and then again in 1978 while driving for Junior Johnson. Since then, no driver had led every single lap of a NASCAR Winston Cup Series race until Jeff Burton's display of total domination at New Hampshire.

But now, that incredible feat was merely another entry in the NASCAR Winston Cup Series record book, and it was back to "business as usual" as teams arrived at the Monster Mile in Delaware's capital city.

Burton's third victory of the season couldn't have come at a better time. With Exide leaving the sport as a primary sponsor after seven years, Burton's team was in search mode for new colors for the 2001 season, and there are few better sales tools to persuade a prospective company than a 300-lap victory. The win also pushed Burton back into second place in the point standings, 168 points behind Bobby Labonte, and kept the Virginian's flickering title hopes alive.

Labonte, however, continued his march toward his first career title with a fighting second place at New Hampshire. Race after race, Labonte was putting good finishes in the book and, at the rate he was going, challengers would be hard pressed to make any serious inroads. Dale Jarrett trailed

Carl Long's crew gets the NoopCo Paint Remover Ford ready for competition.

Labonte by 174 points, while Dale Earnhardt's 12th place at New Hampshire put him 201 behind. With just eight races left in the season, it was looking more and more like a Pontiac driver would win the championship for the third time in history and the first time since Rusty Wallace claimed his title in 1989.

Wallace and Ricky Rudd were tied for fifth place in the standings as teams began work at Dover, with Tony Stewart in seventh, just 15 points behind. Mark Martin was eighth, 18 behind Stewart, while Ward Burton and Jeff Gordon held down the final two posi-

(Top) Kurt Busch made his NASCAR Winston Cup Series debut at Dover in the John Deere Ford and got a little competition from John Andretti. Busch had a sparkling qualifying run to a 10th-place start.

(Right) Tire management always plays a key role in racing, but it's particularly important on the punishing, high-banked concrete at Dover.

(Below) It took him six tries, but Carl Long was all smiles after he qualified for his first major-league race.

tions in the top 10. Matt Kenseth, Mike Skinner and Steve Park remained locked in their torrid battle for 11th place, while Johnny Benson continued his impressive season, now just 43 points behind Park. Ken Schrader held a 12-point bulge over Dale Earnhardt Jr. in their battle for 15th place.

"Silly Season" continued to grab headlines at Dover, with the talk of the garage area focused on none other than Richard Childress and his Mike Skinner effort. After meeting with officials from Lowe's on Wednesday and receiving assurances that the sponsorship would continue for the remaining two years of their contract, Childress was told that on the following day, Lowe's employees received an internal memo stating the company would not sponsor the "31" car next year. By the end of the weekend, it became apparent that Childress would have another company's name on Skinner's Chevrolet at Daytona in 2001.

At the same time, word leaked out that CITGO appeared ready to move to Jeff Burton's "99" team. With United Parcel Service expected to sponsor Dale Jarrett next year, it seemed that Ford Credit and, perhaps, Motorcraft would be on the Wood Brothers' Fords for Elliott Sadler next season. Michael Holigan's sponsorship of Jerry Nadeau was also going away, although Holigan said he would have a NASCAR Busch Series and NASCAR Craftsman Truck Series team for next year. Almost immediately, rumor circulated that Lowe's would be on the "25" car next season.

Travis Carter nodded when asked if Todd Bodine was his choice to replace Darrell Waltrip in the Big Kmart "66" next year. Petty

Enterprises used the days between New Hampshire and Dover to announce that Georgia Pacific would be the primary sponsor of the team's "44" car next season with Georgian Buckshot Jones stepping up from the NASCAR Busch Series, Grand National Division to become the Dodge's driver.

In first round qualifying, Jeremy Mayfield claimed his third Bud Pole of the season and the first of his young career at Dover by cranking a lap at 159.872 miles per hour. Rick Mast surprised many by putting A.J. Foyt's Pontiac on the outside of the front row to claim just his third top-10 starting position of the season. Benson continued his strong performance by earning the inside of the second row, while Rusty Wallace plunked his Miller Lite Ford in the fourth starting position. Mark Martin and Ward Burton claimed the third row ahead of Bill Elliott and Dale Jarrett, with Jeff Gordon and

(Above) Tony Stewart went into the MBNA.com 400 seventh in NASCAR Winston Cup Series points and, after winning the race, moved up to fifth.

(Left) Johnny Benson leads the way for Steve Park (1), Dale Earnhardt Jr. (8), Ricky Rudd (28) and Kurt Busch (97). Benson started third in the Aaron's Pontiac, led twice for seven laps and finished second, tying the career best he posted earlier this year on the concrete at Bristol.

rookie Kurt Busch, making his first NASCAR Winston Cup Series start, filling out the top 10.

Rain washed out second-round qualifying, forcing Dale Earnhardt, Sterling Marlin, Stacy Compton, Brett Bodine, Dave Marcis, Carl Long and Steve Grissom to use provisionals to make the starting lineup. That left Hut Stricklin and Joe Bessey out of the field for the MBNA.com 400.

After using restrictor-plate engines for the New Hampshire race, everyone was back to full power at Dover. At the same time,

Dale Jarrett waits patiently in the garage while his crew makes repairs to his Quality Care Ford after he and Ward Burton tangled very early in the race (left). Jarrett got back into the race and finished under the checkered flag, but took a huge hit to his championship hopes.

every driver knew that the 400-lap event would be a long and difficult race, with tires taking a pounding on the concrete oval. Since the first race was held at Dover in 1969, the events have been some of the most grueling on the tour, and no one expected this year's MBNA.com 400 to be any different. As it turned out, they were right.

Jeff Burton, Jarrett and Earnhardt all hoped to chop into Bobby Labonte's point lead, but by the time the Monster Mile chewed at their tires and cars throughout Sunday afternoon, their hopes were

dashed. Jarrett was the first to feel the track's bite, coming together with Ward Burton on lap 26 and needing lengthy repairs in the garage area. He could manage only a 32nd-place finish. Burton led 37 laps before the midpoint of the race, but he cut a right-front tire and whacked the wall. His day was finished after just 186 laps, and the Virginian was listed 36th in the final rundown. Earnhardt had the best day of the three but lost two laps and finished 17th, dropping 48 points to Labonte in the process.

While all this was going on, Labonte simply made the best he could of the afternoon and finished fifth. He was able to lead one lap and pick up the five bonus points for doing so, but he was never a contender to win. His performance, however, was rock-solid yet again — the type that leads to titles.

His Joe Gibbs Motorsports teammate was the star of the Dover show, and when the checkered flag fall on the MBNA.com 400, Tony Stewart had completed a sweep of the Dover races this year and claimed his fourth victory of the season.

The Home Depot Pontiac driver spent the first half of the event fine-tuning his car's handling and then led 163 laps on the way to his seventh career victory. At the end, he won by margin of 6.75 seconds in a strong display of driving and teamwork on pit road. Behind him, Benson matched the best performance of his brief career with a runner-up finish, while Ricky Rudd nailed down his ninth top-five finish of the year by taking third. Steve Park was fourth ahead of point leader Labonte, and Mark Martin grabbed sixth place. Joe Nemechek edged Rusty Wallace for seventh place, with Gordon, the final driver on the lead lap, in ninth. Rick Mast claimed 10th place, one lap behind.

(Above) Quick pit work helped Ricky Rudd to a third-place finish and his ninth top-five finish of the year.

(Right) Stewart's bunch, however, was just a tad quicker with its driver service, which included multiple chassis adjustment throughout the race en route to a strong, winning finish.

MBNA.COM 400 • final results

Jeff Burton walks away from his bent-up Ford after the "Monster Mile" got him, too. His accident was costly: Burton fell from second to fourth in points after the event.

Fin. Pos.	Start Pos.	Car No.	Driver	Team	Fin. Pos.	Start Pos.	Car No.	Driver	Team
1	27	20	Tony Stewart	Home Depot Pontiac	23	33	01	Ted Musgrave	BellSouth Chevrolet
2	3	10	Johnny Benson	Aaron's Pontiac	24	19	7	Michael Waltrip	Nations Rent Chevrolet
3	14	28	Ricky Rudd	Texaco/Havoline Ford	25	35	4	Bobby Hamilton	Kodak Chevrolet
4	28	1	Steve Park	Pennzoil Chevrolet	26	22	21	Elliott Sadler	CITGO Ford
5	17	18	Bobby Labonte	Interstate Batteries Pontiac	27	43	44	Steve Grissom	Hot Wheels Pontiac
6	5	6	Mark Martin	Valvoline/Cummins Ford	28	41	71	Dave Marcis	Realtree Chevrolet
7	12	33	Joe Nemechek	Oakwood Homes Chevrolet	29	39	9	Stacy Compton	Kodiak/Cougar Ford
8	4	2	Rusty Wallace	Miller Lite Ford	30	18	36	Ken Schrader	M&M's Pontiac
9	9	24	Jeff Gordon	DuPont Automotive Finishes Chevrolet	31	36	66	Darrell Waltrip	Route 66/Big Kmart Ford
10	2	14	Rick Mast	Conseco Pontiac	32	8	88	Dale Jarrett	Quality Care/Ford Credit Ford
11	24	31	Mike Skinner	Lowe's Chevrolet	33	11	25	Jerry Nadeau	MichaelHoligan.com Chevrolet
12	31	17	Matt Kenseth	DeWalt Tools Ford	34	26	26	Jimmy Spencer	Big Kmart/Route 66 Ford
13	25	5	Terry Labonte	Kellogg's Chevrolet	35	1	12	Jeremy Mayfield	Mobil 1 Ford
14	15	77	Robert Pressley	Jasper Engines Ford	36	21	99	Jeff Burton	Exide Batteries Ford
15	23	55	Kenny Wallace	Square D/Cooper Lighting Chevrolet	37	38	40	Sterling Marlin	Coors Light Chevrolet
16	13	8	Dale Earnhardt Jr.	Budweiser Chevrolet	38	30	16	Kevin Lepage	FamilyClick.com/TV Guide Ford
17	37	3	Dale Earnhardt	GM Goodwrench Chevrolet	39	16	93	Dave Blaney	Amoco Ford
18	10	97	Kurt Busch	John Deere Ford	40	6	22	Ward Burton	Caterpillar Pontiac
19	7	94	Bill Elliott	McDonald's Ford	41	42	85	Carl Long	NoopCo Paint Remover Ford
20	40	11	Brett Bodine	Ralphs Supermarkets Ford	42	34	32	Scott Pruett	Tide Ford
21	32	75	Wally Dallenbach	TBS Dinner & A Movie Ford	43	20	27	Mike Bliss	Pfizer/Viagra Pontiac
22	29	43	John Andretti	Cheerios Pontiac					

NAPA AUTOCARE *500*

(Left) Maybe that little bit of extra attention to detail — that personal touch — helped Tony Stewart take the pole at Martinsville with a track record speed of 95.371 miles per hour, lead the race three times for 79 laps and score his fifth win of the 2000 NASCAR Winston Cup Series season.

(Right) The racing is always close at the Henry County, Va., half-mile oval.

With seven races remaining on the schedule, Dale Earnhardt, Dale Jarrett and Jeff Burton were not about to give up the chase for the NASCAR Winston Cup Series championship. Yet, each of the three challengers knew the results from the preceding week's battle at Dover made the quest even more difficult.

Jarrett's collision with Ward Burton and the subsequent work in the garage area by the Quality Care Ford team resulted in a 32nd-place finish, while Jeff Burton's incident against the wall brought an even worse result of 36th place in the final rundown. Earnhardt fared the best of the challengers by claiming 17th at Dover, but once again, Bobby Labonte countered with a well-judged and rock-solid fifth-place finish and gained points on his closest pursuers.

Now, as teams arrived at the splendid Martinsville Speedway for the final short-track race of the season, Labonte was a comfortable 249 points ahead of Earnhardt and led Dale Jarrett and Jeff Burton by 267 and 268 points, respectively.

Labonte frowned for a moment when the word "comfortable" was used to describe his point bulge. With seven races left and Earnhardt in pursuit, Labonte pointed out, things were far from comfortable.

Hut Stricklin, making his sixth start of the 2000 season, got car owner Junie Donlavey's Hills Brothers Ford into the race at Martinsville.

Comfortable, according to the Texan, meant the championship had been mathematically won, and that was not the case at Martinsville.

Tony Stewart's victory at Dover marked his fourth win of the season and, when combined with Ricky Rudd's third place and Rusty Wallace's eighth, pushed the Home Depot Pontiac and Texaco Ford drivers past the 1989 NASCAR Winston Cup Series champion. Stewart and Rudd now found themselves tied for fifth place in the standings, trailing Jeff Burton by 191 points. Wallace was now in seventh place, 28 points behind the Stewart/Rudd tie and just 20 points in front of Mark Martin. It appeared the four drivers would battle for fifth place until year's end.

(Above) One neat thing about Martinsville Speedway is that the standing-room-only crowds of fans get to see everything — including pre-race festivities.

(Left) East Northport, N.Y., native Steve Park was caught here just relaxing and perhaps wondering if Martinsville would be the site of his second career NASCAR Winston Cup Series victory. The best he could do on Oct. 1, though, was to finish 11th on the lead lap.

(Below) Tony Stewart completes getting into his business attire prior to beginning a long day in his "office." In this case, Stewart took care of business in just 3 hours, 33 minutes and 39 seconds.

Ward Burton, after finishing 40th at Dover, maintained ninth place, while Jeff Gordon was 10th, well clear of the furious battle behind him. In a weekly, four-driver struggle for 11th place, Matt Kenseth held a 12-point lead over Mike Skinner, with Steve Park just 18 points behind the Lowe's Chevrolet driver. Johnny Benson's solid performances, including his second place at Dover, had rocketed the Aaron's Rents Pontiac driver up through the points, and he now trailed Park by 28. Dale Earnhardt Jr. held down 15th place, 98 points behind the streaking Benson.

The garage area at Martinsville was packed with competitors as the clock ticked down toward the beginning of Bud Pole qualifying. Kyle Petty was on hand with a Sprint-sponsored entry and carrying number 45, while Casey Atwood was behind the wheel of a Motorola Ford entered by Ray Evernham. Rich Bickle was entered in Joe Bessey's Power Team Chevrolet, while Carl Long hoped to make the field with his own Ford.

Most observers expected Rusty Wallace to add another Bud Pole to his pile of awards this season, but Tony Stewart ran a lap just seven-thousandths of a second faster than the Miller Lite Ford driver to claim his second pole of the season and the fourth of his brief career. It was a surprise to Stewart who said before the event that

Rusty Wallace (2) snatched the lead away from Tony Stewart (20) on the second circuit around Martinsville Speedway and stayed in front through lap 54. From there, though, things like tire problems beset the driver of the Miller Lite Ford. Wallace finished 24th, two laps in arrears.

Martinsville was one of his most difficult tracks and one he felt he had yet to master. Brothers Jeff and Ward Burton gave Virginia fans something to cheer for by grabbing the second row, while Jeff Gordon qualified fifth fastest, beating Kenny Wallace for the inside of the third row. Bobby Hamilton and Mike Skinner claimed the fourth row for the start of the NAPA Autocare 500, with Brett Bodine and Steve Park taking the fifth row ahead of Rudd and Dale Earnhardt.

Ricky Craven was the only driver to run in the second round of qualifying and his lap was good enough to grab 36th place. That left Matt Kenseth, Terry Labonte, Ken Schrader, Kurt Busch, Kevin Lepage, Michael Waltrip and Elliott Sadler using provisionals to make the field, while Carl

Long, Rich Bickle, Dave Marcis, Scott Pruett and Steve Grissom were forced to the sidelines. Sadler, by making the race in the final provisional position, allowed the Wood Brothers team to celebrate its 1,000th start in front of its home state Virginia fans.

Jimmy Spencer (26) and Rusty Wallace get up close and personal on the tight Martinsville track, with Wallace's hot rod routinely spitting fire through the turns.

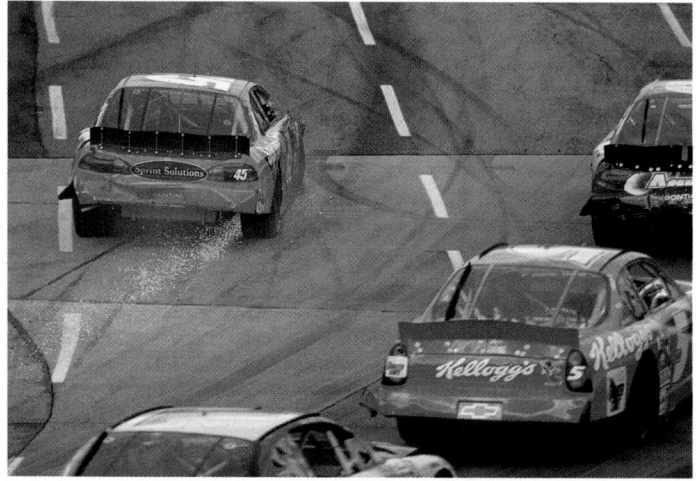

After he was bumped by another car, Kyle Petty's No. 45 Sprint Chevrolet was never in contention for the win. Petty finished 31st after starting 27th.

Although he claimed the pole for the event, few — including himself — chose Stewart as a pre-race favorite to notch his fifth victory of the season. After all, in his previous three outings at Martinsville, he finished 20th, 41st and 6th. Yet, by the time the Sunday afternoon event was completed, Stewart had conquered Martinsville and added his name to the list of winners that stretched back to the first race held at the historic old bullring in 1956.

Stewart fought with Rusty Wallace in the early going, but by claiming the pole, he received his choice of pit positions and took the pit box at the end of pit road, where he would merely have to roll a few feet out of his box to cross the line that determines the order on restarts after caution flags. That decision by Stewart and crew chief Greg Zipadelli would eventually be one of the turning points that led to victory for the Home Depot team. With 13 cautions marking the day, Stewart's choice of pits earned him good positions on restarts time and again, and on his final pit stop of the day, his crew zipped him back into action in position to seal the victory.

Jeff Burton did his best to close the point gap on Bobby Labonte by leading the most laps in the race, and he appeared to have the victory in hand with 35 laps to go. But then the yellow waved again and Stewart's Home Depot crew did their work admirably, putting

What a difference a year makes! In 1999, Martinsville Speedway was definitely a place of problems for Tony Stewart. In three previous races, he needed two provisional starts; his best finish last year at Martinsville was 20th. Here, he holds off Dale Earnhardt after the final restart to take the win.

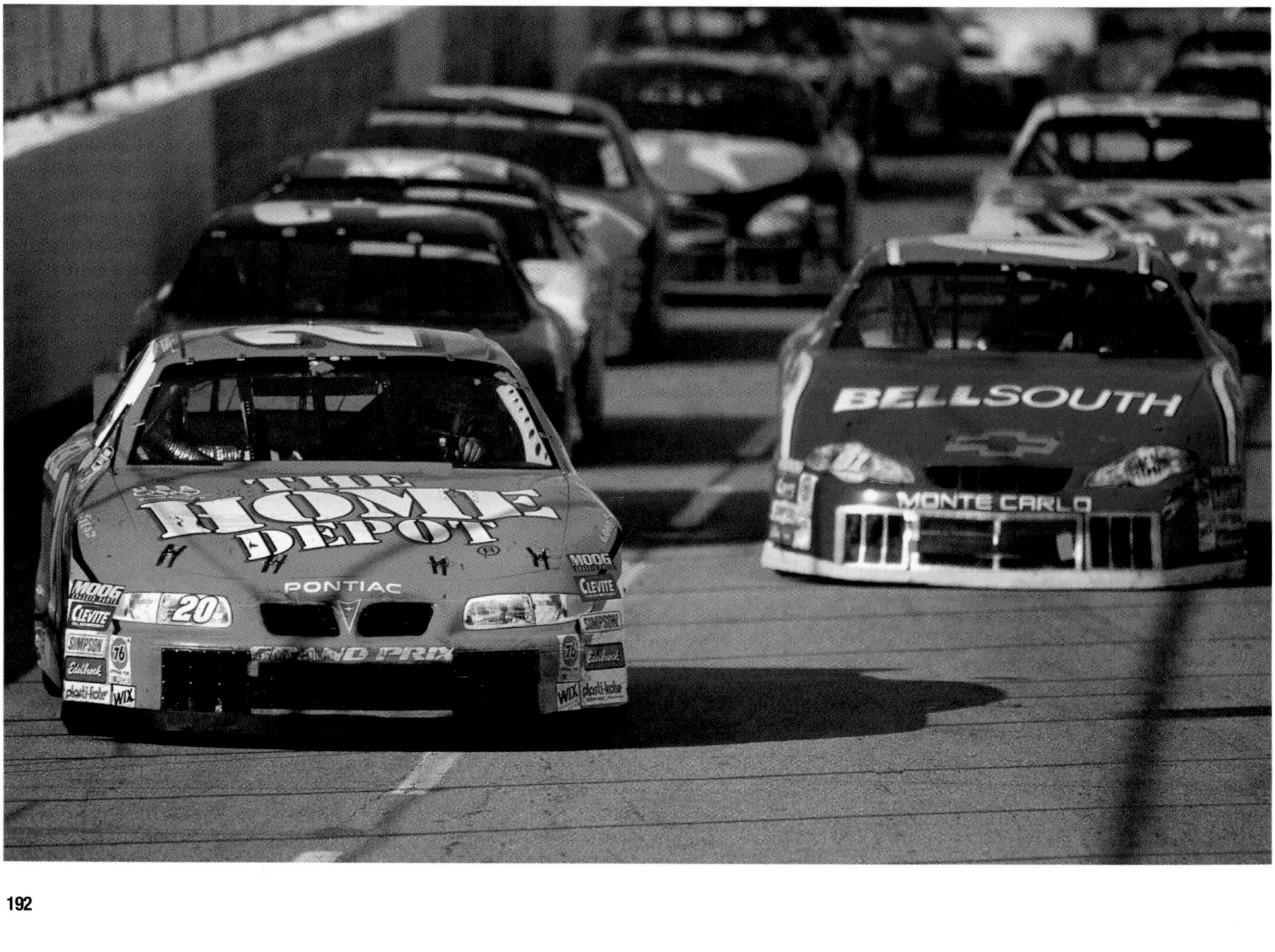

It was crunch time — and a 10th-place finish — for Bobby Labonte in the NAPA Autocare 500. Yet, at the finish he still led in points, some 213 in front of Earnhardt.

four new Goodyears on the Pontiac. Stewart quickly polished off Sterling Marlin, who had gambled with just two new tires, and began to drive away. But his lead was erased by the final yellow flag of the afternoon. He remained on the track, looked in his mirror and saw The Intimidator's GM Goodwrench Chevrolet and shuddered. The last car anyone wants behind him on a restart with 10 laps to go is that one.

Tens of thousands of fans expected to see Stewart moved aside by the chrome horn of the black Monte Carlo, but when the green flag dropped, Earnhardt could not get close enough to Stewart to make a move. Tony kept his concentration and focus, and he rolled to a six-car-length victory. Earnhardt was second ahead of Jeff Burton, while Ricky Rudd posted another top five with his fourth-place finish. Gordon was fifth ahead of Dale Jarrett and Jimmy Spencer, while Skinner and Marlin were eighth and ninth.

Point leader Labonte survived two scary moments — a spin on the racetrack and a minor collision on pit road. He lost points to his pursuers but was pleased to emerge from the Martinsville grinder with a 10th-place finish. It was the kind of afternoon championships are made of.

NAPA AUTOCARE 500 • final results

It's another NASCAR Winston Cup Series first-place trophy for the young tiger from Indiana. The victory marked the second time Stewart posted back-to-back wins this season, with both doubles beginning at Dover.

Fin. Pos.	Start Pos.	Car No.	Driver	Team	Fin. Pos.	Start Pos.	Car No.	Driver	Team
1	1	20	Tony Stewart	Home Depot Pontiac	23	2	2	Rusty Wallace	Miller Lite Ford
2	12	3	Dale Earnhardt	GM Goodwrench Service Chevrolet	24	42	7	Michael Waltrip	Nations Rent Chevrolet
3	3	99	Jeff Burton	Exide Batteries Ford	25	22	19	Casey Atwood	Motorola Ford
4	11	28	Ricky Rudd	Texaco/Havoline Ford	26	19	14	Rick Mast	Conseco Pontiac
5	5	24	Jeff Gordon	DuPont Automotive Finishes Chevrolet	27	18	66	Darrell Waltrip	Route 66/Big Kmart Ford
6	31	88	Dale Jarrett	Quality Care/Ford Credit Ford	28	26	27	Mike Bliss	Pfizer/Viagra Pontiac
7	25	26	Jimmy Spencer	Big Kmart/Route 66 Ford	29	41	16	Kevin Lepage	FamilyClick.com/TV Guide Ford
8	8	31	Mike Skinner	Lowe's Chevrolet	30	21	93	Dave Blaney	Amoco Pontiac
9	34	40	Sterling Marlin	Coors Light Chevrolet	31	27	45	Kyle Petty	Sprint Chevrolet
10	14	18	Bobby Labonte	Interstate Batteries Pontiac	32	43	21	Elliott Sadler	CITGO Ford
11	10	1	Steve Park	Pennzoil Chevrolet	33	16	77	Robert Pressley	Jasper Engines Ford
12	13	25	Jerry Nadeau	MichaelHoligan.com Chevrolet	34	37	17	Matt Kenseth	DeWalt Tools Ford
13	28	43	John Andretti	Cheerios Pontiac	35	7	4	Bobby Hamilton	Kodak Chevrolet
14	24	33	Joe Nemechek	Oakwood Homes Chevrolet	36	32	8	Dale Earnhardt Jr.	Budweiser Chevrolet
15	20	94	Bill Elliott	McDonald's Ford	37	40	97	Kurt Busch	John Deere Ford
16	39	36	Ken Schrader	M&M's Pontiac	38	35	12	Jeremy Mayfield	Mobil 1 Ford
17	38	5	Terry Labonte	Kellogg's Chevrolet	39	30	9	Stacy Compton	Kodiak/Cougar Ford
18	23	6	Mark Martin	Valvoline/Cummins Ford	40	17	75	Wally Dallenbach	RotoZip Tools Ford
19	33	10	Johnny Benson	Aaron's Pontiac	41	9	11	Brett Bodine	Ralphs Supermarkets Ford
20	36	50	Ricky Craven	Midwest Transit Chevrolet	42	29	90	Hut Stricklin	Hills Brothers Coffee Ford
21	15	01	Ted Musgrave	BellSouth Chevrolet	43	4	22	Ward Burton	Caterpillar Pontiac
22	6	55	Kenny Wallace	Square D/Cooper Lighting Chevrolet					

UAW-GM QUALITY *500*

(Left) "It's alive! It's alive!" Nobody messed with Bobby Labonte and his "Frankenstein" car at Lowe's Motor Speedway. Labonte started second, led the UAW-GM Quality 500 on 12 occasions and tightened his hold on the point lead by winning his fourth race of the year.

(Right) Mike Skinner gets out of shape amidst heavy traffic in the fourth turn, but he managed to gather in the Lowe's Chevrolet without major incident. He eventually finished 20th, the first of the lap-down cars.

A look into the eyes of Dale Earnhardt, Jeff Burton and Dale Jarrett in the garage area at Lowe's Motor Speedway left no doubt about the mission at hand. If any of the three were to mount a last-ditch challenge to overcome Bobby Labonte's stranglehold on first place in the NASCAR Winston Cup Series point standings, it would have to begin this weekend in the UAW-GM Quality 500.

Only six races remained on the schedule, and at Martinsville, Va., each of the challengers had been given a little taste of success. Labonte's hard-fought 10th place allowed Earnhardt (second at Martinsville), Burton (third at the paper clip-shaped short track) and Jarrett (sixth) the opportunity to gain a few points. The problem for each of the three hopefuls was that it was, in their estimation, far too little — and perhaps too late.

Earnhardt now trailed by 213 markers, while Burton moved past Jarrett into third place, where he found himself 14 points behind "The Intimidator." Jarrett trailed Burton by 24 markers, while Tony Stewart, in fifth place but 162 behind Jarrett, rolled into Charlotte looking for his third straight victory after wins at Dover, Del., and Martinsville.

Jerry Nadeau qualified in third, took the point on the third lap and led the next 32 circuits, but his day ended in disappointment after he was caught up in an accident and could not finish the race.

Ricky Rudd held down sixth place, although he was 15 points behind Stewart, while Rusty Wallace and Mark Martin continued their battle for seventh place, separated by just 10 points. Jeff Gordon held down ninth place, 82 points ahead of Ward Burton, while Mike Skinner moved back into 11th place in the topsy-turvy battle with Steve Park and Matt Kenseth that seemed to change after every race. Johnny Benson was 14th, still with hopes of finishing as high as 11th in the standings at year's end, while Ken Schrader eased back into 15th place after his Martinsville finish.

The fall Charlotte event always features press announcements as teams present new sponsors, drivers and colors to the public, heralding new associations for the coming year. That tradition continued, with CITGO unveiling its new paint scheme as the primary sponsor

Jeff Burton, showing off his new sponsor's logo for the first time, had to take a provisional starting spot but powered all the way to a strong, sixth-place finish in the race.

Jeff Gordon continued his LMS mastery by notching his seventh pole in 16 outings at the track, while Hendrick Motorsports teammate Jerry Nadeau claimed the inside of the second row next to Jimmy Spencer. Robert Yates Racing teammates Jarrett and Rudd shared the third row, with Bill Elliott turning in another fine qualifying run with his McDonald's Ford to grab the inside of the fourth row. Martin, Benson and Jeremy Mayfield completed the top 10, nudging Rick Mast and Ward Burton back into the sixth row.

During the second round of qualifying, eight drivers attempted to make the field, but none went fast enough to qualify on speed. Dale Earnhardt, along with Jeff Burton, Steve Park, Terry Labonte, Sterling Marlin, Kurt Busch and Ted Musgrave used provisionals to join the fastest 36 drivers for the race. Those failing to qualify were Carl Long, Scott Pruett (working without crew chief Brad Parrott who did not come to the track), Steve Grissom, Stacy Compton and Ricky Craven. Kerry Earnhardt, the older of Dale Earnhardt's two sons, was scheduled to drive a Chevrolet entered by Dave Marcis but crashed during Saturday practice. Marcis was unable to get his backup car into the event during second-round qualifying and had to go home.

A Sunday morning delivery of right-side tires to the race track alleviated fears of a tire shortage for teams, and any related

---

(Left) Jeff Gordon (24) handily collared the pole for the event. It was his seventh No. 1 start at LMS in 16 races, but that was the extent of Gordon's good fortune on Oct. 8. He led only the first lap and then faded back.

(Below) Matt Kenseth, May's winner at LMS, recorded a ninth-place finish and padded his lead in the race for Rookie of the Year honors. He left Lowe's Motor Speedway with 263 rookie points, 26 more then Dale Earnhardt Jr. and 76 in front of Dave Blaney.

of Jeff Burton's No. 99 Roush Racing Ford. The CITGO sponsorship would begin immediately, but the company would also continue its commitment to back the Wood Brothers Racing team through the 2000 season.

The Woods also had their day in the spotlight, displaying the red, white and black of Ford's Motorcraft division the team would race for beginning in 2001. Also appearing in public for the first time in new colors was Chip Ganassi's 2001 silver Dodge, with Coors Light sponsorship continuing for driver Sterling Marlin.

Few teams entered the weekend with more confidence at the 1.5-mile track than the Interstate Batteries Pontiac effort owned by Joe Gibbs. Bobby Labonte finished second in the three previous events at Lowe's Motor Speedway, and when Bud Pole qualifying was completed, Labonte had plunked his specially painted "Frankenstein" car on the outside front row. Labonte showed he was not merely racing for points with his qualifying speed. He was here to win the race — if he could.

(Top) This altercation brought out the sixth of the race's nine caution flags and involved Rusty Wallace (2), Jeff Gordon (24), Robert Pressley (77) and Dale Jarrett (88). Ted Musgrave (01) got through it unscathed, but the damage to Jarrett's Ford effectively ended his challenge for the championship.

(Middle) Jeremy Mayfield's crew elected to put just two new tires on the No.12 Mobil 1 Ford on the final stop, which worked to Bobby Labonte's advantage.

(Bottom) Labonte tracked down Mayfield with seven laps to go and drove off to victory.

problems Bobby Labonte may have anticipated for the end of the race disappeared when Eel River Racing's Mike Bliss was eliminated from the event after just five laps. Bliss' crew chief, Barry Dodson, was the crew chief for Rusty Wallace's Blue Max effort in 1989, where Jimmy Makar (Labonte's crew chief) served as the team's chassis specialist. Old bonds run deep, and Dodson sent his unused tires to Makar's Interstate Batteries team to help in the battle for the championship.

Jarrett's challenge — and in reality his hopes for a second straight championship — ended on lap 159 when Rusty Wallace tagged the Quality Care Ford and sent it into the wall. Earnhardt's hopes faltered when he slid backward after leading eight times for 58 laps in the first 200 laps of the race. Labonte suddenly had even more breathing room, and as the race ground toward its finish, the Texas native found himself in the position to make a run at his fourth victory of the season.

The event, as several others had already this season, turned on the final pit stop. Wally Dallenbach tagged the third-turn wall, and the yellow flew for debris on the track on lap 307, erasing Rudd's lead. On pit road, crew chiefs made the decision to put on either two tires — for track position — or four tires. Makar, calling the shots in the point leader's pit, chose to mount "stickers" all the way around on the Interstate Batteries Pontiac for the final run to the flag. As it

A win at last! Bobby Labonte had several good reasons to whoop it up after the race. One, his previous three races at LMS resulted in second-place finishes; two, it was the first win for Pontiac at the track since 1990; three, he left there with 4,405 points, 252 more than Jeff Burton, who was No. 2 in the chase for the championship.

turned out, the four new tires came from the Eel River batch sent over at the beginning of the race by Dodson.

Bobby restarted in eighth on lap 311, and with 12 laps to go, he had moved all the way to second, passing Martin to trail Mayfield by just over a second. Mayfield had taken two tires during the stop and was no match for Labonte. Within five laps, Bobby moved "Frankenstein" to the point, and he eased away to win by more than a second.

The victory was the first for a Pontiac at Charlotte since 1990 (by Wallace) and further strengthened Labonte's lead in points. Mayfield finished second, while Rudd took third place. Tony Stewart's Home Depot Pontiac claimed fourth place ahead of Mark Martin, while Jeff Burton fought all the way from his provisional start to give his new CITGO colors a sixth place in their first outing on his "99." Steve Park and Johnny Benson were seventh and eighth, with Matt Kenseth and Ward Burton grabbing the final top-10 positions.

UAW-GM QUALITY 500 • final results

With nine pit stops for 51 laps spaced evenly throughout the 334-lap event, pit stops played an important role in the UAW-GM Quality 500.

Fin. Pos.	Start Pos.	Car No.	Driver	Team	Fin. Pos.	Start Pos.	Car No.	Driver	Team
1	2	18	Bobby Labonte	Interstate Batteries Pontiac	23	35	60	Dick Trickle	Power Team Chevrolet
2	10	12	Jeremy Mayfield	Mobil 1 Ford	24	19	4	Bobby Hamilton	Kodak Chevrolet
3	6	28	Ricky Rudd	Texaco/Havoline Ford	25	20	36	Ken Schrader	M&M's Pontiac
4	17	20	Tony Stewart	Home Depot Pontiac	26	33	96	Andy Houston	Ronald McDonald House Charities Ford
5	8	6	Mark Martin	Valvoline/Cummins Ford	27	40	5	Terry Labonte	Kellogg's Chevrolet
6	38	99	Jeff Burton	CITGO SUPERGARD Ford	28	29	93	Dave Blaney	Amoco Pontiac
7	39	1	Steve Park	Pennzoil Chevrolet	29	43	01	Ted Musgrave	BellSouth Chevrolet
8	9	10	Johnny Benson	Aaron's Pontiac	30	34	66	Darrell Waltrip	Route 66/Big Kmart Ford
9	26	17	Matt Kenseth	DeWalt Tools Ford	31	41	40	Sterling Marlin	Coors Light Chevrolet
10	12	22	Ward Burton	Caterpillar Pontiac	32	31	11	Brett Bodine	Ralphs Supermarkets Ford
11	37	3	Dale Earnhardt	GM Goodwrench Service Chevrolet	33	24	75	Wally Dallenbach	Dinner & A Movie Ford
12	16	16	Kevin Lepage	FamilyClick.com/TV Guide Ford	34	7	94	Bill Elliott	McDonald's Ford
13	42	97	Kurt Busch	John Deere Ford	35	15	77	Robert Pressley	Jasper Engines Ford
14	21	33	Joe Nemechek	Oakwood Homes Chevrolet	36	3	25	Jerry Nadeau	MichaelHoligan.com Chevrolet
15	4	26	Jimmy Spencer	Big Kmart/Route 66 Ford	37	32	55	Kenny Wallace	Square D/Cooper Lighting Chevrolet
16	23	21	Elliott Sadler	CITGO Ford	38	25	13	Robby Gordon	Team Menard Ford
17	11	14	Rick Mast	Conseco Pontiac	39	1	24	Jeff Gordon	DuPont Automotive Finishes Chevrolet
18	28	43	John Andretti	Cheerios Pontiac	40	5	88	Dale Jarrett	Quality Care/Ford Credit Ford
19	13	8	Dale Earnhardt Jr.	Budweiser Chevrolet	41	27	98	Jeff Fuller	MacPherson Motorsports Ford
20	18	31	Mike Skinner	Lowe's Chevrolet	42	36	90	Hut Stricklin	Hills Brothers Coffee Ford
21	22	2	Rusty Wallace	Miller Lite Ford	43	30	27	Mike Bliss	Pfizer/Viagra Pontiac
22	14	7	Michael Waltrip	Nations Rent Chevrolet					

WINSTON 500

OCTOBER 15, 2000 • TALLADEGA SUPERSPEEDWAY

(Left) Following his incredible ride at Talladega Superspeedway, Dale Earnhardt shared his joy with crew chief Kevin Hamlin (left) and team owner Richard Childress. It was "The Intimidator's" 10th career victory at the Alabama speedplant.

(Right) In a race that featured 21 race leaders, Earnhardt went to the point seven times for 34 laps.

Thunk. Thunk. THUNK.

One by one, month after month, important race after important race, Bobby Labonte drove nails into the lid, destroying the momentum of his rivals and proving time and again the Joe Gibbs Racing Interstate Batteries team was not about to yield in the pressure-packed stretch run to the NASCAR Winston Cup Series championship.

Leading Dale Jarrett by 53 points, Labonte hammered out victory in the Brickyard 400 in August. In September at Darlington, he claimed the Pepsi Southern 500 after entering the classic event just 91 points ahead of Dale Earnhardt. Now, after Earnhardt arrived at Charlotte with high hopes despite trailing by 213 points, Labonte once again slammed the door on the competition by emerging the victor in the UAW GM Quality 500.

The victory at Lowe's Motor Speedway provided Labonte with a 252-point cushion as teams arrived at Talladega Superspeedway, and although the Texan had not mathematically clinched the title, he was truly in the driver's seat. Finally, if his team wanted to, Bobby could start counting points.

"Team Conseco" principals crew chief Philippe Lopez (left), general manager Tommy LaMance (center) and owner A.J. Foyt confer before the race.

Jeff Burton's sixth-place finish in his first outing in CITGO SUPERGARD colors moved the Virginian to second place in the standings entering Talladega, while Earnhardt's 11th-place effort dropped him to third, six points behind the Ford driver. Jarrett, with a disastrous weekend at LMS, dropped 37 points and now found himself just 40 points ahead of Labonte's teammate, the streaking Tony Stewart. Ricky Rudd was sixth, five points behind the Home Depot Pontiac driver, while Mark Martin and Rusty Wallace swapped places, with Martin moving to seventh. Ward Burton held onto ninth place, but in reality was in a dead heat with Jeff Gordon, who was just a single point behind the Caterpillar Pontiac driver.

The battle for 11th place raged on. Steve Park rode his seventh place at LMS to a 13-point bulge over Mike Skinner, while Matt Kenseth found himself 29 points behind Skinner after his ninth place at the 1.5-mile track. Johnny Benson held 14th, 14 points behind Kenseth, with Ken Schrader clinging to 15th place.

Technical modifications like taller deck-lid spoilers (above) and roof-mounted "disturbance strips" (right) were put into effect to enhance safety and improve competition. Along with a 15/16-inch restrictor plate, they seemed to do the job, as demonstrated below by Steve Grissom (44), Terry Labonte (5) and Mark Martin (6).

Scenes like this — four-abreast racing — kept the overflow crowd at Talladega on its feet most of the day. Here, the Fords of Darrell Waltrip (66) and Mark Martin (6) put the squeeze on the Chevrolets of Jeff Gordon (24) and Bobby Hamilton (4).

The event at the massive Talladega Superspeedway would be the last one called the "Winston 500." R.J. Reynolds officials announced before the race the company would not sponsor the event after 2000, ending a relationship that began with the first Winston 500 in 1971.

The "final edition" of the event would be held under revised aerodynamic rules for the cars. The new specs included raising the nose ride height, a larger rear spoiler for Pontiacs and Fords with a much higher "attack" angle for all, a raised metal piece running across the width of the car roof and a one-inch restrictor plate. All of the modifications were aimed at slowing the cars down and making them more responsive to driver input. Several cars were forced to go through technical inspection more than once as crew chiefs and fabricators

tried to push the envelope with the changes.

The teams of Joe Nemechek and Bill Elliott showed they had the new rules figured out the best when Bud Pole qualifying was completed for the Winston 500. Nemechek claimed the sixth pole of his

Pole winner Joe Nemechek and No. 2 starter Bill Elliott lead the field under the flagman's green banner and get the final "Winston 500" off to a great start.

Typical Talladega. Things got just a little bit hairy toward the end of the Winston 500 when teammates Mike Skinner (31) and Dale Earnhardt (3) ran side by side and felt the heat from Dale Earnhardt Jr. (8), Kenny Wallace (55) and Joe Nemechek (33). Bobby Labonte (18) got caught in the shuffle and finished 12th but still held on to his lead in points.

career and the first of the year, earning the Oakwood Homes Chevrolet a spot in the February Bud Shootout at Daytona. His lap time of 50.326 seconds (190.279 mph) was six-hundredths of a second faster than Elliott's, who also claimed the outside of the front row here in the spring event. Elliott's lap was his 18th top-10 qualifying effort of the season.

Dale Earnhardt Jr. and Jerry Nadeau grabbed the second row starting positions, while Stewart celebrated a three-year extension of Home Depot's sponsorship with the fifth-fastest lap. Bobby Labonte was on his right as the Joe Gibbs-owned Pontiacs swept the third row. Gordon and Dave Marcis made up the fourth row ahead of

Park and Rudd, while Jeff Burton, Rusty Wallace, Chad Little, Jeremy Mayfield, Robert Pressley, Brett Bodine and Mike Bliss were the provisional starters. Wally Dallenbach, Blaise Alexander and Hut Stricklin failed to make the field.

After seeing faster than expected speeds during the final practice session, NASCAR officials immediately swapped the one-inch restrictor plates for 15/16th-inch plates, and from the drop of the green flag, it was evident that the technical changes were working. The rainbow-hued pack of cars roared around the 2.66-mile oval, and for more than three hours, few of the spectators in the huge throng sat in the seats they paid for.

It was incredible stuff. Cars three and four wide, a pack of 30-40 cars intact, hurtling around the track and drivers doing whatever they had to do to move toward the front. White-knuckled, breath-defying tactics behind the wheel? Absolutely! Incredible racing and spectating for the fans that included 49 lead changes among 21 drivers? You betcha!

And when it was show time, who else could please the enormous crowd than the old "airmeister" himself, who strode to the front from a 20th-place start by splitting the pack and running right up the gut?

Yup.

Earnhardt.

Beep! Beep! Scott Pruett (32) can't seem to make a move as long as Steve Grissom (44), Rich Bickle (60), Bobby Labonte (18) and his brother, Terry (5), hog the road!

Earnhardt does a bit of a victory-lane dance as he marks winning the season's final No Bull 5 event. It was the first time he'd won the special million-dollar bonus.

From 22nd place with 10 laps to go — and with an assist from Kenny Wallace — "The Intimidator" made his run. He couldn't describe how he did it. Others couldn't, either. With 182 laps in the books and six to go he was 16th. With two circuits remaining, he had split, fought, gouged, clawed, shimmied, slithered, rocketed and pounded his way past teammate Mike Skinner to take the point. Even the most grizzled Earnhardt fan in the stands, after watching every move the black Chevrolet made on the track, couldn't recount the way the seven-time champion got to the front.

And in the end, when Earnhardt flashed under the checkers for his 10th victory at the massive track, every fan stood and cheered one of the most incredible performances seen at Talladega since Bill Elliott made up nearly two laps under the green flag in 1985 on his way to eventually winning the Winston Million.

This one was worth $1 million from Winston as well. The Winston 500 was the final No Bull 5 event of the season, and although Earnhardt had been eligible for the bonus several times in the past, this was the first time he won the money.

Kenny Wallace tried hard to find a way to pass Earnhardt in the final two laps but was forced to settle for second place ahead of teammate Nemechek. Gordon, Terry Labonte and

Skinner were fourth, fifth and sixth ahead of Martin, Rusty Wallace, Mike Bliss and Matt Kenseth.

But where was Bobby Labonte? In the final four laps, Labonte got involved in a wild scramble for position and came out on the short end of it. He slid from second place to 12th, but when the point leader emerged from his Pontiac after the race, he had a smile on his face. The damage was limited, and he still had a lead of more than 200 points with four races remaining in the 2000 NASCAR Winston Cup Series season.

Joe Gibbs watches NASCAR Winston Cup Series point leader Bobby Labonte get the worst of a late race scramble. Labonte came home 12th while stablemate Tony Stewart could not work his way to the front, finishing 27th.

WINSTON 500 • final results

Ward Burton spent time with the leaders and even led at Talladega, but he really had nothing to celebrate at the end of the day, except that he was running at the finish!

Fin. Pos.	Start Pos.	Car No.	Driver	Team
1	20	3	Dale Earnhardt	GM Goodwrench Service Chevrolet
2	7	55	Kenny Wallace	Square D/Cooper Lighting Chevrolet
3	1	33	Joe Nemechek	Oakwood Homes Chevrolet
4	8	24	Jeff Gordon	DuPont Automotive Finishes Chevrolet
5	17	5	Terry Labonte	Kellogg's Chevrolet
6	24	31	Mike Skinner	Lowe's Chevrolet
7	27	6	Mark Martin	Zerex/Cummins Ford
8	38	2	Rusty Wallace	Miller Lite Ford
9	43	27	Mike Bliss	Pfizer/Viagra Pontiac
10	36	17	Matt Kenseth	DeWalt Tools Ford
11	11	28	Ricky Rudd	Texaco/Havoline Ford
12	6	18	Bobby Labonte	Interstate Batteries Pontiac
13	4	25	Jerry Nadeau	MichaelHoligan.com Chevrolet
14	3	8	Dale Earnhardt Jr.	Budweiser Chevrolet
15	12	88	Dale Jarrett	Quality Care/Ford Credit Ford
16	31	44	Steve Grissom	Hot Wheels Pontiac
17	25	21	Elliott Sadler	CITGO Ford
18	39	97	Chad Little	John Deere Ford
19	10	1	Steve Park	Pennzoil Chevrolet
20	15	43	John Andretti	Cheerios Pontiac
21	28	60	Rich Bickle	Power Team Chevrolet
22	21	22	Ward Burton	Caterpillar Pontiac

Fin. Pos.	Start Pos.	Car No.	Driver	Team
23	13	9	Stacy Compton	Kodiak/Cougar Ford
24	2	94	Bill Elliott	McDonald's Ford
25	41	77	Robert Pressley	Jasper Engines Ford
26	42	11	Brett Bodine	Ralphs Supermarkets Ford
27	5	20	Tony Stewart	Home Depot Pontiac
28	33	93	Dave Blaney	Amoco Pontiac
29	37	99	Jeff Burton	CITGO SUPERGARD Ford
30	26	50	Ricky Craven	Midwest Transit Chevrolet
31	29	14	Rick Mast	Conseco Pontiac
32	30	01	Ted Musgrave	BellSouth Chevrolet
33	23	10	Johnny Benson	Aaron's Pontiac
34	18	7	Michael Waltrip	Nations Rent Chevrolet
35	34	66	Darrell Waltrip	Route 66/Big Kmart Ford
36	19	4	Bobby Hamilton	Kodak Chevrolet
37	14	36	Ken Schrader	M&M's Pontiac
38	22	26	Jimmy Spencer	Big Kmart/Route 66 Ford
39	35	32	Scott Pruett	Tide Ford
40	9	71	Dave Marcis	Realtree Chevrolet
41	32	40	Sterling Marlin	Coors Light Chevrolet
42	40	12	Jeremy Mayfield	Mobil 1 Ford
43	16	16	Kevin Lepage	FamilyClick.com/TV Guide Ford

POP SECRET MICROWAVE
POPCORN *400*

(Left) Dale Jarrett had a couple of good reasons to smile. The Pop Secret 400 was his first-ever win at "The Rock," and it was his first victory since he notched the Daytona 500 back in February. Also, his winner's purse of more than $125,800 would keep him in plenty of popcorn for a long time to come!

(Right) Pole winner Jeremy Mayfield led eight times for 169 laps, but electrical problems ruined a potentially great day.

Dale Earnhardt Jr. checks in with Dad prior to the race's start.

After the rousing battle at Talladega, where 21 drivers swapped the lead 49 times, everyone needed a chance to take a deep breath. But with the NASCAR Winston Cup Series season headed for the conclusion of a pressure-packed stretch of 12 consecutive races, there was little time for kickin' back and coolin' off.

Since the run had begun at The Brickyard in early August, teams watched as the pretenders were sorted from the contenders. And through that run of 11 straight races, Bobby Labonte and the Interstate Batteries crew, led by crew chief Jimmy Makar, stood the test. Labonte entered the string of events leading by just over 50 points, and he now entered the final race of the "series" with a 210-point margin over Dale Earnhardt.

The cushion built by the No. 18 team was punctuated by three victories — but more important, Labonte had taken every point he could earn during the stretch. It was the way championships are won.

Jeff Burton, hurt by a 15-second penalty at Talladega when two members of his pit crew went over the wall too soon during a stop (and a resulting 29th place finish), now was third in the standings,

(Right) Bobby Labonte and his crew chief, Jimmy Makar, go over strategy before the start of the Pop Secret 400. The important thing was to keep the advantage in points they'd maintained since the start of a 12-race stretch in August.

(Below) Mayfield jumped out to an early lead and withstood pressure from Jeff Gordon's DuPont Chevrolet and Labonte's Interstate Batteries Pontiac.

(Bottom) A late-race pit stop worked against Jeff Burton, who finished fourth.

98 points behind Earnhardt. Dale Jarrett was 94 points behind the CITGO Ford driver after finishing 15th at Talladega. For all intents and purposes, the battle for the championship was down to Labonte and Earnhardt — and Bobby had a huge advantage heading into the final four races of the season.

Ricky Rudd moved past Tony Stewart in the battle for fifth place in the standings, while Mark Martin and Rusty Wallace continued their struggle for seventh place. Jeff Gordon parlayed his fourth place at Talladega into ninth place in the standings. He moved past Ward Burton after a flat tire left the Caterpillar Pontiac struggling to a 22nd-place finish in the Winston 500.

Mike Skinner moved back into 11th place on the strength of his sixth-place finish at Talladega, with Steve Park falling to 12th ahead of Matt Kenseth and Johnny Benson. Dale Earnhardt Jr. reclaimed 15th place in his battle with Joe Nemechek and Ken Schrader.

After notching his fourth Bud Pole of the season by lapping the 1.017-mile Rockingham track at 157.342 mph, Jeremy Mayfield tried to put an end to the rumors surrounding his future with the Mobil 1 team. In the days prior to Talladega, Roger Penske bought partner Michael Kranefuss' interest in the organization, and "Silly Season" gossip had Mayfield headed for Morgan-McClure Motorsports and the vacant No. 4 Kodak Chevrolet for the coming season. Mayfield

and crew chief Peter Sospenzo told media members they each planned to stay with the Mobil 1 team, with Mayfield noting he had two years remaining on his contract with what had become Penske Racing.

Point leader Labonte again showed he would be competitive in the Pop Secret Microwave Popcorn 400, grabbing the outside of the front row, with Jeff Gordon and Bill Elliott claiming the second-row starting slots. Roush Racing teammates Jeff Burton and Mark Martin were in the third row, with Nemechek and Skinner lined up behind them. Ward Burton and Kenny Wallace beat Rick Mast and Jerry Nadeau for the final top-10 starting positions.

With tire wear a problem due to the abrasive surface of the race track, teams scrambled trying to find the right suspension combinations to give their drivers a chance at victory. Over the years, Dale Jarrett has had chances to conquer "The Rock." Each time, though, it seemed other crews made the right decisions in the closing laps that gave their drivers the edge needed to post the victory. Jarrett had finished second a half-dozen times at Rockingham and had yet to find his way to victory lane.

Not this time, however.

With his team cranking out a sub-15-second pit stop during the final caution period of the afternoon, Jarrett emerged

(Above) While Tony Stewart (20) and Ricky Rudd (28) came in with top-10 finishes, Dale Earnhardt (3) could do no better than 17th at the end.

(Right) A really quick pit stop late in the going helped clinch the race for Dale Jarrett.

(Below) Jarrett beat Gordon (24) to the checkered flag by a bit over two seconds.

Dale Earnhardt Jr., along with Elliott Sadler, John Andretti, Scott Pruett, Robby Gordon, Dave Marcis and Carl Long, used provisional starts to make the field, while Ted Musgrave, Rich Bickle, Steve Grissom, Hut Stricklin and Stacy Compton all failed to gain a starting position in the event.

Once the green flag fell on the field, Mayfield wasted no time underscoring the fact that he had the fastest car on the race track. He led eight times for 169 laps, but once again, his race ended in the garage area. A broken alternator and electrical problems forced a stop to change the battery in his Ford, and he finished six laps behind in 29th place.

Jeff Burton appeared headed toward another victory for the Roush Racing juggernaut. He, however, was foiled when a late-race pit stop dropped him from second to fifth place. He fought back to fourth, but that was the best the Virginian could muster in the remaining laps.

Ricky Rudd's Ford sticks on the bottom to work past the Pontiac of Ward Burton. Rudd took the lead in the middle of the race, but could not challenge Dale Jarrett or Jeff Gordon at the end and finished third. Ward Burton came home in eighth.

at the point for the sprint to the flag. Behind him was teammate Ricky Rudd, while Jeff Gordon lined up behind Rudd's Texaco Ford. And when Gordon fought his way past Rudd, Jarrett looked in his mirror and grimaced. In the past, Gordon had found ways to catch Jarrett and pass him to win. Jarrett took one look this Sunday afternoon and hoped he had what was needed to keep the Quality Care Ford ahead of Gordon's DuPont Chevrolet.

He started working the high line around the track, and when Gordon finally closed and tried to make his move, Jarrett had the momentum he needed hold onto the lead. As the laps wound down, Jarrett eased away from Gordon's challenge and went on to win by more than two seconds.

It had been a long dry spell since Jarrett opened the defense of his championship by winning his third Daytona 500 in February. He was in the heat of the point battle for most of the year, falling away only in the last four events. His hopes of defending his title were

now history, but he was back in the winner's circle for the 24th time in his career and the second time this season.

Gordon held off Rudd to grab second place, while Jeff Burton finished fourth. Rusty Wallace fought to fifth place ahead of Steve Park, with Tony Stewart seventh and Ward Burton eighth. Bobby Hamilton brought the Kodak Chevrolet home in ninth place ahead of Joe Nemechek, who rounded out the top 10.

POPSECRET MICROWAVE POPCORN 400 • final results

By winning, Jarrett also clinched the Manufacturers' Championship for Ford. This was the Blue Oval's 13th visit to victory lane during the 2000 season.

Fin. Pos.	Start Pos.	Car No.	Driver	Team		Fin. Pos.	Start Pos.	Car No.	Driver	Team
1	21	88	Dale Jarrett	Quality Care/Ford Credit Ford		23	38	43	John Andretti	Cheerios Pontiac
2	3	24	Jeff Gordon	DuPont Automotive Finishes Chevrolet		24	24	97	Kurt Busch	John Deere Ford
3	13	28	Ricky Rudd	Texaco/Havoline Ford		25	28	17	Matt Kenseth	DeWalt Tools Ford
4	6	99	Jeff Burton	CITGO SUPERGARD Ford		26	25	11	Brett Bodine	Ralphs Supermarkets Ford
5	15	2	Rusty Wallace	Miller Lite Ford		27	12	25	Jerry Nadeau	MichaelHoligan.com Chevrolet
6	17	1	Steve Park	Pennzoil Chevrolet		28	30	96	Andy Houston	Ronald McDonald House Charities Ford
7	18	20	Tony Stewart	Home Depot Pontiac		29	1	12	Jeremy Mayfield	Mobil 1 Ford
8	9	22	Ward Burton	Caterpillar Pontiac		30	40	32	Scott Pruett	Tide Ford
9	35	4	Bobby Hamilton	Kodak Chevrolet		31	42	71	Dave Marcis	Realtree Chevrolet
10	7	33	Joe Nemechek	Oakwood Homes Chevrolet		32	43	85	Carl Long	ST Wooten Ford
11	14	10	Johnny Benson	Aaron's Pontiac		33	23	40	Sterling Marlin	Coors Light Chevrolet
12	26	77	Robert Pressley	Jasper Engines Ford		34	37	8	Dale Earnhardt Jr.	Budweiser Chevrolet
13	11	14	Rick Mast	Conseco Pontiac		35	20	7	Michael Waltrip	Nations Rent Chevrolet
14	8	31	Mike Skinner	Lowe's Chevrolet		36	16	16	Kevin Lepage	FamilyClick.com/TV Guide Ford
15	29	50	Ricky Craven	Midwest Transit Chevrolet		37	31	66	Darrell Waltrip	Route 66/Big Kmart Ford
16	4	94	Bill Elliott	McDonald's Ford		38	32	5	Terry Labonte	Kellogg's Chevrolet
17	27	3	Dale Earnhardt	GM Goodwrench Service Chevrolet		39	34	26	Jimmy Spencer	Big Kmart/Route 66 Ford
18	19	36	Ken Schrader	M&M's Pontiac		40	5	6	Mark Martin	Valvoline/Cummins Ford
19	39	21	Elliott Sadler	CITGO Ford		41	41	13	Robby Gordon	Team Menard Ford
20	2	18	Bobby Labonte	Interstate Batteries Pontiac		42	22	93	Dave Blaney	Amoco Pontiac
21	36	27	Mike Bliss	Pfizer/Viagra Pontiac		43	10	55	Kenny Wallace	Square D/Cooper Lighting Chevrolet
22	33	75	Wally Dallenbach	Redcell Batteries Ford						

CHECKER AUTO PARTS/DURA LUBE *500*

NOVEMBER 5, 2000 • PHOENIX INTERNATIONAL RACEWAY

(Left) Jeremy Mayfield led the 500-kilometer race twice and gave his sponsor, Mobil 1, some valuable "TV time." He came up just a little bit short, though, and finished second to Jeff Burton (Right), who made his fourth trip into victory lane in 2000. Burton was still third in points after Phoenix but was just eight markers behind second-place Dale Earnhardt.

Phew! One could hear the sigh of relief all the way to the top row of the grandstands at North Carolina Speedway at the conclusion of the Pop Secret Microwave Popcorn 400.

It came from the green-and-black-clad Interstate Batteries Pontiac team and its driver, Bobby Labonte, after the point leader managed to escape from a near trap and ease away from the Sandhills with a lead of 201 points over Dale Earnhardt.

Earnhardt needed some poor luck by Labonte to create a battle for the championship, and it looked as though "The Intimidator" was going to get that gift. A cut tire and lost lap had put Labonte back in the field — exactly the opportunity needed by Earnhardt to close the gap. But in the closing laps, Earnhardt lost the handle on the black GM Goodwrench Chevrolet and drifted backward, losing position after position. He could post just a 17th-place finish, and with Labonte finishing 20th, Earnhardt's point gain was minimal.

Now, with three races left in the season, Labonte was truly in command of the battle. The tide had turned in September following his Pepsi Southern 500 victory at Darlington Raceway. By the end of that month, at Dover, he had moved to his biggest point lead of the season. Race after race, Labonte

Ryan Newman made his NASCAR Winston Cup Series debut at Phoenix in a Penske Racing Ford and qualified an impressive 10th quickest.

and the Joe Gibbs-owned team had refused to be dislodged from the top of the standings. Now the Texan found himself in the position of needing only to finish 14th or better in the remaining three events to join older brother Terry and become the first brothers in history to win NASCAR Winston Cup Series titles.

Earnhardt's back was against the wall. He needed poor finishes from Labonte and strong results at Phoenix, Homestead and Atlanta to have any chance of winning an unprecedented eighth title. Now, with Labonte so far ahead in points, Earnhardt knew his chances were slim at best.

Dale Jarrett's victory at Rockingham, his second of the season, was not enough to move him out of fourth place in the standings, where he now trailed Jeff Burton by 79 markers. Jarrett's Robert Yates Racing teammate, Ricky Rudd, finished third at "The Rock" and lost a few points but still held onto fifth, 43 points behind his teammate and 62 ahead of Tony Stewart. Rusty Wallace moved from eighth to seventh in the standings following his fifth place at Rockingham, while Mark Martin's disastrous 40th-place showing dropped him to eighth place, where he held a 138-point bulge over Jeff Gordon. Ward Burton was solidly in 10th place, nearly 300 points ahead of Mike Skinner. It appeared the elder Burton brother was assured of an invitation to the stage at the Waldorf-Astoria in December.

(Above Left) Brett Bodine and his crew chief, Mike Hillman, relax after getting their Ralphs Supermarkets Ford into the event. Bodine finished 20th, his best showing of the season.

(Left) Dale Earnhardt (center) seems to enjoy socializing with Darrell and Stevie Waltrip. Did the Waltrips take "Route 66" to get to the track?

(Below) They don't call the Phoenix area the "Valley of the Sun" for nothing. Ideal fall weather always helps bring out record crowds at Phoenix International Raceway.

The driver of the No. 31 Lowe's-sponsored Chevrolet, however, was hardly in control of 11th place. Steve Park moved to within two points of Skinner, while Matt Kenseth was just 78 markers behind. Johnny Benson now trailed Kenseth by just 47 points, while Joe Nemechek retained 15th place via his 10th-place finish at Rockingham.

(Right) Rusty Wallace, after capturing his third pole position at Phoenix, went after his second career victory at the desert one-miler. He put the Miller Lite Ford out front five times for 86 laps and finished fourth.

(Below) Sterling Marlin's Coors Light crew hustles to service his Chevrolet. Marlin finished 15th.

"Silly Season" unveiled its latest chapter at Phoenix, as Robert Pressley re-upped with Jasper Motorsports for another year. A.J. Foyt made a decision about his driver for next season official: He named Ron Hornaday to drive the Conseco Pontiac for the 2001 season, which made Rick Mast a free agent for the coming year. Within minutes, a rumor ran through the garage area that Mast would be the driver for Chip Ganassi's BellSouth Dodge for 2001, but no official confirmation was made.

Jerry Nadeau's new sponsors — the United Auto Workers and Delphi Automotive Systems — also came to light during the Phoenix weekend, with new contract by plunking the Jasper Ford on the inside of the second row. Johnny Benson, working hard and looking for his first pole of the season, settled for the fourth starting position, while Steve Park and Ken Schrader shared the third row. Kenny Wallace and Mark Martin made up the fourth row ahead of Bobby Labonte and 22-year-old Ryan Newman, who was making his NASCAR Winston Cup Series debut in a Penske Racing Ford.

Despite being head and shoulders faster than any other driver in testing at Phoenix, Tony Stewart was forced to use a provisional start to get into the race, as did Terry Labonte, Joe Nemechek, Jerry Nadeau, Ted Musgrave, Michael Waltrip and Rich Bickle. Those who failed to make the field were Stacy Compton, Steve Grissom, Robby Gordon, Dave Marcis and Hut Stricklin.

After winning Saturday's NASCAR Busch Series, Grand National Division race, Jeff Burton headed for his CITGO Ford Sunday morning as the "Desert King." He had swept the NASCAR Busch Series and NASCAR

(Left) While the "race" in the pits is controlled by speed limits, it can be as competitive as the one on the track!

(Below) Ah, those first-year blues! Rookie Scott Pruett spun out in the fourth turn but finished the race three laps down.

UAW and Delphi replacing Michael Holigan Homes on the No. 25 Hendrick Motorsports Chevrolet. Holigan himself, it appeared, wanted to become a NASCAR team owner in his own right.

For the ninth time in the season, Rusty Wallace's Miller Lite Ford claimed the Bud Pole Award, and this time, Wallace needed every single ounce of speed he could wring from the blue-and-white Taurus. He beat Jeff Burton by just 15-thousandths of a second for the inside of the front row, while Pressley celebrated his

One of the most sought-after "seats" at Phoenix International Raceway is the hill overlooking the track and facing the third and fourth corners.

luck reared its ugly head once again. On the 294th circuit, Rudd was collected after Mike Bliss rear-ended Rick Mast on the backstretch, and Bliss' blue-and-silver Pontiac slid right into Rudd's path.

Rudd's Texaco Ford suffered front-end damage, and his hopes for victory were over. With nearly every lead-lap car stopping for tires and fuel for the final sprint, Mark Martin gambled on 90-lap tires. He stayed on the track and held the point when the event restarted with 11 laps to go. It was his only

Winston Cup Series races earlier in the season at Las Vegas and was now three for three for the year. Could he make it a clean sweep and give CITGO its first victory since joining the team at Charlotte?

For the longest time Sunday, it appeared Ricky Rudd was finally on the way to his first victory lane celebration in over two years. He worked through the field from his 17th-place starting position while improving his car on each stop in the pits, and took the lead on lap 253. With Jeff Burton running second and beginning to close lap after lap, Rudd still looked as though he had the race in hand. Then bad

chance for victory, but the old tires on the Valvoline Ford could not provide the edge he needed. Burton swept past and rolled to his fourth win of the season.

Jeremy Mayfield fought to second place ahead of Steve Park and Rusty Wallace, while point leader Bobby Labonte did exactly what he needed to and finished fifth. Martin faded to sixth ahead of Jeff Gordon, and Dave Blaney posted a solid eighth-place finish in his Amoco Pontiac. Dale Earnhardt was ninth and lost more points in his quest for an eighth title, while Dale Jarrett finished in 10th.

CHECKER AUTO PARTS/DURA LUBE 500 • final results

Tony Stewart turned a 37th-place start into a 14th-place finish. Stewart moved up one spot in points from sixth to fifth.

Fin. Pos.	Start Pos.	Car No.	Driver	Team	Fin. Pos.	Start Pos.	Car No.	Driver	Team
1	2	99	Jeff Burton	CITGO SUPERGARD Ford	23	40	25	Jerry Nadeau	MichaelHoligan.com Chevrolet
2	25	12	Jeremy Mayfield	Mobil 1 Ford	24	39	33	Joe Nemechek	Oakwood Homes Chevrolet
3	5	1	Steve Park	Pennzoil Chevrolet	25	41	01	Ted Musgrave	BellSouth Chevrolet
4	1	2	Rusty Wallace	Miller Lite Ford	26	35	94	Bill Elliott	McDonald's Ford
5	9	18	Bobby Labonte	Interstate Batteries Pontiac	27	18	8	Dale Earnhardt Jr.	Budweiser Chevrolet
6	8	6	Mark Martin	Valvoline/Cummins Ford	28	29	43	John Andretti	Cheerios Pontiac
7	24	24	Jeff Gordon	DuPont Automotive Finishes Chevrolet	29	26	97	Kurt Busch	John Deere Ford
8	13	93	Dave Blaney	Amoco Pontiac	30	33	21	Elliott Sadler	CITGO Ford
9	31	3	Dale Earnhardt	GM Goodwrench Service Chevrolet	31	3	77	Robert Pressley	Jasper Engines Ford
10	36	88	Dale Jarrett	Quality Care/Ford Credit Ford	32	42	7	Michael Waltrip	Nations Rent Chevrolet
11	30	31	Mike Skinner	Lowe's Chevrolet	33	34	66	Darrell Waltrip	Route 66/Big Kmart Ford
12	19	22	Ward Burton	Caterpillar Pontiac	34	21	32	Scott Pruett	Tide Ford
13	14	26	Jimmy Spencer	Big Kmart/Route 66 Ford	35	43	60	Rich Bickle	Power Team Chevrolet
14	37	20	Tony Stewart	Home Depot Pontiac	36	32	96	Andy Houston	Ronald McDonald House Charities Ford
15	27	40	Sterling Marlin	Coors Light Chevrolet	37	17	28	Ricky Rudd	Texaco/Havoline Ford
16	4	10	Johnny Benson	Aaron's Pontiac	38	15	27	Mike Bliss	Pfizer/Viagra Pontiac
17	38	5	Terry Labonte	Kellogg's Chevrolet	39	28	14	Rick Mast	Conseco Pontiac
18	11	50	Ricky Craven	Midwest Transit Chevrolet	40	6	36	Ken Schrader	Pedigree/Uncle Ben's Pontiac
19	7	55	Kenny Wallace	Square D/Cooper Lighting Chevrolet	41	10	02	Ryan Newman	ALLTEL Ford
20	23	11	Brett Bodine	Ralphs Supermarkets Ford	42	12	17	Matt Kenseth	DeWalt Tools Ford
21	22	16	Kevin Lepage	FamilyClick.com/TV Guide Ford	43	16	4	Bobby Hamilton	Kodak Chevrolet
22	20	75	Wally Dallenbach	Redcell Batteries Ford					

PENNZOIL *400* PRESENTED BY DISCOUNT AUTO PARTS

(Left) Tony Stewart and his crew chief, Greg Zipadelli (left), had plenty to smile about in victory lane at Homestead-Miami Speedway. They'd just clinched their sixth victory of the year and second straight at the South Florida superspeedway. While still fifth in NASCAR Winston Cup Series points, Stewart did pick up 73 markers on fourth-place Dale Jarrett, who finished 17th in the race.

(Right) Stewart started 13th in the Pennzoil 400 and led for the first time on lap 53. He ended up going to the front four times for 166 of the event's 267 laps, beating runner-up Jeremy Mayfield by over 4-1/2 seconds.

Just days after the nation voted for its new president — an election that ended up "stalled in the pits" — Bobby Labonte and his Interstate Batteries Pontiac team arrived at Homestead-Miami Speedway determined to be sure the result of this year's NASCAR Winston Cup Series championship chase was anything but "too close to call."

Labonte's rock-solid performance in the desert at Phoenix the previous weekend put him in total command of the point battle. As a result, the Texan needed only a top-five finish in the Pennzoil 400 to claim the title and write his name into the NASCAR record book as the only NASCAR Busch Series, Grand National Division champion to go on to win the NASCAR Winston Cup Series title.

That top-five finish would also give the Labontes — Bobby and older brother Terry — the distinction of becoming the only brothers in history to claim stock car racing's most prestigious title.

While the nation waited in suspense to see whether George W. Bush or Al Gore would claim Florida's electoral votes and with it the presidency, there was no drama left in the NASCAR Winston Cup Series point battle. Dale Earnhardt's ninth-place finish at Phoenix had not been the kind of effort needed to put him into a challenging position in the final two events of the season. Instead, Earnhardt was now locked in a ferocious battle with Jeff Burton for second place in the year-end standings. Burton's Phoenix victory had moved him within eight points of second place.

Jeff Burton's battle with Dale Earnhardt in the points continued at Homestead, where Jeff's 11th-place finish was good enough to push him up to second place with a 19-point lead over the former champ.

(Above) While his younger brother was busy wrapping up the 2000 NASCAR Winston Cup Series championship, Terry Labonte seemed to be stuck in "Whoville." The 1996 champion started 39th and finished 25th.

(Left) While Stewart (20) smoked the field at Homestead, young Casey Atwood (19) continued to pick up valuable experience. He was the fifth-fastest qualifier and brought the Motorola Ford home in 10th place.

the Quality Care Ford driver by 113 markers and was returning to the Florida track as the defending race champion. Anything could happen.

Just ask Ricky Rudd. Seemingly headed for his first victory in two years, Rudd was collected at Phoenix and forced to a 37th-place finish. It dropped him to sixth place in the standings, seven points behind Stewart and just 49 points ahead of Rusty Wallace. Mark Martin held eighth place, 83 points behind Wallace, while Jeff Gordon hoped to move up from ninth place. He trailed Martin by

In 1999, Dale Jarrett headed for Homestead-Miami in the same position as Bobby Labonte a year later. And Jarrett responded by clinching the NASCAR Winston Cup Series title in Florida.

This year was a different story. Like many others, Jarrett had been unable to successfully defend his title and now found himself in a struggle to keep fourth place in the standings. Tony Stewart trailed just 147 points. Ward Burton held down 10th place, 114 behind Gordon, but it appeared the Caterpillar Pontiac driver had clinched an invitation to the stage at the NASCAR Winston Cup Series Awards Banquet at the Waldorf-Astoria Hotel. He held a 254-point bulge over 11th-place Steve Park after the Pennzoil Chevrolet driver posted an outstanding third-place finish at Phoenix.

Park's surge through the point standings following his victory at Watkins Glen International in August gave the yellow-and-black-clad Pennzoil team a great deal of confidence entering the Homestead-Miami event. With the race also sponsored by Pennzoil, no effort would be wasted by the team to produce results. Park underscored the growing competitiveness of the team when he rocketed to the fastest lap of the Bud Pole qualifying session to snatch the fastest lap from Ricky Rudd and claim the inside of the front row for the second time in his young career.

(Right) The recent frustrations of his driver seem to be reflected in the brake dust-covered face of Bobby Burrell, the front tire changer on Ricky Rudd's No. 28 Texaco/Havoline Ford. Rudd started second, led the race on six occasions but could muster just a sixth-place finish.

(Below) Steve Park (1) and Ricky Rudd (28) lead Bobby Labonte (18) and Jimmy Spencer (26) as the event gets underway. Park, riding a string of strong performances over the second half of the season, scored his second career pole with a track record lap at over 156 mph.

The margin between the two drivers was a mere seven-thousandths of a second, adding even more frustration to Rudd's team after the Phoenix result. Park was the final driver to take his lap, and until that point, it appeared Rudd's black-and-red Texaco Ford would be on the pole.

Bobby Labonte claimed the third-fastest lap, while Jimmy Spencer qualified fourth ahead of young Casey Atwood and Joe Nemechek. Jarrett and Ward Burton made up the fourth row for the start of the race, with Brett Bodine turning in another fine qualifying run to beat Kurt Busch for the inside of the fifth row. Mark Martin and Dale Earnhardt Jr. barely missed obtaining top-10 starting positions for the Pennzoil 400.

Darrell Waltrip grabbed a first-day qualifying spot, and Rick Mast's Conseco-sponsored team also shone, using a backup car to grab 25th place after Mast damaged the primary car during the first practice session. Dale Earnhardt, Matt Kenseth, Terry Labonte, Ken Schrader, Michael Waltrip, Kenny Wallace and Bobby Hamilton used provisionals to make the field. Two of the three Petty Enterprises Pontiacs — driven by Kyle Petty and Steve Grissom —

failed to run fast enough in qualifying to make the field, with the two drivers joining Hut Stricklin, Ricky Craven, Dave Marcis, Norm Benning, Hermie Sadler and Ted Musgrave on the sidelines for the Pennzoil 400.

Still, there were two father-son combinations in the field (Dale Earnhardt Jr. and "Big. E" and Bobby Hamilton Sr. and Jr.), as well as five sets of brothers (the Burtons, Labontes, Brett and Geoffrey

(Right) Rudd's late-season spate of bad luck certainly wasn't the fault of the "Star Car" crew, which, as always, hustled and performed well in the pits.

(Below) Movin' on up? It looks like there might be another second-generation namesake on the circuit next year. Bobby Hamilton Jr. (57), here going side by side with Wally Dallenbach, ran this unsponsored Chevrolet owned by his dad. Bobby Sr. thought it was time for his son to get some track time with the big boys.

While Bobby Labonte's future in the Interstate Batteries Pontiac is almost certainly assured for years to come, the same couldn't be said for Kevin Lepage's. With no sponsor in sight for 2001, the future of the Jack Roush-owned team was up in the air.

Bodine, Kenny and Rusty Wallace and Darrell and Michael Waltrip).

Although five days after America went to the polls, the outcome of the race for the nation's chief executive was still in doubt, Tony Stewart wasted little time displaying the "presidential" form that took him to victory here last year. The Home Depot Pontiac driver rocketed through the field from his 13th starting position, and although he was dislodged from the point from time to time during pit stops, there was no doubt he had the fastest car in the field.

No one had anything for Stewart, and after he took the lead for the final time on lap 219, he eased away from the field to post a 4.5-second victory over Jeremy Mayfield. Mark Martin fought to third place, and behind him, Bobby Labonte turned in the race that won his NASCAR Winston Cup Series title.

Labonte fought his way to a solid fourth place, ahead of Jimmy Spencer and Rudd, and claimed the championship. At the conclusion of the race, he joined Stewart in a side-by-side victory lap around the track. The two Joe Gibbs Racing stablemates exchanged thumbs-up gestures to each other after outstanding performances that brought the race victory and the coveted championship to the Huntersville, N.C.-based team.

Three-time champion Jeff Gordon took seventh place, a lap behind, while Park continued his torrid pace with an eighth-place effort. It was his ninth top-10 finish in the last 13 races. Dave Blaney was ninth, the highest-finishing rookie driver, while Atwood, who will drive one of Ray Evernham's Dodges next season, rounded out the top 10.

PENNZOIL 400 PRESENTED BY DISCOUNT AUTO PARTS · final results

Champagne jam - Tony Stewart style!

Fin. Pos.	Start Pos.	Car No.	Driver	Team	Fin. Pos.	Start Pos.	Car No.	Driver	Team
1	13	20	Tony Stewart	Home Depot Pontiac	23	18	31	Mike Skinner	Lowe's Chevrolet
2	22	12	Jeremy Mayfield	Mobil 1 Ford	24	42	55	Kenny Wallace	Square D/Cooper Lighting Chevrolet
3	11	6	Mark Martin	Valvoline/Cummins Ford	25	39	5	Terry Labonte	Kellogg's Chevrolet
4	3	18	Bobby Labonte	Interstate Batteries Pontiac	26	15	40	Sterling Marlin	Coors Light Chevrolet
5	4	26	Jimmy Spencer	Big Kmart/Route 66 Ford	27	33	16	Kevin Lepage	FamilyClick.com Ford
6	2	28	Ricky Rudd	Texaco/Havoline Ford	28	27	21	Elliott Sadler	CITGO Ford
7	28	24	Jeff Gordon	DuPont Automotive Finishes Chevrolet	29	25	14	Rick Mast	Conseco Pontiac
8	1	1	Steve Park	Pennzoil Chevrolet	30	14	10	Johnny Benson	Aaron's Pontiac
9	19	93	Dave Blaney	Amoco Ultimate Pontiac	31	43	4	Bobby Hamilton	Kodak Chevrolet
10	5	19	Casey Atwood	Motorola Ford	32	40	36	Ken Schrader	M&M's Pontiac
11	31	99	Jeff Burton	CITGO SUPERGARD Ford	33	30	57	Bobby Hamilton Jr.	Bobby Hamilton Racing Chevrolet
12	21	25	Jerry Nadeau	MichaelHoligan.com Chevrolet	34	41	7	Michael Waltrip	Nations Rent Chevrolet
13	12	8	Dale Earnhardt Jr.	Budweiser Chevrolet	35	32	75	Wally Dallenbach	Rotozip Ford
14	9	11	Brett Bodine	Ralphs Supermarkets Ford	36	24	66	Darrell Waltrip	Route 66/Big Kmart Ford
15	17	2	Rusty Wallace	Miller Lite Ford	37	16	43	John Andretti	Cheerios Pontiac
16	26	77	Robert Pressley	Jasper Engines Ford	38	20	9	Stacy Compton	Kodiak Ford
17	7	88	Dale Jarrett	Quality Care/Ford Credit Ford	39	8	22	Ward Burton	Caterpillar Pontiac
18	6	33	Joe Nemechek	Oakwood Homes Chevrolet	40	35	27	Mike Bliss	Pfizer/Viagra Pontiac
19	10	97	Kurt Busch	John Deere Ford	41	36	98	Geoffrey Bodine	Miccosukee Indians Ford
20	37	3	Dale Earnhardt	GM Goodwrench Service Chevrolet	42	29	96	Andy Houston	Ronald McDonald House Charities Ford
21	38	17	Matt Kenseth	DeWalt Tools Ford	43	34	32	Scott Pruett	Tide Ford
22	23	94	Bill Elliott	McDonald's Ford					

NAPA 500

(Left) Jerry Nadeau's crew kept him among the leaders throughout the afternoon, then fitted their driver with two new tires during the last caution. That put Nadeau in second place for the final sprint to the checkers.

(Right) Within a lap after the final restart, Jerry Nadeau powered to the point and led the final seven circuits of the NAPA 500 to claim his first career NASCAR Winston Cup Series victory.

As Bobby Labonte began to enjoy his first few days as the newest NASCAR Winston Cup Series champion, the circuit moved to Atlanta Motor Speedway for the final event of the long season.

Labonte's title, salted away with his fourth-place finish at Homestead, Fla., allowed the Joe Gibbs Racing/Interstate Batteries Pontiac team the opportunity to take a few chances and experiment a bit with chassis and engine combinations in the final race of the season. While Labonte and his crew of "Battery Chargers" readied for the first race in their new role as champions, Atlanta's NAPA 500 marked the end of several eras in NASCAR Winston Cup Series racing.

The 34th point race of 2000 would be the "last hurrah" in Darrell Waltrip's storied career; it would see the conclusion of a 25-year relationship between Bill Elliott and Ford Motor Co.; it would be the end of Alabama native Larry McReynolds' long career as crew chief, and it would mark the finale of decades of work by ESPN and its incredibly talented and hard-working production crew.

For Waltrip, the Atlanta weekend was one of highly charged emotion. Many of the sport's newest fans had not seen his incredible battles of the past with the likes of Richard Petty, Bobby Allison, David Pearson, Neil Bonnett, Dale Earnhardt and others. They knew of his three championships but had not been witness to his fender-to-fender wars fought in the 1980s and early 1990s. His career was now

Among the announcements that took place during the weekend for the 2001 season was that of driver Robby Gordon (left) and Larry McClure, owner of the No. 4 Kodak Film Chevrolet. They agreed to team up for 2001.

(Above, left) Darrell Waltrip prepares to compete for the last time in the 2000 season finale at Atlanta. After leading the field around the track during parade laps, Waltrip took the green flag to begin the 809th start of his storied career.

(Top and Above) Over the weekend, fellow competitors — some of who had been fierce rivals with Waltrip at various points during his career — had an opportunity to participate in "A Day of Champions Honoring Darrell Waltrip." Among a "bounty" of farewell gifts for "Ol' D.W." was a wooden rocker, which, judging by his gesture will be a welcome change from the tight confines of his driver's seat.

(Left) In his last race, Darrell took his Route 66/Big Kmart Ford to a 34th-place finish, capping a stellar career that spanned 29 seasons and included three NASCAR Winston Cup Series championships, 84 wins, 276 top-five and 390 top-10 finishes, 59 poles and nearly $20 million in winnings.

THANKS FOR THE MEMORIES D.W. WE'LL MISS YOU.

reaching an end. The final time he would slide through the window of a race car would be at Atlanta.

Elliott first appeared on the NASCAR Winston Cup Series scene in February 1976 at Rockingham, N.C., where he piloted a Ford owned and prepared by his family team. He became one of the superstars of the sport, winning 40 times and notching 49 poles, all in Fords. His 1988 NASCAR Winston Cup Series championship was the first for a Ford driver since David Pearson won in 1969 in a Ford prepared by Holman-Moody.

Fourteen times the sport's most popular driver, Atlanta would be the final race for Elliott in a Blue Oval.

McReynolds first appeared on the NASCAR Winston Cup Series scene

(Right) Scott Wimmer raised some eyebrows while driving the No. 23 AT&T-sponsored Pontiac in his NASCAR Winston Cup Series debut. Scott qualified for the race, on his speed, in the 31st position, led once for nine laps, and finished 22nd, three laps off the leader's pace.

(Below) Preparing for a full-time run in the 2001 NASCAR Winston Cup Series season driving a Dodge for Petty Enterprises, Buckshot Jones (00) suited up for the NAPA 500 and had occasion to race with veteran Brett Bodine (11).

Throughout the season, several of NASCAR's broadcast partners completed their final race telecasts, but perhaps none was more emotional than the Atlanta race. ESPN would cover a NASCAR Winston Cup Series event for the final time, completing the cycle that began with the network's first live, flag-to-flag presentation of a race at Atlanta in 1981. In two decades, ESPN had been instrumental in building the sport to the level it enjoys today. For the likes of Bob Jenkins, Ned Jarrett, Benny Parsons, Dr. Jerry Punch, John Kernan,

Bill Weber, producer Neil Goldberg and director Mike Wells, as well as the others working the telecast, Atlanta was bittersweet.

With those eras coming to an end, the sport's new look for the 2001 season continued to take shape. Dale Jarrett and Robert Yates Racing announced their new sponsorship with United Parcel Service, and Petty Enterprises unveiled aptly appropriate new Georgia Pacific sponsorship for the team's "44," to be driven by Georgia native Roy "Buckshot" Jones. Hershey's joined Dale Earnhardt as an associate sponsor on the GM Goodwrench Chevrolet for next season, and Morgan-McClure Motorsports announced

in 1981 as a truck driver and mechanic on a three-person team. Five years later, he got his first shot as a crew chief when he was named to head up a new team owned by drag racer Kenny Bernstein. He claimed 23 victories over the years, and the Atlanta race marked his final event, where he called the shots for driver Mike Skinner and the No. 31 Lowe's Chevrolet.

Robby Gordon would pilot its Kodak Chevrolets in 2001.

With the "Siberian Express" sweeping down from Canada, and with crewmembers bundled into their parkas, Bud Pole qualifying began under leaden skies on Friday. When the session was complete, Jeff Gordon had rocketed to a lap at more than 194 mph to claim the final pole of the season. His Hendrick Motorsports teammate, Jerry

(Left) The guys who serviced Buckshot Jones' No. 00 Pontiac — especially the jackman — really got into their work. The Georgia driver started 29th and finished 37th.

(Below, left). It was the move that made the difference for Jerry Nadeau (25). When he passed Ward Burton (22) after the race went green for the final time on lap 319, he shot away to his first series victory.

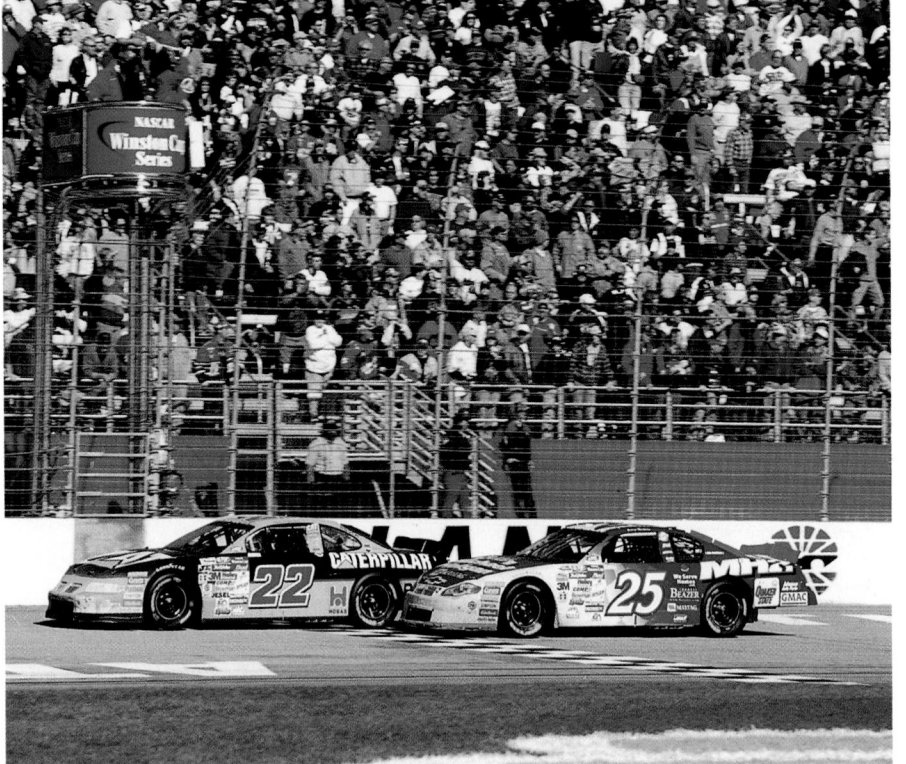

Champion's provisional to start the final race of his career.

That left the "unlucky 13" — Stacy Compton, Hermie Sadler, Hut Stricklin, Dick Trickle, Blaise Alexander, Morgan Shepherd, Tim Sauter, Larry Foyt, Kevin Lepage, Carl Long, Mike Bliss, Steve Grissom and Norm Benning — on the sidelines for the NAPA 500.

Rain and sleet blanketed the Atlanta area late Saturday and continued through Sunday. Shortly after 1 p.m., it was apparent the weather would not clear enough by the end of the day to permit the event to be run on its scheduled day, so the race was rescheduled to begin at 10 a.m. Monday.

Under blue skies and bundled against the 38 degree temperature, crews pushed the cars to the line for the start of the final race of the season. For Ricky Rudd, Mike Skinner, Johnny Benson and others, the NAPA 500 marked the last chance to win a race this year. For others, the race results would determine the outcome of the final point standings — and the size of the bonus checks from the NASCAR Winston Cup Series point fund.

With Jeff Gordon dropping back due to handling problems in the opening laps of the race, Jerry Nadeau had the stage to show what he had in his Michael Holigan-sponsored Chevrolet. It turned out there was plenty under the hood.

Although others challenged — and at times it appeared that Ward Burton had the fastest car on the track — Nadeau and his Hendrick Motorsports team were about to share the sweet taste of victory.

Mark Martin's and Elliott Sadler's challenges ended with engine failure, Michael Waltrip, Tony Stewart and Geoffrey Bodine hit the wall, and as the race wore on, Atlanta's rain-washed surface took its toll in tire wear. With the Caterpillar Pontiac enjoying a healthy lead, the final caution flag of the race flew on lap 311 when Scott Pruett spun on the backstretch. The nine cars on the lead lap headed for pit road, and when they emerged, Burton held the point.

Nadeau, made it a Chevrolet sweep of the front row, while Jarrett pleased the UPS execs in attendance by notching the third-fastest lap. Rookie Dave Blaney was on Jarrett's right, while Todd Bodine, entered in a third Haas-Carter Motorsports-owned Ford, surprised many by grabbing the inside of the third row. Mark Martin was sixth fastest ahead of Jeremy Mayfield and Dale Earnhardt, while Bobby Labonte and Wally Dallenbach beat Rick Mast and Ward Burton for the final top-10 qualifying positions.

In second-round qualifying, Elliott delighted his legions of fans by turning the fifth-fastest lap in the field and grabbing the 26th starting spot. Jeff Burton, Ricky Rudd (after damaging his primary car in Friday's first qualifying session), Mike Skinner, Dale Earnhardt Jr., John Andretti and Robert Pressley used provisionals to make the field. And in his final race, "Ol' D.W." used the Former

Burton, Nadeau, Rusty Wallace and Dave Blaney all took two tires, while behind them, Skinner, Earnhardt, Bobby Labonte, Jeff Gordon and Sterling Marlin took four. When the green flag dropped with seven laps remaining, Nadeau made his move, dropping to the inside and passing the yellow-and-black Pontiac. With Earnhardt and Gordon blasting their way toward the front, Nadeau used every ounce of power in his blue-and-white Chevrolet, withstanding Earnhardt's charge.

In his 103rd start, Nadeau cruised to victory, becoming the fourth first-time winner this season, tying a mark last matched in 1988 when Ken Schrader, Lake Speed, Phil Parsons and Alan Kulwicki posted their first career wins. He became the 14th different winner this year, equaling the mark from 1991. And he became the first driver to win his first NASCAR Winston Cup Series race at Atlanta

since Jim Hurtubise drove Norm Nelson's Plymouth to victory in the spring of 1966.

More important to Nadeau, he provided Hendrick Motorsports with the first victory for the "25" team since Ken Schrader won two races in 1991 in a Kodiak-sponsored Chevrolet.

Earnhardt finished second, cementing his second place in the final point standings, while Ward Burton slipped to third. Gordon was fourth across the line, with Bobby Labonte claiming fifth place. Skinner, in his last outing in the Lowe's colors, was sixth ahead of Rusty Wallace and Sterling Marlin. Matt Kenseth claimed ninth, a lap behind but ahead of Benson.

Darrell Waltrip, who had led the field on a parade lap to begin his final event, was 34th.

Jeff Burton's 12th-place finish dropped him to third place in the final standings, while Dale Jarrett held on to claim fourth place. Tony Stewart's Atlanta problems allowed Ricky Rudd to move into fifth place in the final standings, where Rudd claimed the position by five points. Rusty Wallace nearly moved past Stewart also, but was forced to settle for seventh in the final tally, just 26 points behind the Home Depot Pontiac driver. Mark Martin, Jeff Gordon and Ward Burton completed the top 10, while Steve Park beat Mike Skinner for 11th place. Johnny Benson claimed 13th over NASCAR Rookie of the Year Matt Kenseth by just five points, while Joe Nemechek edged Dale Earnhardt Jr. for 15th by just 18 points.

NAPA 500 • final results

Elliott Sadler and his Wood Brothers Ford were decked out in their new Ford Motorcraft colors for the NAPA 500.

Fin. Pos.	Start Pos.	Car No.	Driver	Team	Fin. Pos.	Start Pos.	Car No.	Driver	Team
1	2	25	Jerry Nadeau	MichaelHoligan.com Chevrolet	23	35	55	Kenny Wallace	Square D/Cooper Lighting Chevrolet
2	8	3	Dale Earnhardt	GM Goodwrench Service Chevrolet	24	38	28	Ricky Rudd	Texaco/Havoline Ford
3	12	22	Ward Burton	Caterpillar Pontiac	25	15	33	Joe Nemechek	Oakwood Homes Chevrolet
4	1	24	Jeff Gordon	DuPont Automotive Finishes Chevrolet	26	13	36	Ken Schrader	M&M's Pontiac
5	9	18	Bobby Labonte	Interstate Batteries Pontiac	27	33	13	Robby Gordon	Turtlewax/Team Menards Ford
6	39	31	Mike Skinner	Lowe's Chevrolet	28	22	11	Brett Bodine	Ralphs Supermarkets Ford
7	20	2	Rusty Wallace	Miller Lite Ford	29	10	75	Wally Dallenbach	Redcell Ford
8	19	40	Sterling Marlin	BellSouth Chevrolet	30	32	50	Ricky Craven	Midwest Transit Chevrolet
9	23	17	Matt Kenseth	DeWalt Tools Ford	31	28	01	Bobby Hamilton Jr.	Coors Light Chevrolet
10	21	10	Johnny Benson	Aaron's Pontiac	32	30	32	Scott Pruett	Tide Ford
11	26	94	Bill Elliott	McDonald's Ford	33	16	26	Jimmy Spencer	Big Kmart/Route 66 Ford
12	37	99	Jeff Burton	CITGO SUPERGARD Ford	34	43	66	Darrell Waltrip	Route 66/Big Kmart Ford
13	42	77	Robert Pressley	Jasper Engines Ford	35	11	14	Rick Mast	Conseco Pontiac
14	5	46	Todd Bodine	Kmart Ford	36	24	97	Kurt Busch	John Deere Ford
15	3	88	Dale Jarrett	Quality Care/Ford Credit Ford	37	29	00	Buckshot Jones	Crown Fiber Pontiac
16	27	4	Bobby Hamilton	Kodak Chevrolet	38	17	20	Tony Stewart	Home Depot Pontiac
17	14	5	Terry Labonte	Kellogg's Chevrolet	39	25	7	Michael Waltrip	Nations Rent Chevrolet
18	4	93	Dave Blaney	Amoco Ultimate Pontiac	40	6	6	Mark Martin	Valvoline/Cummins Ford
19	41	43	John Andretti	Cheerios Pontiac	41	7	12	Jeremy Mayfield	Mobil 1 Ford
20	40	8	Dale Earnhardt Jr.	Budweiser Chevrolet	42	34	21	Elliott Sadler	Motorcraft Ford
21	18	1	Steve Park	Pennzoil Chevrolet	43	36	35	Geoffrey Bodine	Bari Italian Foods Chevrolet
22	31	23	Scott Wimmer	AT&T/TDS Pontiac					

REFLECTIONS *2000*

NASCAR racing was saddened by the loss of two potential stars, Kenny Irwin (right) and Adam Petty (below) in separate racing accidents. Adam, 19, was a blossoming driver in the NASCAR Busch Series, Grand National Division, as well as being the scion of the famed Petty family of Randleman/Level Cross, N.C. The Petty racing dynasty, founded by Lee Petty (who also passed away in 2000), was made famous by Richard Petty, Adam's grandfather, while his dad, Kyle (bottom) had recently assumed command of the family business. Kenny, 31, of Indianapolis, came out of the open-wheel ranks of USAC. He ran his first NASCAR Winston Cup Series race in 1997 and was named the circuit's Raybestos Rookie of the Year in 1998. The motorsports community mourned the loss of these two fine competitors.

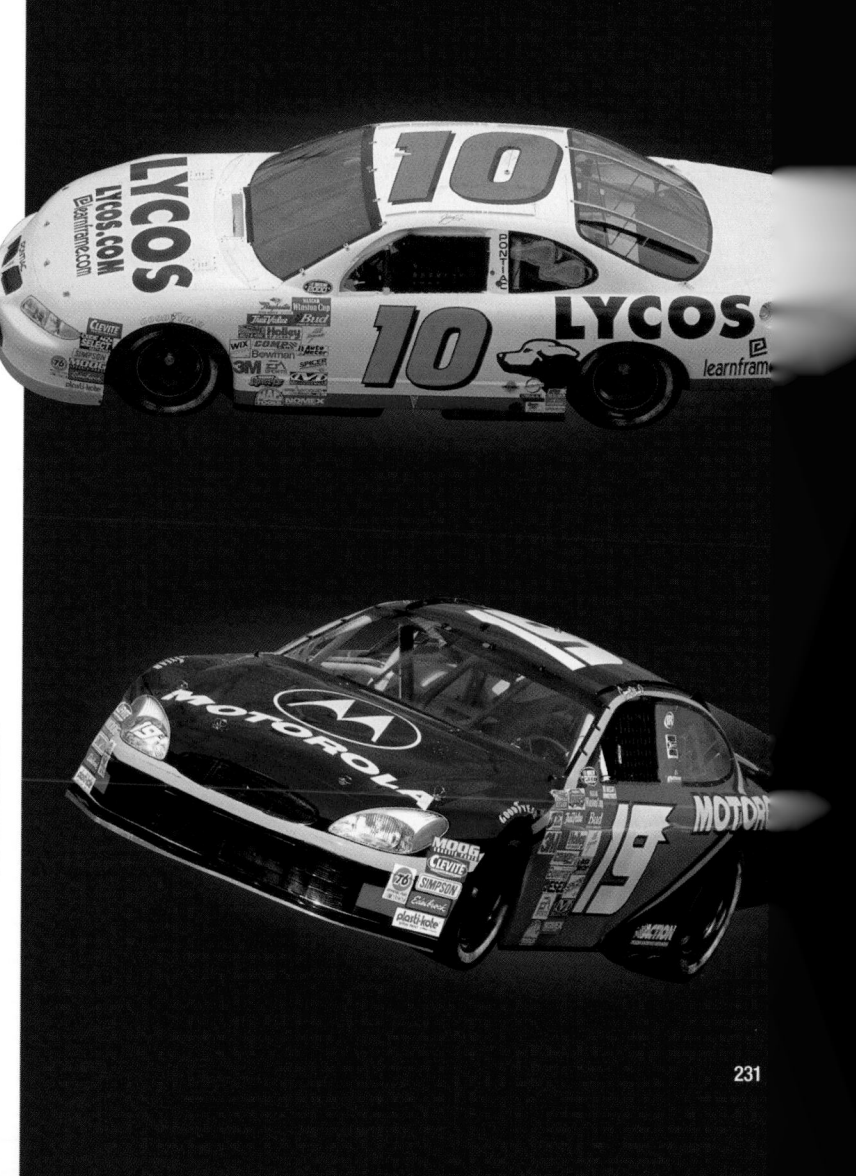

(Above) Matt Kenseth and Dale Earnhardt Jr. respected each other's talents but raced each other hard for the Raybestos Rookie of the Year title. Between them, they won races at Concord, N.C., Fort Worth, Texas, and Richmond, Va., took several pole positions, while Earnhardt also scored big by winning The Winston non-points special event in May at Lowe's Motor Speedway.

(Right) Two of the year's "Cinderella" stories involved Johnny Benson (10) and Casey Atwood (19). Benson's team picked up sponsorship from Lycos, an online service provider, at Daytona Beach, Fla., in February, where Benson came close to winning the Daytona 500. Later in the season, Lycos "went away" and team owner Tim Beverly sold his team to MB2 Motorsports. Valvoline then agreed to sponsor the Benson car in 2001 and ended up buying a 50-percent stake in the organization. Atwood, a young NASCAR Busch Series standout from Tennessee, was tapped by Ray Evernham to join the new Dodge racing program for the 2001 season. Evernham, Dodge's motorsports "boss," decided Atwood could use a bit of NASCAR Winston Cup Series exposure and put him behind the wheel of a Ford for three races.

(Below) Paul Sawyer (left), founder and former owner of Richmond International Raceway, created a showplace he sold to the International Speedway Corp. Sawyer became the track's chairman of the board while Douglas Fritz (right) was named RIR's new president.

(Left) As illustrated by Scott Pruett (32), Jerry Nadeau (25) and Bobby Hamilton, the competition in 2000 was oftentimes nail-bitingly close. While pursuing the Raybestos Rookie of the Year Award, Pruett found the transition from open-wheel Indy Cars to full-bodied sedans was sometimes difficult; Nadeau, a roofer by trade before he became a professional racer, seemed to find the perfect sponsor in MichaelHoligan.com, an Internet-based home improvement corporation; Hamilton's season was less than "picture perfect," and he and the Morgan McClure team agreed to split up after a three-season run.

(Below) Terry Labonte went through a trying season, too, at Hendrick Motorsports and failed to register a win.

(Bottom) Michael Waltrip, Ricky Rudd and Bobby Labonte found time to check on the welfare of fellow driver Bill Elliott, who injured a knee after taking a fall at his Blairsville, Ga., home. Elliott missed a couple of races but recovered from the mishap.

(Above/Above Right) The Indiana wonder! Team owner Joe Gibbs was able to celebrate being a championship team owner thanks to the efforts of Bobby Labonte. Gibbs' season, however, turned out even better because of his other NASCAR Winston Cup Series driver, Tony Stewart. In fact, had the No. 20 Home Depot Pontiac driver's overall record been a bit more consistent, it might have been him at the head table at the Waldorf-Astoria instead of his teammate. Stewart was able to collect more victories than anyone else — six — and that included back-to-back wins at Dover, Del., and Brooklyn, Mich., in the spring and Dover and Martinsville, Va., in the fall. He also won the first race of the year at New Hampshire International Speedway and the November event at Homestead, Fla., for the second straight year. The Homestead triumph was especially sweet for Gibbs because that's where Labonte officially wrapped up the championship. However, finishes of 23rd or worse at places like Atlanta, Bristol, Pocono and Talladega did crimp Stewart's style a bit, and he ended up fifth in overall points.

(Right) The 2000 season was one of transition for veteran competitor Bill Elliott. His six-year stint as a team owner and driver for sponsor McDonald's restaurants, and a "lifetime" association with the Ford marque, would come to an end. Elliott had chosen to drive for Evernham Motorsports in 2001 and help represent the return of Dodge to NASCAR Winston Cup Series racing.

(Right) Dale Jarrett will undoubtedly, for several good reasons, remember the 2000 Daytona 500 for years to come: One, it was the third time he'd won one of the world's most famous races; two, he finished the event in the same position from which he started it — first; three, the 500 was a "No Bull 5" event, and as an eligible driver, Jarrett collected a $1 million bonus. His total winnings were $2,277,975, a single-season record for a NASCAR Winston Cup Series event; four, Jarrett got into a crash during a "happy hour" practice session the day before, and his crew labored the rest of the day and then early Sunday morning to repair the car. Jarrett called the massive effort by his team-mates an "incredible job."

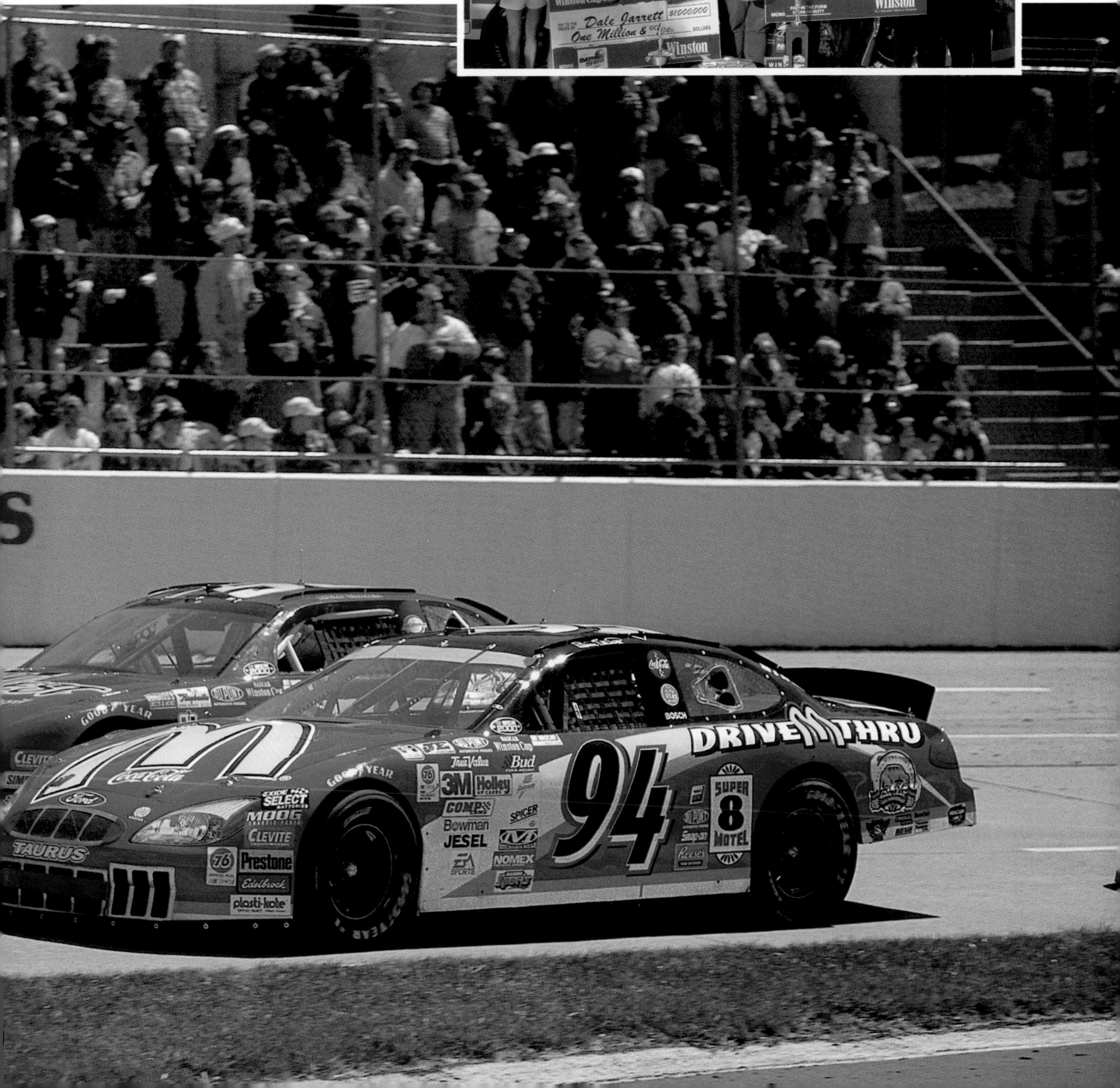

A master of self-motivation, Rusty Wallace, early in the year, apparently convinced himself he was going to make his 2000 NASCAR Winston Cup Series season a lot more productive than the one he had the year before. (Top left) Wallace said, for one, the spirit of cooperation between his Penske Racing South team and that of the Penske-Kranefuss organization of driver Jeremy Mayfield would have to increase. The Mobil 1 driver's year was highlighted by four pole wins and two race victories.

(Bottom left) Wallace himself went on a tear, especially with No. 1 starts. He notched his first Bud Pole Award at Rockingham, N.C., in late February and his ninth at Phoenix, Ariz., in November. The accomplishment earned Wallace an extra $80,000 from sponsoring Anheuser-Busch, Inc. Wallace would also celebrate winning both races at Bristol, Tenn., as well as events at Brooklyn, Mich., and Pocono, Pa.

(Right) The display of pyrotechnics at Daytona International Speedway in July heralding the nation's Independence Day was impressive and patriotic, to say the least. (Above) Jeremy Mayfield's personal fireworks display at Richmond, Va., in early September served to illustrate an up-and-down year of personal highs offset by low points. Mayfield missed two races because of injury, and late in the season, Mayfield's co-team owner, Michael Kranefuss, relinquished his part of the organization to Roger Penske.

"We did it! Finally ... it's ours!"

AUTOGRAPHS 2000